The Chronological History of the Roanoke Missionary Baptist Association and Its Founders from 1866-1966

Volume 1

DR. LINWOOD MORINGS BOONE. D. MIN.

authorHOUSE®

AuthorHouse™
1663 Liberty Drive
Bloomington, IN 47403
www.authorhouse.com
Phone: 1-800-839-8640

Published by AuthorHouse   09/04/2012

ISBN: 978-1-4634-2195-3 (sc)
ISBN: 978-1-4634-2196-0 (e)

Any people depicted in stock imagery provided by Thinkstock are models, and such images are being used for illustrative purposes only.
Certain stock imagery © Thinkstock.

This book is printed on acid-free paper.

Because of the dynamic nature of the Internet, any web addresses or links contained in this book may have changed since publication and may no longer be valid. The views expressed in this work are solely those of the author and do not necessarily reflect the views of the publisher, and the publisher hereby disclaims any responsibility for them.

CONTENTS

LIST OF ILLUSTRATIONS DIAGRAMS

LIST OF PORTRAITS

DEDICATION

William A. Boon

William Aldred Boon was born on January 15, 1845 in the Reynoldson District of Gates County, North Carolina to John C. Boon (1814) and former Martha "Patsy" Reid of Nansemond County, Virginia. William A. Boone was the grandson of Joseph "Joe" Skeeter, an English land surveyor who settled Skeetertown, near the Dismal Swamp. Joe Skeeter had two interracial marriages. His daughter, Patsy, was William's mother. In 1850 six year old William "Orren (translated as Orange and thus his nickname") was living in the Reynoldson District of Gates County with his black father, John Boon, and his mulatto mother, Patsy, and his mulatto siblings Jason, Francis and Parmelia. William's other siblings were: Ada, Preston, Frank (1830), Anthony (1836), Andrew (1851), and Sarah Jane (1860). William BOON (son of Patsy BOON, deceased) was listed among those allowed to work in the Great Dismal Swamp. He was a member and secretary of the Stony Branch Baptist Church, Gates, N. C., When he moved to Somerton, located in the southernmost part of Nansemond County, Virginia in 1878, he became a member of the Palm Tree Missionary Baptist Church. William Aldred Boon married three times. He first married was to Phereby Chalk of Nansemond County, Virginia. His second marriage was to Nancy Duck of Nansemond County, and his third marriage was to Edith Victoria Caroline Boon, Reynoldson, North Carolina, (February 1858) daughter of Mills Parker and Mary Ann Boon Parker. His October 1888 marriage to Edith Victoria Caroline Boon was performed by Rev. W. B. Waff in Reynoldson, N. C. William & Edith's (fondly known as Caroline) mulatto house hold consisted of Otis (1882), Daisy (May 1884), John Wesley (Jan 1887), Canzina (September 1892), Saphronia (September 1894), Mary Iona (April 1898), Elnora (April 1900), and Constantinople (1903), and sometimes her grandparents, Dempsey & Anzilla Boon. Boon was the official photographer of the Stony Branch Missionary Baptist Church. Many of his black and white type pictures have survived. Boon's work depicted the religious life and activities of the week to week services at Stony Branch. A picture possibly taken by William "Orange" during one of its Odd Fellow Meetings on the Stony Branch Church campus is displayed in Chapter 11 under the heading of Stony Branch.

The ideal of black men donning military uniforms gained public support after the summer of 1862. In April of that year, the Confederacy had begun conscription, and the necessity for a draft in the North became plain when states took months to answer the president's call in July for three hundred thousand more volunteers. In January, 1863—the month of Lincoln's Emancipation Proclamation and the second year of the Civil War—the United States began allowing black soldiers to enlist in the Union army. The army needed more manpower or, as African-American soldier James Henry Gooding put it with bitter eloquence, "more food for its ravenous maw."

William A. Boon's inclinations and favoritism towards the Union Army may have resulted from an initial contact with the secessionist Confederates on July 29, 1863. It was not a pleasant meeting. Col. Samuel P. Spear of the 11th Pennsylvania Volunteer Cavalry arrived on the east bank of the Chowan River, across from Winton, North Carolina. The 11th Pennsylvania had come from their camp at Bowers Hill, which is near Suffolk, VA, and traveled and stopped on William's property on the North Carolina, and Virginia boarder. While there, they forcefully and unmercifully commandeered his valuables, and properties, and one horse. Boone would later recount the experience on his application to the Southern Commission. Boone had witnessed the Confederate defeat and the Union's victory during the seizure at Suffolk. He had seen the Union army meet its objectives at Hill Point and at Backwater in the Nansemond County, district of Suffolk, Virginia. It was widely circulated that the Union Army campaign had been to hold Suffolk, which they had done. Boon stated that he visited with a cousin in Norfolk, Virginia in 1864, and while there was induced to enlist in the Army by a recruiting officer who, according to a written statement by Boon, "laid upon me unless I enlist I would be drafted into the service in a very few days. He said the government wanted every able body, young colored man that they could get. Therefore, when I returned back to Gates County from the visit, I returned to Suffolk, Virginia a few days after and enlisted in the Union Army on August 4, 1864 in Norfolk, Virginia., and without my knowledge or consent was assigned to Company "H," 1st Regiment of the U. S. Col Cav." The 1st Regiment of the United States Colored Cavalry was organized at Camp Hamilton, Virginia, Dec. 22, 1863. Camp Hamilton was located on the mainland opposite Fort Monroe (where the downtown section of Phoebus is today).

Colored Men across the width and the depth of the United States of America yearned to serve in any capacity within the Union Army. Their motives were complex, but revolved around a desire to "prove" them worthy of equal citizenship. They knew that the war meant the death of slavery, but not necessarily the birth of freedom or equality. They hoped to prove, to the racist white population, their worth in the crucible of battle. Once admitted to enter the Union Army, the white Union soldiers often treated the black soldier with derisions of all kinds. Despite these decisions and obstacles the Black Union Soldier were determined to serve their country and to fight for their rights. Inspection reports indicate that black troops did well in drill, took pride in their uniforms, and suffered less than white troops from such camp vices as drinking and swearing. Boone declared on an affidavit dated April 16, 1894 that: "There was not a Gates County man in my regiment; there was not a Gates County man in the whole company. They were all strangers, to me. The company was composed of slaves; nearly everyone had run away from their owners and enlisted. These men had come from different sections of the country. When the war was over and they were discharged from the army, they did not have a home to go to. Hence they went all over the country. All but 50,000 of the 186,000 black Union soldiers were escaped slaves from Southern states. Boon stated in another affidavit dated the 16th of May 1894 that "At the time I was hurt, I was with a detailed of 8 or 10 men from the Regiment; only 2 from my company, according to my recollections Benjamin Flythe an escaped slave, now dead, John Williams, who then said that he was escaped from the Eastern Shore of Virginia and I knew about my complaining of being hurt at the time."

Boon agreed, against all odds, obstacles, derisions, and ill and abusive treatments by the White Union Soldiers, the Negro Soldiers composed of former run-away slaves, and the Free Born Man held their own. Although, at first the Black Union Soldier received no pay at all; when offered half-pay, they refused saying that they would volunteer service to their country, rather than be treated as less than full soldiers. Boon's August 27, 1864 army mustered record shows that he was committed to 3 years of volunteer service. However, he did not receive the 30c due him until March-April 1865. There are notations on his records for 30c due him for May-August 1865 for service rendered at Saban Knot. Boon received no pay for his service in Brazos Santiago, Texas. He was there from February 4, 1864 to July 1, 1864. He was paid $100.00 for this period of time on August 31, 1865. A special note is affixed to the bottom of this muster record stating that: William A. Boon joined as Recruit force previous to April 19, 1861. (Boon very possibly passed as a white man doing that period of time in the army.) Boon's regiment eventually received full pay due to the persistence of the men.

Boon's attachment served in southern Virginia from early 1864 to June 1865. They were attached to Fort Monroe, Virginia, Department of Virginia and North Carolina, to April, 1864. Unattached Williamsburg, Va., Department of Virginia and North Carolina, to June, 1864. 1st Brigade, 3rd Division, 18th Corps, Army of the James, to August, 1864. His mustered record verifies that he was at the Newport News, Virginia from August 1, 1864 to August 30, 1864. His company held the Defenses of Portsmouth Virginia, District of Eastern Virginia, to May, 1865. Cavalry Brigade, 25th Corps, Department of Virginia and Department of Texas, to February, 1866. William Aldred Boon was at Fort Monroe and Williamsburg, Virginia until May, 1864. He and his battalion conducted reconnaissance in Kings and Queens County February, 1864. Butler's operations on south side of James River and against Petersburg and Richmond May 4-28. Capture of Bermuda Hundred and City Point May 5. Swift Creek May 8-10. Operations against Fort Darling May 12-16, Actions at Drury's Bluff May 10-14-15 and 16; In trenches at Bermuda Hundred until June 18. Bayler's Farm June 15. Assaults on Petersburg June 16-19, Siege of Petersburg until August. Action at Deep Bottom July 27-28. He was ordered to Fort Monroe August 3. Duty at Newport News and at Portsmouth and in District of Eastern Virginia until May, 1865. Cos. "E" and "I" Detached at Fort Powhatan and Harrison's Landing August, 1864, to May, 1865, then to City Point, Va. By 1865, he and approximately one tenth of his fellow Union soldiers and sailors about 80% of these came from the slave states. Black soldiers fought with notable valor. When captured they faced much greater brutality from Confederate soldiers than did their white comrades. Union service, for Boon and the other 5,723 Virginia United States Colored Troops did not guarantee equal treatment. Black soldiers in the Union army served in segregated troops, often faced menial assignments, and received lower pay—$10 per month to white soldiers' $13. He was honorably discharged from Cedar Point, Virginia during February 1865 due to an injury to the face, eye and head.

Some Blacks held commissions in the Union Army. Two regiments of General Butler's *Corps d' Afrique* were entirely staffed by Black officers, including Major F. E. Dumas and Captain P. B. S. Pinchback. An independent battery at Lawrence, Kansas, was led by Captain H. Ford Douglas and 1st Lt. W. D. Matthews. The 104th Regiment had two black officers, Major Martin R. Delany and Captain O. S. B. Wall. Among the Black chaplains with commissions were John Bowles, Samuel Harrison, William Hunter, William Jackson, Henry M. Turner, James Underdue, William Waring.

Blacks performed all kinds of services in the Union Army. Organized into raiding parties, they were sent through Confederate lines to destroy fortifications and supplies. Since they knew the Southern countryside better than most white soldiers and could pass themselves off as slaves, they were extensively used as spies and scouts. White officers relied upon information secured by Black spies for Union troops at many points of the eastern seaboard. Naturally the Confederacy was outraged by the Northern use of Black troops. The question immediately arose as to whether they should be treated as soldiers of the enemy or slaves in insurrections. The vast majority of white Southerners viewed Blacks soldiers as rebellious slaves and insisted that they should be treated as such. In 1862 the Confederate President Davis ordered that all slaves captured in arms were to be delivered to the state from which they came, to be dealt with according to state laws. President Lincoln responded in kind, declaring that for every Union soldier killed in violation of the laws of war, a Rebel soldier would be put to death, and that for every Union soldier enslaved, a Rebel soldier would be placed at hard labor on the public works. This ideal was accepted by the Confederates in 1864.

William A. Boon suffered a back injury on September 1865 while working with others in unloading a ship, taking off heavy building timbers, such as Scanting from the Hatch Hold. He added, I did not feel it at first. However, its intensity has increased during 1868-1869 when it became too bad. Alfred Parker and B. W. Gatling signed an affidavit stating the same. He reported on the "Call for History of Claimant Disability Form" that he was discharged from the U. S. Service in February 1866. He located and lived near Nurmeysville, Virginia, and as best as I can remember, left Nurmeysville in 1872 and came to Gates County, and lived about 4 years (1876) before returning to Virginia and located near Somerton Virginia, where I remained for 5 years (1881), I think. I then removed to Gates County again, and located after living 2 years (1883) at William Everett just over the Virginia and North Carolina, then to Dort. I have been living in Gates County every since, more or less 8 or 10 years (1898). He stated that his usual employment had been light farming or day work on the farm.

During the year of 1872 William Aldred Boon made a claim against the Southern Claims Commission as a "Loyalist." The "Loyalist of North Carolina opposed the succession of the States in order to form the Confederate States of the United States of America with the rights to continue to traffic in human slavery. The Union Loyalist fought against slavery and the dissolution of the Union because they knew that Negro slavery had been different than any other form of slavery. The African-Negro had been seized a prisoner of war, unarmed, bound hand and foot, and conveyed to a distant country among what to him were worse than cannibals; brutally beaten, half-starved, closely watched by armed men, with no means of knowing their own strength or the strength of their enemies, with no weapons, and without a probability of success.

The following statements were extracted from his 1871 & 1872 claims: William Boon is a free colored man, was born free-resident of Gates County, N. C., He was in no way connected with the succession government, was never in Confederate employment. His sympathies were at all times with the Union Army. His loyalty is well outlined. About the last day of July 1863 a force came by claimant place on their way to Suffolk, Virginia where they were stationed. When they were at the claimant house one of them took the claimant house. The securement and the payment of $100.00. The application form reads: Before the Commissioners of Claims: In the matter of the claim of William A Boon of Gatesville, in the County of Gates and State of North Carolina. "COMES NOW THE CLAIMANT," and represent that he has hereto forth filed with the above named commission a Petition for the allowance of a claim for the property taken for the use of the army of the United States. The said property, the claimant believes was BY DAMAGED, DESTRUCTION and/or LOSS, and NOT he use, of property by unauthorized or unnecessary DEPREDATION of troops and other persons upon the property, or rent or compensation for the occupation of building, grounds or other real estate, is as follows: 1 horse valued at $200.00.

According to Boon these soldiers were acting under the direction of a "General Veil." An unidentified cavalry spearman of the 11 Pennsylvania Calvary was actually responsible for his loss of valuables, one horse and home in the Reynoldson District of Gates County, North Carolina. Boon was able to sufficiently verify that he held American citizenship, resided in North Carolina after it succeeded from the union, could document loyalty to the federal government throughout the conflict; and had suffered official confiscation of goods from his Reynoldson, North Carolina property. He was paid a reasonable amount for his loses and for his loyalty. On his January 30, 1895 pension application, William made the following statement:

> "I do solemnly swear that I spell my name in full and foresaid, William Aldred
> Boon. I do solemnly swear that I could not read or write when I listed in the army.
> What I know about reading and writing, and all I know about it, I learned during
> the war, while I was in the army. I think it proper to state that my name "Aldred"
> is sometimes began with an "E", but not by my authority. I will also state that the
> name "Boon" is sometimes spelled as Boon "e", but not by me. I spell it Boon.

Boon's statement about his literacy is unquestionable. His statement accurately described the illiteracy rate of many of the Union solders when they first entered the Union Army. Although most were illiterate ex-slaves, several thousand were well educated, free black men from the northern states. A religious worker in Virginia was astonished to find a host of black soldiers who could speak Spanish, Italian, and Portuguese, and several were able to read Latin, Greek, and Hebrew.

The surrender of the Confederate army in 1865 meant victory not only for the powerful military forces of the North but also for the indestructible Union. Once and for all the question of whether states had a right to secede from the Union was settled. States were now bound to recognize the superior sovereignty of the federal government., and were required to participate in the reconstruction of the Union. William A. Boon knew from personal experience that Reconstruction did not end abruptly as the result of congressional or presidential action. Rather it came to a gradual end as restraints were relaxed and stringent legislation repealed. Just as Reconstruction had begun long before the war was over, so it drew to a close long before the final withdrawal of troops from the Southern soil. As early as 1865 many Confederate whites had resumed their places at home as respected citizens of their communities, and they resumed political activities on taking the oaths of office.

After the Civil War ended with the complete defeat of the Confederates many United States Colored Troops veterans struggled for recognition and had difficulty obtaining the pensions they were due. Since the United Stated Colored Troops was considered an auxiliary force, its members were not considered veterans by the Department of War's standards. Although the Veterans of the Union army who were disabled as a result of their service during the Civil War were eligible for a federal pension as early 1868. The Federal government did not address the inequality until 1890, and many of the veterans did not receive service and disability pensions until the early 1900s. On March 4, 1870 Boon provided a claimant's testimony that while at Key West, Florida he contacted an "affection" of the eyes caused by exposure to the white sand and the glare thereof. He reapplied twice a year until 1879 or 1880. On that application Boon stated that he believed that such injury to his eye was due to exposure while in the United States Army as a member of Company H, 1st U. S. C. Cavalry. He added, "I first experienced painful sensations in my eyes that caused a partial failure of sight, which I first noticed by my inability to read. My left eye is especially affected, inflamed and sore at times." He resubmitted claims for Invalid Pensions on January 17, 1894, February 5th, 1895, and February 15, 1901. On February 4, 1905, 58 year old Boon made a Declaration for Increase of Pension. He listed five reasons for needing an increase in his pension: stated the disease of eyes, rheumatism, and an injury to back, kidney trouble and general disability. He made additional remarks that he had one very bad eye and the other is defective, and had only married once, to the former Mrs. Caroline Parker. The application was signed by C. Frank Eleanor and John Darius Boon. His printed signature was affixed to his application.

The story is told of a young Confederate soldier captured during a battle in the western theater. The Rebel found to his surprise that one of his Union captors was his brother, whom he had not seen since the beginning of the war. After a brief reunion, the captured soldier was led away and his brother returned to the battle. The captured Reb called back to his brother, "Don't shoot that-a-way no more—Father's over there!"

William Aldred Boon brothers, Anthony, Frank, Andrew and Jason Boon both served in various support roles during the Civil War. William, Andrew, and Frank served the Union cause and Anthony and Jason served the cause of the Confederates to hold Negroes in slavery and in servitude. The following graphic account of the accidental meeting of two brothers, former residents of Princess Anne, after a separation of nearly forty years, is given by the Newport News correspondent of the Baltimore Sun. The stories highlights the similarities and difficulty that these divided loyalties presented to the soldiers and to the Boon family. This notable incident occurred in the streets of Phoebus, (Hampton, Virginia) when an ex-confederate soldier ignored his brother, a Union veteran, whom he had not seen since the outbreak of the Civil War. The family of Kings, in Princess Anne, Somerset County, Maryland was divided.

The father and his son, Albert King, cast their lot with the South, as did Jason and William Boon, and joined the First Maryland Regiment of the Western Shore, Colonel Herbert commanding. John King, sympathizing with the North as did William Aldred Boon, joined the First Maryland regiment of the Eastern Shore, commanded by Col. James Wallace. The regiments went to the front, joining the respective armies of the North and South. At the Battle of Gettysburg both were engaged and it is said at one time the one clashed with the other. In the engagement the father was killed. His son, the Confederate, bore the body from the field. When the war ended the family remained divided. Albert King, having lost all his property, left Maryland for the Pacific Slope. After 41 years' separation he returned east and settled at Old Point in present day Hampton, Virginia. While walking in the streets of old Phoebus, he entered into conversation with some old soldiers. One of the veterans gave a brief account of his career. King, to his astonishment, found it was his brother, still clad in blue and an inmate of the Soldier's Home. Without disclosing his identity he hurriedly walked away and took the next car for Old Point. Here, when he was interviewed, he broke down and cried like a child. There might have been forgiveness, he said, if he had not found him an inmate in the home. This seemed to strike him as worse than his brother fighting against him.

William A. Boon was an outstanding person in the community. Giles Eure and Moses Boon stated on a General Affidavit signed on April 7, 1894, each speaking for himself that he had known William A. Boon long before the late Civil War. I believe that he is a man of good character. I know him to be a sober and upright man, and a member of the Baptist Church, and in regularly attendance. Moses Boon stated that he believed William A. Boon to have no vices, and he is a good citizen. W. H. Cross and Mills Parker both stated on an Affidavit dated February 15, 1901 that they had known William A. Boon for the last forty years, and have never even heard of him having any vices; although he has been suffering for a long time. During March 27, 1901 John J. Melton and C. J. Boon acknowledged in a letter to the Department of the Interior, Washington D. C., that William A. Boon was a yellow man of Dort, North Carolina can be identified by a mark under his left eye. He is an outstanding person. On February 5, 1935, Mrs. Bettie Morgan, the next door neighbor to the veteran stated that Mr. Boon is receiving the full benefits of his pension. Mr. Abe Lassiter who has known Mr. William A. Boon for a number of years was of the opinion that William A. Boon was receiving good attention and that his pension check was being used to good advantage.

Field Examiner, J. O. Howard of the Public Administration Office, Washington, D. C. addressed William A. Boon's mental acuity and entered the following report about Boon's mental intellect.

> I contacted the above captioned Civil War Veteran and found him in bed from an illness which was not of a serious nature. It was some sort of Bowel ailment for which Dr. Thomas L. Carter had prescribed that morning. I found an old colored man about 92 years of age. He was hard of hearing and it was necessary to shout

for him to understand what was said. However, his mind was clear and he gave intelligent answers to all the questions I asked him. He told me that he paid his daughter, Mrs. Rayfield Boon $42.50 per month to take care, prepare his meals and look after his welfare. He lives to himself in a small one room building in the back yard of the home of his daughter. It is his preference to reside there.

Mr. G. G. Gatling went with me to see this veteran and the veteran remembered Mr. Gatling very well and also incidents which had happened more than twenty-five years before. Those two renewed acquaintances and discussed mutual friends and relatives that they knew. Veteran's mind seemed to be clear and he stated that he handled his own money and that Rayfield Boon his son-in-law and Rayfield Boon's brother Pat Boon help him attend to his affairs. Veteran stated that Rayfield Boon brought his mail to him and got his check cashed for him and her then paid his daughter the $42.50 per month and then got Pat Boon to deposit some money in the Gatesville Bank, Gatesville, N. C. so that he would have enough to bury him when he died. I contacted Rayfield Boon, the son-in-law of veteran and he told me practically the same story that the veteran had told me, veteran is getting very good treatment and is well satisfied with his treatment.

He does not appear to need a guardian and he knows what he is doing and seems to be able to handle his own affairs with the help of his sons-in-law Rayfield Boon and the brother of Rayfield Boon, Pat Boon, who are not related to veteran by blood. Rayfield Boon and Pat Boon bear good reputations in the community, are intelligent and industrious farmers. Rayfield owns his own farm. Dr. Thomas L. Carter, Gatesville, N. C. was contacted and attached herewith his statement and in view of his statement and my observations I do not think the Clerk of Superior Court, Gatesville, N. C. would appoint a guardian.

However, Mr. S. E. Ellenor, County Commissioner of Gates County, North Carolina communicated with the Chief Attorney and Contact Representative in Washington, D. C., requesting that in his opinion Mr. Boon is more or less mentally unbalance. Mr. Ellenor asked if the agency would file a petition for a lunacy hearing. He disagreed with the Field Examiner, J. O. Howard of the Public Administration Office, Washington, D. C. William A. Boon remained intellectual stimulated although he was confined to his bed for the last two years of his life. He managed his own affairs until the last year of his life at which time a special guardian was appointed for the retired Civil War Veteran. He died November 18, 1937 at the age of 93. He was interned in the Boon family plot in south most part of Nansemond County, Virginia. He received no official recognition for his achievement and valor as a Cavalryman in Company H. 1st Regiment of the Colored U. S. Union Army. If there were any recommendations for service they were filed away and ignored. There is no headstone or tombstone to mark his final resting place.

The story of William Aldred Boon's exploits on the behalf of the Union Army is a continuation of the first appearance of the Negro in the military affairs of this country beginning with the Virginia militia of 1652, and from the French and Indian Wars to the present conflict in the Middle East. The Free People of Color exploits have been numerous. While the death of Crispus Attucks in the

Boston Massacre is often recalled, the deeds of Lemuel Hays, a native of Massachusetts and one of the Minute Men is recalled during Black History month, the names of William Aldred Boon and James Jenkins of Gates County, North Carolina have been nearly buried in the forgotten history of the past.

A committee consisting of William A. & Caroline Parker Boon's great-grand children: Linwood Morings Boone (Amanda), D. MIN., chairman, Lisha Boone-Johnson (Jimmy), assist chairperson, Melvin Boone, Ollie Boone, Rose Camm, Willie Leroy Hunter, Catheryn Hunter-Woodard (C. B.); and great great grandchildren, Sherri Boone & Carla Saunders Jones, and great-great-nephew Earl Boone, D. MIN., planned a May 9, 2012 Memorial and Dedication Ceremony. In preparation for the Memorial Service and Dedication the team's research included the U. S. National Archives and Records Administration, Washington, D. C., state archives in North Carolina and Virginia; Harrison B. Wilson Archives and Gallery at the Norfolk State Library, Norfolk, Virginia, the Special Collections at the Peabody Archives at Historic Hampton University, Hampton, Virginia, Shaw University, Raleigh, North Carolina, Baptist Collection at the Z. Smith Reynolds Archives at Wake Forest University, Greensboro, North Carolina, G. R. Little Archives, Elizabeth City, North Carolina, and the Outer Bank History Center, Manteo, North Carolina.

On Saturday May 9, 2012 more than one hundred twenty-five people including descendents, family friends and re-enactors assembled at the Stony Branch Missionary Baptist Church, Gates, North Carolina for a motorcade led by Brian Parker, and the *Next To Nun Bike Club* to the family cemetery ten minutes away in old Nansemond County, Virginia. With lights flashing, horn blowing, and a motorcade of seventy-five cars, being led by twenty five bikers, dressed in their club colors, black and purple to pay homage to William A. Boon by dedicating his new Union Tombstone.

Deacon Ollie Boone, a great-grandson of William A. Boon and deacon of Union Baptist Church, Pughsville, Virginia offered the Invocation. Dr. Earl Boone, the dean of Religion and Religious Studies at the Pentecostal Inc, Suffolk, VA was the William Aldred Boon Memorial Speaker. Dr. Boone immortalized the following words:

> "the souls of the righteous are in the hands of God, and no torment shall touch them. In the eyes of the foolish they seem to have died; and their departure is accounted to be their hurt; and their journeying away to their ruin; but they are in peace. Their hope is the fullness of immortality."

In additional to the above remarks Dr. Boone explicated several of William A. Boon's accomplishments in light of the world in which he lived. Dr. Earl Boone's remarks reverberated the words of William Loyd Garrison, as an additional reason for William A. Boon's service in the Union army.

"I am in Earnest!
I will not Equivocate!
I will not excuse!
I will not retreat a single Inch!
And, I will be Heard!"

Thomas L. Grub Jr. Commander of the James D. Brady Camp #63 stated: "the march of this soldier is over. Let us remember comrade Boone, as it is our duty as Sons of the Union Veterans of the Civil War to honor the memory of the men who stood shoulder to shoulder on the battlefields. He fought for liberty and the dear old flag."

The Commander, Chaplain and Brethren of the Sons of the Union conducted the Acts of Dedication. The following participated in the Memorial:

The Laying of the Wreath of ever green	Donald E. Wells
The laying of a single rose on the grave	Charles B. Hawley
The laying of the Laurel on the grave	Mark Day
The placing of the United States flag on the grave	Thomas L. Grub, Jr.
The reading of the poem "The Unknown Dead"	Chaplain Charles B. Hawley

The tombstone reads: "William A. Boon, Pvt. Co. H. 1st Regiment-USCT (United States Colored Troops), January 15, 1846-November 18, 1937. The Sons of Union Veteran's members laid two wreaths, a rose and a U. S. Flag, followed by a three-volley military gun salute and the playing of taps.

Brian Parker and the *Next to Nun Bike Club* led the recessional and motorcade back to Stony Branch Missionary Baptist Church where the social hour began with a short program under the direction of Great-grand daughter Rose Camm. Joyful music and singing was led by Dr. Linwood Morings Boone at the piano.

Dressed in cloths from the period, Deloyce Maria "Ria" Camm-Glass, great-granddaughter, re-enacted the role of her great-grandmother Caroline Parker Boone, wife of William Aldred Boon. She wore a profusely ornamented black bonnet with a beige sash accented with a long silk dress that flowed from sided to side as she mincingly shahayed up the center aisle. Her silk blouse was breath taking. A beautifully well chosen old-fashioned brass brooch tied the outfit together. She was a little woman, not five feet tall, and proportioned to her height. She stood erect. She seem'd a part of joyous spring: She look'd so lovely, as she entered the fellowship hall. She swayed the congregation with dainty finger tips. She was led through the fellowship hall and introduced to her grandson, 95 year old James Hunter, Franklin, Virginia. Caroline sashayed through the hall, stopping momentarily to make lavish comments about her great-grandchildren, family members, and friends. The Apex of Caroline's visit from the grave was the unveiling of a black a white portrait of William Aldred Boon. This was an awakening moment as only a few decedentants had ever seen a picture of William Aldred Boon. The Memorial Service and Tomb Dedication concluded with the same fanfare as it commenced. The following unit's participants in the ceremony:

Colonel James D. Brady Camp
Department of the Cheseapeake
Sons of the Union Color Guard
54th Massachusetts Infantry
63rd New York Infantry
Next to Nun Bike Club

Aldred Boon finally received the homage due him for his years of service to the Union Army. His story is forever memorialized in the May 13, 2012 edition of the Suffolk News Herald, Suffolk, Virginia; the May 28, 2012 edition of the Virginia Pilot-Suffolk-Sun, Suffolk, Virginia, and in this book, *The Chronological History of the Roanoke Missionary Baptist Association and Its Founders from 1866-1966 Volume I.,* and on more than twenty WWW sites. Each can be accessed by inputting the keywords: William A. Boon Union Soldier in the search engine of your choice. Therefore, the beloved of our Lord and Savior, Jesus Christ, Be Ye Steadfast, unmovable, always abounding in work of the Lord, forasmuch as ye know that your labor is not in vain in the Lord. (I Corinthians 15: 58 KJV)

Loyalty to Christ

On to Victory! On to Victory! Cries our great Commander, On!
We'll move at His command-We'll soon possess the land,
Thru loyalty, loyalty, yes, loyalty to Christ.

From over hill and plain there comes a signal strain-
'Tis loyalty, loyalty, loyalty to Christ;
Its music rolls a long, the hills takes up the song,
'Of loyalty, loyalty, loyalty to Christ;

O hear, ye brave, the sound that moves the earth around-
'Tis loyalty, loyalty, loyalty to Christ;
Arise to dare and do, ring out the watchword true,
'Of loyalty, loyalty, loyalty to Christ;

Come join our loyal throne-we'll rout the giant wrong-
'Tis loyalty, loyalty, loyalty to Christ;
Where Satan's banners float we'll send the bugle note,
'Of loyalty, loyalty, loyalty to Christ;

The strength of youth we lay at Jesus' feet today-
'Tis loyalty, loyalty, loyalty to Christ;
His gospel we'll proclaim throughout the world's domain,
Of loyalty, loyalty, loyalty to Christ.

On to Victory! On to Victory! Cries our great Commander, On!
We'll move at His command-We'll soon possess the land,
Thru loyalty, loyalty, yes, loyalty to Christ.

ACKNOWLEDGMENTS

The persons listed below provided me with invaluable assistance and services as I was locating Sources for the research and documentation. This poem is dedicated to them and their families.

<u>Show me the way</u>

Not to fortune and fame Not
how to win laurels Or Praise
for my name But show me
the way

To spread "the great Story" That
Thine is the kingdom
And the power and the glory.

Archives

Alex Artis, System Manager at the William & Mary Swem Library, Williamsburg, Virginia.

Sonja Basknight, Research Assistant, Peabody Collection, Hampton University.

Gladys Smiley Bell, Director of the Special Collections, Peabody Collection, Hampton University, Hampton, VA.

Mrs. R. Collina, Moorland-Spingarn Research Center, Howard University, Washington, D. C.

Gaynell Drummond, Archivist at Hampton Public Library Virginian Genealogy Room, Hampton, Virginia.

Julia W. Bradford, Coordinator—Baptist Collection at the Z. Smith Reynolds Library, Wake Forest University.

Lucious Edwards, Archivist at Virginia State University. Petersburg, Virginia

Janis G. Holder, University Archivist. University Archives and Record Services. The Wilson Library at the University of North Carolina at Chapel Hill.

Lynn (Roslyn) Holdzkom, Head of Technical Services, Assistant Curator, and Manuscripts Department, Wilson Library at the University of North Carolina at Chapel Hill.

Beatheia Jackson of the Albemarle Pasquotank Regional Library, Elizabeth City, North Carolina.

Dr. Shelia Mingo-Jones, Ph. D., Hampton University.

Mrs. Darlene Slater Herod, Research Assistant, Virginia Baptist Historical Society.

Marcia Kirby, Library Assistant for Services, William & Mary Swem Library, Williamsburg, Virginia.

Dr. Deborah Majett, Ed. D., G. R. Little Library, Elizabeth City State University, Elizabeth City, North Carolina.

Donzella Maupin, Assistant Archivist. Hampton University Museum, Hampton University.

Ms. Annette Montgomery, Assistant Archivist Harrison B. Wilson Archives & Gallery at Norfolk State University, Norfolk, Virginia.

Charlotte L. Strum, Archivist at the Rockefeller Archive Center, Sleepy Hollow, New York.

Bill Youngmark, Ed. D., Archivist at Southeastern Baptist Theological Seminary Library {Baptist Room}, Wake Forest, North Carolina.

Churches

New Middle Swamp Missionary Baptist Church, Corapeake, North Carolina.

Mount Ararat Missionary Baptist Church, Cow Track Road, Windsor, North Carolina

Saint John Baptist Church, Portsmouth, Virginia

Organizations

Howard Hunter, III, Hunter's Funeral Home, Ahoskie, N. C.

Mrs. Elsie Horton Lassiter, Past President of the Roanoke Missionary Baptist Association Women

Missionary & Education Union

North Carolina Department of Cultural Resources Office of Archives & History, Raleigh, N. C.

The late Dennis L. & Marion Collins Stallings of the Stallings Funeral Home, Elizabeth City, N. C.

Outer Banks History Center, Manteo, N. C.

Individuals

Rev. Caray Banks, Palmyria Baptist Church, Elizabeth City, N, C.

Haywood L. Bond, Ryan's Grove Missionary Baptist Church, Edenton, N. C.

Mrs. Amanda B. Boone, My best friend and my wife of twenty-two years.

Rev. Jerry Boone, Jr., New Olive Branch Baptist Church, Suffolk, Virginia.

Rosa Eley Vaughan Boone

Rev. James Kenneth Brown, New Hope Missionary Baptist Church, Gatesville, N. C.

Rev. Maurice V. Fowler

James Ronell Gatling, Suffolk, Virginia

Cennie Penny Gilliam, Windsor, North Carolina

Rev. Lycrugus & Mrs. Carla Chavis Harrell, Sandy Branch Church, Roxbel, N. C.

Dr. Billy J. Hill, D. MIN-Baptist Church, Mosley Memorial Baptist Church Richmond, Virginia

Rev. Hallie Richardson, Little Bethel Baptist Church, Hampton, Virginia

Deacon John Riddick, Pineywood Chapel Baptist Church, Bertie County, N. C.

Rev. James Rodgers, past-moderator of the Roanoke Missionary Baptist Association

Rev. John S. Shannon-Providence Missionary Baptist Church, Edenton, N. C.

Dr. James Sherin, D. MIN., Jordan Grove Baptist Church, Winton, North Carolina

Deacon John Spivey, Lebanon Grove Missionary Baptist Church, Gatesville, North Carolina

Fannie Matthews-Spivey-New Hope Missionary Baptist Church, Gatesville, North Carolina

Corithym Thomas, granddaughter of Cora P. Thomas.

Dr. Carl L. Sweat, D. MIN., Laurel Hill United Church of Christ, Suffolk, Virginia.

Rev. & Mrs. Stanley Wiggins, Drum Hill, North Carolina.

PREFACE

In the Roanoke Missionary Baptist Association from 1866-1966, Dr. L. Morings Boone has done a tremendous job of restoring a history and legacy of African American clergy who established a ministerial alliance against the backdrop of racial oppression and dismal circumstances. These Founding Fathers and men of faith and courage led their congregations in such a way as to establish the Roanoke Institute to educate the children of northeastern North Carolina. Dr. Boone has searched tirelessly into the history of the Association to discover the passionate work that drove these men against the tyranny of southern discrimination to elevate their communities through public education.

With limited financial resources, these men were able to succeed against the odds due to their willingness to work together; they persevered and endured hardness as good soldiers as they made progress despite powerful opposition. The work of institution-building is never easy and the history of this association and institute has never been forgotten. However, as the founders and organizers passed on from earth to heaven it became very evident that their historical work needed to be written down and understood for future generations! Their work could serve as inspiration for those who would later take their rightful place as servants in these meaningful institutions. These preacher-teachers, inspired by God, recognized the power in educating the African American community. As the preachers became more educated, they saw the need to educate their congregations. For advancement of the race, solvent and influential religious institutions, a stronger community politically, socially and economically, the Roanoke Institute became the fertile soil from which African American youth were educated. The African American Church was the center of life for African Americans who were denied equal access to education, jobs, justice, political inclusion and housing by white supremacy.

Dr. Boone has taken the Bataan from others who knew that this important historical contribution needed to be gathered, appreciated, shared and celebrated for a job well done. Unfortunately, no one was able to consistently pursue this great endeavor before Dr. Boone's extensive and exhaustive work represented here. He has put in place a solid foundation that can be built upon as new information becomes available.

The visionary Founding Fathers and leaders of the Roanoke Missionary Baptist Association make very plain the fact that no challenge is too great nor opposition too strong that it cannot be overcome through faith in God and committed team effort! Dr. Boone has displayed the same visionary commitment, faith and focus needed to bring such a relevant piece of Christian history back to life!

Dr. Boone's skillful research, insightful scholarship and unyielding determination have unearthed a rich harvest of ministry well done for the people of faith and the community at-large. He has contributed greatly through this labor of love to further expose the reality of African American sacrificial service to the Kingdom of God!

Billy J. Hill, D. MIN.
Friend, Colleague, Preacher of the Gospel

INTRODUCTION

The *Heroic Age* of the Roanoke Association did not begin with the "cease firing" order of 1865 between the Northern and Southern States;[1] or with the founding of the Roanoke Association in 1865 but in the bush arbor churches, in caves, valleys, and in dug-outs in northeastern North Carolina during the slavery. The Heroic Age of Roanoke continued throughout the dark and dismal days of the Reconstruction Period. The *Heroic Age* and the epoch of these times were filled with many proscriptions against the Negro's personal freedoms and liberties which resulted in hundreds of revolts in northeastern North Carolina. There were thousands of these black Americans who never yielded in their hearts to the conditions of slavery; but nowhere in our school histories do you find a really un-biased treatment of these revolts. Nowhere in these books do you find the true story of the heroic roles played by the men and women treated in this work. For these true stories you will have to hunt far and wide in musty volumes that are kept in a mere scattering of libraries and research centers throughout the country. In many instances scholars and research students have found that pages which give an unbiased and accurate picture of the Negro's contribution to a particular period have been torn from these volumes by prejudiced persons bent on blotting out forever the high courage of our people during these terror-laden years in our history.

Herbert Apotheker, an American writer who has done considerable research in this field, has this to say about the treatment of Negro slave revolts in America:

> "Nothing in America historiography has been more neglected, nor, when treated, more distorted, than the story of these revolts. Out of Channing's thousands of pages, about five touch this subject and his treatment is, among the standard histories of Beard, McMaster, Rhodes, Hundredth, Schuler, Osgood, Bancroft, the most extensive. Sectional histories, with rare exceptions (exceptions are R. Scarbowwrough, Opposition to Slavery in Georgia: and H. S. Cooley, A Study of Slaves in New Jersey) are worse, and Negro writers (Journal of Negro History, Volume, VII, p. 361; XV, p. 112) are hardly better. The scores of pages devoted to slave revolts by U. B. Phillips still remain the most complete record of this important chapter in American history. But his pretentiously "objectivity" account is actually a subtle apology for the Southern Barbons."

During this period every device known to man was employed by slave holders to keep the Negro from revolting. They were not allowed to learn to read or write. They required passes from the slave over-lords in order to move about. They were only allowed to worship at certain times, and under strict supervision. A wide gap between white indentured servants, who were little more than slaves, and the Negro slaves was maintained. Anti-slavery agitation was beaten down with the aid of the rifle, the rope and imprisonment. Everywhere they were watched and kept in the most inarticulate condition to prevent their uprising up to break their chains.

We are constantly amazed, as we put together the story of these heroic men and their accomplishments during the slave revolt period. As these men come to life and rise out of the pages of obscure reports, faded and discontinued journals, long lost love letters and correspondences, their achievement is difficult to believe that these Founding Fathers worked against the incalculable harm that had been done to the cause of bringing the Negro up to his full stature in the day to day life of our country. The Committee on Education consisting of Rev. James A. Harrell, R. R. Cartwright, J. H. Perkins, and C. C. Felton made the following Resolution about the history of the Founding Fathers to the 1906 Annual Roanoke Association.

Resolution No. 1. Whereas, the fathers and founders of this Association are rapidly passing away to reap their eternal reward for faithful services and whereas, their work and worth in this Association have been inestimable, and whereas, nothing is kept and reserved to perpetuate in the minds of the present and coming generations, their noble work and sacrifices for the great cause of the Baptist Church and the unalterable principals for which she stands, and whereas, it is possible to collect some facts regarding their toil and struggle now, that it will be impossible to collect in after years, be it resolved—1). That this Association now in session take such steps as she may deem proper in getting up a brief history of the fathers and founders of this Association and also of the Association. [2]). That after the cancellation of such expenses as may occur in the preparation of this history, the proceeds from the sale of the same go to Roanoke Institute. 3). That in event such steps are taken that the work be commenced at once and prosecuted until completed. G. D. Griffin.[3] Rev. B. W. Dance stated during the Fifty-First {1917} Annual Session of the Roanoke Missionary Baptist Association that it was highly important that the history of the Association be recorded and given to the world. Rev. Thomas Sharp said that much valuable data may be found in his library.[4] The Roanoke Missionary Baptist Association has widely used the "Roanoke Alumni Hour" as an ongoing part of the Association. This segment of time is supposedly set aside to discuss, the lives and the accomplishments of the faculty and students of Roanoke Institute. To the writers knowledge this has not happened. This statement is based upon the writer's attendance at the Association for periods of 1977-2001.

The need to complete histories of the *Heroic Age* of the Roanoke Association was always in the forefront of Rev. Joseph Tillett's preview. At the 75th Diamond Church Anniversary of the Providence Missionary Baptist Church, Edenton, North Carolina, Rev. Tillett spoke from the subject, "Spiritual Unrest." He used this topic to trace the advancement of African People of Color and the progress of the Church since its organization in 1865.[5] Ten years later, {1950} President Joseph E. Tillet in 1950 make the following observation and recommendation: "In view of the fact that much of our history has been lost and by reason of which unborn generations have sustained an irreparable loss, I therefore recommend that a short history of this Association be written, embracing the names of as many founders and their contributions as it is possible to ascertain and the same become a permanent part of our minutes."[6]

Rev. Joseph Edward Tillet was very aware that the African origin of religion and philosophy was revealed and concealed; many of the Roanoke members rejected their own legacy. It was Herodotus that stated: "Almost all the names of the gods came into Greece from Egypt." Therefore, Tillet skillfully wove the Egyptian concept of god as seen in the African Diaspora into the fabric of his anniversary message, thereby tracing the founding and advancement of the Roanoke Association and Institute. Consequently, he expected to refute the fact that early centuries of Ancient Greek history are often called the "*Heroic Age*," because of the number of great men of heroic statue whose names have been preserved for us in the *Iliad* and the *Odyssey*. Tillet showed that the Ancient Egyptians had developed a very complex religious system, called the Mysteries, which was also the first system of salvation.

Fifteen years following Rev. Joseph Edward Tillet's recommendation that a brief history be compiled for succeeding generations, another recommendations was made by the Recommendations Committee of the Roanoke Missionary Baptist Association composed of W. H. Trotman, William H. Davis, A. W. Lamb, Charles F. Graves and Joshua A. Nimmo to the Ninety-Ninth Annual Session of the Roanoke Missionary Baptist Association {May 18-29th 1965} was 1). We recommend that space be given in our minutes each and every year thereafter and the names of the founders be inserted therein giving the date of birth and death if possible to obtain that information for the benefit of rising generations."2). We recommend that the Trustees be authorized and empowered to investigate the cost of erecting a monument at some suitable spot on the campus of Roanoke Institute to the memory of the Founders of this Association and upon which their names would be engraved, the said trustees to make report at the next Association meeting."[7]

Dr. D. W. Lamb, the historian of the Roanoke Missionary Baptist Association made the Report of the Historian on Thursday, May 22, 1980. His report contained the following observations, "If we look in our Minutes we will see the team of Moderators that has served from 1866-1985, beginning with Moderator Boone which begin at Haven's Creek on down to our present Moderator Rev. J. E. Barnes. Looking at the total minutes all of our work is in each year's minutes. I do not have any minutes beyond 1950. We do not have: 1). The teachers that have taught at Roanoke Institute. 2). I have asked the moderators of the Union Meetings to ask all the churches to give them the history of the ministers or pastors. 3). I've asked Sister Moore to be responsible for getting the entire teachers name who have taught at Roanoke. 4). I need a committee to get the deceased teachers. 5). I have asked Sister Mitchell to compile this into a booklet. These items will bring us up to date to our present teacher Dr. L. Warren Chase. As a family, we will begin to piece together what we have of the total history of the Roanoke Missionary Baptist Association. [8]

A careful review of the Minutes of the Roanoke Missionary Baptist Association from the March 1935 fire to 2010 reveal that the brave, heroic and honorable deeds of the history of the Roanoke Missionary Baptist Association and the Founding Fathers were never reconstructed. The review does show three instances in which a bird's eye view were given concerning the founding of the Roanoke Association and the Roanoke Institute. During the Wednesday Evening Session of the One Hundred and Sixth Annual Session {May 18th-20th 1972} of the Roanoke Missionary Baptist Association, Rev. William Davis recalled the fact that this association was named for Roanoke because it was organized on Roanoke Island. Davis said that the association was split twice; one was called the West Roanoke and the other the Middle Ground.[9]

Rev. Oliver Welch delivered the Inspirational Sermon during the One Hundred and Eight Annual Session of the Roanoke Missionary Baptist Association {May 21st-23rd 1974}. Rev. Welch announced his text from Hebrews 12:1. "Wherefore we are compassed about with such a great cloud of witnesses" Welch stated that his sermon topic was "The Great Cloud of Witnesses." Welch stated in his sermon that to run a race, one must divest himself of things that would hinder him; he must lay aside every weight for we must run to gain the victory. He continued, "we must stay humble at the foot of the cross as we look back at the great cloud of witnesses." Welch spoke of Abel, of Enoch, of Noah, of Abraham, of Stephen and of John. He recalled the past witnesses of the Association—Lemuel Washington Boone, William Reid, Zion Hall Berry, Ivy Boone Roach, Archer, Simon Knight, George Wellington Lee, Daniel Griffin, Benjamin Saunders, Harry H. Norman, David Lamb, Taylor, Rubin R. Cartwright, Joseph Edward Tillett, and Charles S. Mitchell. These men are looking down on us, he said, "To see what we are doing with the arts, religions and sciences bequeathed to civilization by the people of North Africa and not by the people of Greece." Welch urged the Association to carry on." [10] The following day, Dr. O. L. Sherrell, the Executive Secretary of the North Carolina State General Baptist Convention commended the Roanoke Association; he praised the past leadership of the association. He commended the work of J. E. Tillett, J. R. R. McRay, A. W. Lamb, W. H. Trotman, H. L. Mitchell, J. E. Trotman, H. D. Cooper, D. W. Lamb and others. [11] On October 21, 1981, at the request of Dr. L. Warren Chase, the Executive Board created a Board of Education, [12-13] and by motion, during the Thursday Morning Session of the One Hundred Eighteen Annual Session {May 22nd-24th 1984} the Historian Dr. D. W. Lamb reported that all future minutes of the Roanoke Association and the Roanoke Institute would be given in writing in order that it could be published at some future date. [14]

Except for an occasional Rev. Nathaniel "Nat" Turner, Booker T. Washington, or George Washington Carver, the Black man and his religious institutions are missing from the textbooks from which the millions learn their history. The race has bulked large as a theme in American Historiography, but such treatment has largely preoccupied with Negroes "en masse" and as a "problem," and has rarely extended to individuals, creative Negroes and their contributions to American society or education. It may be supposed that white, college bred-Americans can identify very few of the most celebrated African American religionist who attained prominence in "The Roanoke Missionary Baptist Association."

The writing of this book has fulfilled a long cherished desire, not in its best sense to say a history, but to lay some kind of foundation, so that the historian of the future may have something to build upon and may someday give to the world the facts concerning the service, sacrifice and achievements of the Roanoke Missionary Baptist Association. While the difficulty in obtaining information at times has caused discouragement and delay, the writer has never engaged in any task which has brought to him so much satisfaction and pleasure, and he will feel amply repaid if the readers find half so much pleasure and profit in the reading. The writer, too, expresses the hope when some other shall undertake to build on this foundation it will not be so difficult to obtain the necessary information. [15] To all who have responded and have furnished data for this book the writer wishes to express his grateful acknowledgment. There are many distinguished African Americans who deserved an honorable mention in this book, because they impressed the world as preachers of power. They not only built imposing edifices and pastured large congregations, but went from place to place in the State and country impressing the world with the power of God unto salvation. So generally did they ingratiate themselves into the favor of the public that they passed among the people as seers and prophets of a former period?[16] It is a golden opportunity to bequeath to the Roanoke Missionary Baptist Association an unusual legacy of such magnitude that it must be accorded a singular place in the history of African American Education in North Carolina and to fulfill the requests of Moderator Revered Joseph Edward Tillett and President Joshua A. Nimmo that a written history of the leaders of this association and Institute be recorded for future generation.

In the early decades nearly all the leading divines were self taught and education was almost everywhere regarded as an affair of the church; and the clergy were always the most erudite and usually the only teachers.[17] In the free territories, there were more educated Negroes. Negro minister-educators opened schools for the instruction of Negro Youth in conjunction with their religious institutions throughout the antebellum.[18-19] When the Negro minister became more educated, so did his congregation. Thus, did his community. The Negro Church took on the role not only of spiritual center but, in most cases, political, economic, and social center for the Black community, as well as giving Negroes a sense of independence, power and agency. Carter G. Woodson said, "It was in these church schoolhouses that many of the Negroes received their first training in books and dreamed of the future greatness which made them leaders of the race after many years."[20] Augmenting this is the real desire to show the progress made by the Black School under the most servile conditions of the time.

A book dealing with contemporary men can never be made quite complete or exhaustive, for, even while it is being made, some will move or pass from our realm, while others will rise to take their places. An attempt was made to make this work representative dealing with the education, and religious life of the Roanoke Association. An exhaustive study of the subject could not be made because of time and resources. No other study on the Roanoke Missionary Baptist Association could be discovered and no material could be secured in chronological order. Therefore, the discussion of the historical setting in this book is not intended as a comprehensive history of the education of Blacks in the Roanoke Missionary Baptist Association, but rather a brief local prologue to consideration of the religious patterns of educations. Though complete objectivity is impossible, particularly on racial issues that inspire sharp opinion, surrounding the religious life and the educational life in the counties within the Roanoke Missionary Baptist Association, the scholar has endeavored to portray the development of the association in a way that is faithful to the historical record and fair to all involved. This book seeks to examine the founding of the Roanoke Missionary Baptist Association from the perspective of its supports as well as from a larger socio-historical perspective. From the time the Plymouth settlement was founded in by the English colonists, the United States has been run by and in the interest of white people, and consciously so.[21] Though men and women from a variety of other racial and cultural backgrounds have been major participants in shaping of American History, most whites know little and care less about their roles.

It is significant that just at this time of Barack Obama's 2008 historic election to the United States of America Presidency a great deal of attention was being given to the matter of not merely recording the lives of Roanoke Association progress, but also placing them before the public. Certainly, this record will inspire future generation. Alternately used, abused, and ignored by the white majority, African American, Native Americans {Indians} Hispanic Americans, Asian

Americans, and other minorities peoples have had a history of racial oppression, similar to the experience shared by the African and native American residents of those connected to the Roanoke Association.[22] It is often stated that Blacks in America has come further, and faster than any other racial group. It might be added that he has overcome more obstacles than any other group of people. His phenomenal progress alone makes him more of a political asset to his country than a burden. Therefore, it is necessary to retell the story in order to place the Negro in his proper relationship and perspective. The Negro adventures in the United States of America have been structured differently in the United States than in the other parts of the hemisphere. In spite of his adaptability, his willingness and his competence, in spite of his complete identification with the mores of the Unites States, he is excluded and denied. A barrier has never been completely effective, but it has served to deny him the very things that are the greatest value among humanity, equality of opportunity for growth and development as a man among men. Therefore, to have preceded writing without articulating these most basic facts would have been to ignore the indisputable fact that historical forces are all pervasive and cut through the most rigid barriers of race and caste. [23] The Emancipation may have legally freed the Negro, but it failed morally to free the white man, and by this failure it denied the Negro the moral status requisite for effective legal freedom.

The Manson's Yonder

Shall we reach the home in glory
When the years of life are gone?
Shall we sing the dear old story
With redeemed one's round the throne?

Shall we see the blessed Savior
Radiant with eternal light,
Within dwell in heaven forever,
Clothed in robes of purest white?

Shall we share the joys eternal,
And the glory all divine?
Shall we, with the pure and Holy,
In the heavenly city shine?

Yes, we shall reach the mansion's yonder;
If we keep the garments bright,
We will greet our loved immortals
In yon palaces of light.

Yes, we shall reach the mansion's yonder;
If we keep the garments bright,
We will greet our loved immortals
In yon palaces of light.

1

THE FOUNDING FATHERS OF THE ROANOKE MISSIONARY BAPTIST ASSOCIATION

The last thing that white slave owners said to their Negro slaves as they were riding off to fight a war to protect their own rights to have and to hold other human beings in slavery was, "I leave my home and loved ones in your charge." The slave owner was conscious that his victory made the chains that held Negroes in bondage more enduring. Prohibited by law from fighting in the Civil War, the Negro slave was left behind as the sole support and the protection of the families of Confederate soldiers. However, the tenderness between man and master stood firm. A few slaves held that charge sacred through storm and temptation. He became a body guard to his master's family; the observant friend; the silent sentry in the lowly cabin; the shrewd counselor; and when the dead came home, a mourner at the open grave. Others deserted the white slave owners cause and openly communicated and collaborated with the Union soldiers.

No tongue, no pen, nor brush of artist can paint the desolation in the South when General Lee's battle scarred veterans turned their backs on Appomattox, Virginia and faced their old homes after the signing of the January 1, 1863 Emancipation Proclamation. The husband, son, father, who had not fallen in battle, or died of disease, and who, amid flying colors and martial strains, went forth from loving hearts and happy home four years ago, returned tattered and torn, defeated and humiliated, to broken homes and broken hearts. The south had been scattered. Thousands of graves marked the resting places of her white sons. Thousands of black chimneys told where mansions once stood. Dismantled towns, a desolate country, lack, misery, and death everywhere, were in the view of armies which had thundered over her territory and wasted her life.[24]

Georgia's matchless orator, Henry W. Grady, says, "It has been noted repeatedly that history records no more remarkable illustration of loyalty to trust than that manifested by the Negro of the South during the Civil War. I rejoice that when freedom came to him after years of waiting, it was all the more sweeter because the Negro hands from which the shackles fell were stainless of a single crimes against the helpless ones confided to his care."[25]

At the end of the Civil War in 1865, there were few independent Negro churches in Northeastern North Carolina. The Union Chapel Baptist Church, Weeksville, Haven Creek Baptist Church, Manteo, and the New Hope Baptist Church, Gatesville were among the few. One cannot write any portion of the history of the eastern North Carolina African American without at the same time writing the history of the slavery and abolitionist to which they were equally subjected.

During slavery Abolitionist like Moses Wilkerson, who had been a slave in Nansemond County, Virginia in the area of Mineral Springs and Harrell's Grove Baptist Church, Whaleyville, Virginia both churches within the Roanoke Missionary Baptist Association; from where he escaped, even though he was blind and lame embodied these words "I wish to plead my own cause. Too long have others spoken for me." Moses Wilkinson was known as 'Daddy Moses'. His owner was the Suffolk merchant Mills Wilkinson, son of Willis Wilkinson of Pigs Point Nansemond. Wilkerson was a fervent abolitionist, preacher and a stalwart defender of the religion that he loved so well.[26] For Wilkerson, other abolitionist, and the Founding Fathers, preaching was not simply religious ranting or cathartic discharge, it was an act of spiritual release, a celebration of freedom from bondage and oppression, both the human and spiritual kind. Founding Father Hodges and his brother Reverend Willis A. Hodges, Reverend James Jenkins and other abolitionist morally revolutionized the nation with the ideals that God is wholly impartial and that from one blood He created all races and nations. The Abolitionist created a *conscience before God and the world that included the tenants':* God has set no geographical or racial boundaries; there is no divine right of race; the rights of humanity are divine; we are all God's creation; God created the Negro in His own image, which pervaded all the length and the breath of the country, and which could never be appeased while one person remained in slavery. The Abolitionist agitated the whole world! They created a spirit of inquiry existing though out all the extent of the continent, on the subject of Slavery, and the fact that God hath send the Negro on a special errand,[27] to expound the truths that all men, black and brown and white are brothers, varying through time and opportunity, in form and gift and feature, but differing in no essential particular, and alike in soul and the possibility of infinite development.[28] The revolution, the agitation and the Spirit of Inquiry as presented by the abolitionist naturally raise the biblical questions? Are not the dry bones everywhere, being roused up from their sleep of inquiry and mortal death, to life and activity? The United States of America was once dead, now she is alive in moral thought, feeling, and action, and for this life we are under God.

Each of the Founding Fathers was born during slavery and servitude. Founder Lemuel Washington Boone was free born in 1827. Founding Father Hodges was free-born in 1819. The two Reynolds Founding Fathers were free-born in Hertford County, North Carolina. The senior Founding Father Reynolds was free born in Hertford County in 1827, and the Junior Founding Father Reynolds was born about 1835 in Hertford County, North Carolina. There is no available information for the status of Founder Father Berry born 1830. Founder Father Flemings was born a slave in Virginia May 1831. Founding Father Hayes was born in slavery about 1830, in Gates County, North Carolina. There is no available information for Founding Father Harper. Founding Father Holland was born in slavery in Virginian 1833. Founding Father Johnson was born to slave parents in Warrenton, North Carolina in 1833. These men and abolitionist knew from bitter negotiations and agitations' that Lincoln's proposal was a proposal "to conduct the war for the preservation of the status quo which had produced the war."[29] The abolitionist and the parents of the Founding Fathers forged onward in the battle for truth and freedom.

Charles E. Hodges, a Founding Father and activist of the Roanoke Missionary Baptist Association and brother of Willis A. Hodges, abolitionist' both friends and colleagues of John Brown and Frederick Douglas, said "If there is no struggle, there is no progress. Those who profess to favor freedom, and yet deprecate agitation, are men who want crops without plowing up the ground. They want rain without thunder and lightning. They want the ocean without the awful roar of its many waters. This struggle may be a moral one, or it may be a physical one, or it may be both moral and physical, but it must be a struggle. Power concedes nothing without a demand." Frederick Douglas, the Abolitionists and Autobiographer "To those who have suffered in slavery I can say I, too, have suffered. To those who have battled for liberty, brotherhood and Citizenship, I can say I, too, have battered."[30] Father Hodges recalled, "When I thought of slavery, with its democratic whips, its republican chains, its evangelical bloodhounds, and its religious slaveholders, when I thought of all this paraphernalia of American democracy and religion behind me, I was encouraged to press forward, my heart was strengthened and I forgot that I was hungry, and when I look at the future of the Roanoke Missionary Baptist Association, it is so bright it burned by eyes." He continued, "Therefore, I donned my long tail duster and my black beaver hat, grabbed my satchel containing a Bible, a hymn book, and I commenced to travel the long winding roads and muddy streams preaching the gospel of love[31] to men who had been robbed by slavery of himself and made the property of another." [32]

Prior to 1861 there were few Negro ordained pastors in these areas. A Negro could serve as a preacher and deacon. This means that he was appointed by the *white deacons* with the consent of his master, to look after the colored people only, and to hand to them emblems of the Lord's Supper, in the gallery of the white church, after the white people had taken it. These were the only credentials a Negro man could get to preach; he could not be regularly ordained because he belonged to another; it did not matter what his qualifications were, or how loud the Lord called him, it was optional with his master whether or not he should answer the call. These were the days when colored ordained ministers were very few; sometimes not more than half a dozen in a whole county, one would frequently be called upon, as best he could, to take charge of four, six or as many as twelve churches. The Founding Fathers planned their ternary to accommodate the greatest number of churches within a geographical area. Thus, it was not unusually for a Founding Farther to have the charge of 12 churches per month. This included an eleven o clock service, a 1:30 P. M. services and a 7 P. M. O'clock service. A Founding Farther, although he was a pastor in the town of Camden, could be called to serve several country churches which he was largely instrumental in organizing. Thus, he served a church in Camden County, Gates County, Martin County and Tyrell County, preaching to it once a month in the morning. He could be called to a church seventeen miles in the Nansemond County or Princess Ann County, Virginia, or Hertford County, North Carolina. On preaching days he would go and preach to them, and take his horse or horse and buggy ride back to town and preach in the evening. The Founding Fathers were men who made history. They became great. No one can attain to breadth and height and weight who is occupied in thought and heart with trifles. Elihu Burritt was a blacksmith, but he was at the same time a student, and while his arm wielded the hammer his mind was with Plato and Aristotle. Rev. James Jenkins of Lebanon Grove fought in the Civil War with a rifle in one hand and the Bible in the other.

The Founding Fathers intuitively knew that the Freedmen of northeastern North Carolina needed leadership, a leadership that would not allow them to deny their past, and would required them to seriously think about the future and then to fully invest themselves. They wanted something for themselves and for their children. Hence, they took a chance with their lives knowing very well that the ultimate measure of a man is not where he stands in moments of comfort, but where he stands at times of challenge and controversy. Most of problems can be solved. Some of them will take brains, and some of them will take patience, but all of them will have to be wrestled with like an alligator in the swamp. The spirit of the old-time Founding Fathers still fills some pulpits in many communities, and still declared that the day has arrived that you will have to help yourself or suffer the worse. This means that you have to deal with yourself as an individual worthy of respect and make everyone else deal with you the same way. Unless we learn the lesson of self-appreciation and practice it, we shall spend our lives imitating other people and deprecating ourselves. Anytime there is a self loving, self-respecting, and self-determining black man, he is one of the most dangerous folks in America; because it means that you are free enough to speak your mind, you are free enough to speak the truth. When nobody speaks your name, or even knows it, you, knowing it, must be the first to speak it.

Why did the Founding Fathers experience so much success in such a short span of time? One of the important reasons why the Founding Fathers were the first to reach the Negro in the Roanoke Missionary Baptist Association was due in part to an itinerant system. The Founding Fathers and its Board of Elders serving like scouts went out into the wilderness to find the people and bring them in. Unlike the aristocratic Presbyterian church, the Founding Fathers did not disregard the character of experimental religion." They appealed to their intellect through their spirit. While the good Presbyterian and the Methodist were writing their discourses, rounding off the sentences, the itinerant Founding Fathers were traveling from forty to sixty miles with his horse and saddle bags. While other pulpiteers were adjusting their spectacles to read their manuscripts, the itinerant Founding Fathers had given hell and damnation to his unrepentant hearers. The Founding Fathers took to the woods, the water-ways, and to horse back and horse buggy and made them re-echo with the voice of free grace, believing with L.W. Boon, Z. H. Berry, Bryant Lee, "The Groves" were God's first temples.

The second reason that the Founding Fathers experienced so much success was due to the peculiar feature of Baptist policy. In the first place, the Founding Fathers believed that the local Baptist Church was thoroughly independent of any other organization or church. It may become associated with other churches in bodies meeting periodically to devise plans for the common good of the denomination; but it is in no sense bound by the rules and regulations of such bodies; and should an association, moreover, exclude a church from its group, that church is still legally constituted a Baptist church and may join another association or form one of its own in cooperation with other churches similarly disposed. Any group of baptized believers of not less than four, moreover, may exercise the liberty of organizing a church under the direction of a regularly ordained minister of the denomination and ordination in the Baptist Church is not a difficulty. With the tendency of so many members to find fault, to disagree, to follow the advice of ill-designing persons seeking personal ends, it was a decidedly easy matter for Negro Baptist churches under these circumstances to split and thus multiply. [33]

The Founding Fathers believed that the hope of the African race in American was largely in its pulpit. The school house and the newspaper have not substituted the pulpit, as a throne of spiritual power, in any Christian nation. They did not believe that they ever would; but for this race the pulpit must be pre-eminently its teacher. Here they must receive their best counsels and their divine's inspiration. When the Founders Fathers said the pulpit, they meant *its* pulpit; they meant this. White preachers have done much and ought to have done more; they can now do much and ought to do a hundred-fold more than they do; but the great work must be done by preachers of the Negro race. Tongues and ears were made for each other; in each race both its tongues and its ears have characteristics of their own No other tongue can speak to the Negro's ear like a Negro's tongue. All races are so; some missionaries have found this out. In every mission field the "native ministry" does a work that no other can do. How urgent the need and how sacred the duty of preparing those of this race whom God calls to preach to their people! Heaven bless the men and women who have given money and personal service for their education! Heaven bless their "schools of the prophets!" May they ever be under the wisest guidance and the holiest influences![34] The Founding Fathers and succeeding generations of pastors, ministers, deacons and Christian educators of the Roanoke Missionary Baptist Association are weekly confronted with the inescapable consequences of their servitude and the many vicissitudes of slavery which required them and their progenitors to give slavery and servitude their ongoing attention.

The Roanoke Missionary Baptist Association's birth arises from the October 17, 1865 meeting when Reverends Lemuel Washington Boon, Edwards Eagles, Joshua Flemings, H. Grimes, R. H. Harper, C. Johnson, Emanuel Reynolds, R. B. Spicer, William Warrick, and delegates met at Haven's Creek Baptist Church on Roanoke Island, North Carolina and organized the Roanoke Missionary Baptist Association based upon a strict Constitution, By-Laws and Order of Service. Reverend Lemuel Washington Boone was instrumental in establishing the association was asked to preside over the opening meeting, and his cousin Asbury Reid was selected as the first secretary.

In 1870 the Roanoke Missionary Baptist Association list of Ordained Elders included only fifteen names: Elder Lemuel W. Boon, Gatesville, N. C.; Elder Zion H. Berry, Shiloh; Elder Charles S. Hodges, Lake Drummond, VA; Elder Emanuel Reynolds, Winton; Elder Richard R. Creecy, Columbia; Elder Willis Melton, Hertford; Elder Abrum Mebin, Plymouth; Elder Henry Hays, Gatesville; Elder Bryant Lee, Woodville; Elder Benjamin Clark, Woodville; Elder Thaddeus Wilson, Merry Hill; Elder Charles Capps, South Mills; Rev. William Bass, No city or County provided; Elder Robert Valentine, Harrellsville; and Rev. Robert Westcott Roanoke Island.[35] The Roanoke Missionary Baptist Association was composed of land masses from Martin County, North Carolina, northward to the Mineral Springs and Harris Grove Baptist Churches, in Whaleyville, (Nansemond County), Virginia; Tyrell & Washington Counties, to Jamesville, North Carolina to Elizabeth City, North Carolina to Weeping Mary Baptist Church in Creeds, Virginia on ward to several churches in Princess Ann, Virginia; with two or three churches in Norfolk, Virginia.

The average congregant of the Roanoke Missionary Baptist Association seems not to know the Founding Fathers or what the Founding Fathers and the Roanoke Missionary Baptist Associations has contributed to the religious, educational and political world. Thus, not knowing these rudimentary things about the Founding Fathers, the average congregant does not believe it when they hear of the great exploits of the Founding Fathers, and not believing the reports of their great exploits, the average congregant becomes easily persuaded and asserts the belief that the Founding Fathers of the Roanoke Missionary Baptist Association has made no attributable contributions. In order that we may know what the Founding Fathers did, and become, it is well to consider that the Founding Fathers and their congregants were free when they were under the grove together for that togetherness represented and embodied the transplanted African Memory. The Founding Fathers knew that nothing the future could bring would defeat a people who have come through 300 years of slavery and humiliation and privation with heads high and eyes clear and straight. For too long, the lives and legacies of the Founding Fathers of the Roanoke

Missionary Baptist Association have gone over looked, unnoticed, ignored and forgotten. Their path has been lavishly strewn with thrones and with a few roses, and their history has been one of profound pathos. From time immemorial and in all places he has been a burden-bearer, the plaything, the tool and the discarded dupe of his more privileged brother. Throughout most of the Nation's history, and thru no fault of his own-has been considered a problem by our white neighbors. Of all the preachers on earth, there was, there is, and there never will be a greater preacher than the God sent Black preacher of which the Founding Fathers were included. The 1871 the following names were listed as ordained elders. The 1871-1878 Minutes of the Annual Roanoke Missionary Baptist Association provided a list of other ministers who participated in the first twelve years of the Roanoke Missionary Baptist Association. They were also born under slave's cruel bondage.

Year, 1871	Name	City, State
Elder's	Lemuel W. Boon	Gatesville, N. C.
	Zion Hall Berry	Camden Court House, N. C.
	Charles S. Hodges	Lake Drummond, VA
	Emanuel Reynolds	Winton, N. C.
	Richard H. Creecy	Columbia, N. C.
	Willis Melton	Hertford County, N. C.
	Abrum Mebin	Plymouth, N. C.
	Henry H. Hayes	Gatesville, N. C.
	Bryant Lee	Woodville, N. C.
Licentiate's	Anthony Bowling	Merry Hill, N. C.
	John B. Hogood	Windsor, N. C.
	Brown Holly	Colerain, N. C.
	Henry Holly	Colerain, N. C.
	Henry Huggins	Hamilton, N. C.
	William Jarvis	Lake Drummond, VA
	James Lamb	Camden, N. C.
	Alexander Lane	Camden County, N. C.
	Married Marsett	Camden, N. C.
	Levi Mullen	Elizabeth City, N. C.
	Henry Olds	South Mills, N. C.
	Benjamin Oughaw (Outlaw)	Merry Hill, N. C.
	Jeremiah Roten	Coinjock, N. C.
	James Rountree	Colerain, N. C.
	Albert Saunders	Gatesville, N. C.
	Frank Smallwood	Windsor, N. C.
	Thomas Thompson	Hertford County, N. C.
	Grandville Towe	Plymouth, N. C.
	Benjamin Verman	Colerain, N. C.
	Solomon Webb	South Mills, N. C.

1872-1878		
	Unknown Archer	
	Willis Arterbridge	
	Nelson Beamon	
	Charles Capps	
	J. W. Chesson	
	Benjamin Clark	
	R. R. Creecy	
	Edward Freeman	
	Elijah H. Griffin	
	Henry H. Hays	
	Moses Hodges	
	George Jarvis	
	James Jenkins	
	Newman Johnson	
	Alexander Lamb	
	J. K. Lamb	
	Monroe Lane	
	Byrant Lee	
	B. J. Lennox	
	G. A. MeBane	
	Willis Melton	
	Levi Mullen	
	Henry Outlaw	
	Andrew Parker	
	Luke Pierce	
	Ivy Boone Roach	
	N. F. Roberts	
	Alfred Saunders	
	D. L. Simmons	
	Robert Valentine	
	Solomon Webb	
	John Wilkins	
	Thaddeus Wilson	
	Henry Woodley	

CONSTITUTION

SECTION 1. This Association shall be known as the "Roanoke Missionary Baptist Association."

SEC. 2. This Association shall be composed of Pastors and two Messengers from each church composing this body, and Ordained Elders, who shall be entitled to a seat in the same.

SEC.3. This Association shall have a Moderator and Vice Moderator, Secretary, Treasurer, Corresponding Secretary and Historian, who shall be chosen by the pastors and messengers annually.

SEC. 4. Any regular Missionary Baptist church, by application, may join this Association by paying one dollar.

SEC.5. any member of a regular Missionary Baptist church may join this Association by paying one dollar.

SEC. 6. The letters received by this Association from the various churches composing—this body shall express the total number in full fellowship, the number baptized, those received by letter, those excommunicated and those deceased since last Association.

SEC. 7. This Association shall not lord it over God's heritage, nor interfere with the internal rights of the churches.

SEC. 8. The object of this Association shall be to aid Home and Foreign Missions, Ministerial and General Education, the Orphan Asylum and the Academy at Elizabeth City.

SEC. 9. Each church is recommended to pay twenty-five cents per member annually to this Association.

SEC 10. This Association shall supply the several churches with the minutes of its annual session, which shall be directed to the clerks of the churches in care of the pastors.

SEC. 11. This Association shall withdraw from any church, minister or member who may violate its rules on the principle of morality and religion.

SEC. 12. No question is to be discussed until it is moved and seconded and distinctly stated by the moderator.

SEC 13. After a motion is fully before the meeting; the mover cannot withdraw it except by unanimous consent.

SEC. 14. A motion shall contain but one distinct proposition.

SEC 15. The minutes of each day's session of the Association shall he corrected (if need be) an (1 adopted.

SEC 16. This Association shall have the power to inquire into why each church is not represented.

SEC. 17. This Association shall have the power to adjourn to any future time or place most convenient to the churches.'

SEC 18. This constitution shall be subjected to change by a two-thirds vote of the Pastors, Messengers and Ordained Elders composing this body.

BY-LAWS

SECTION 1. The Association shall be opened and closed by prayer. Not more than one shall speak at a time, which shall rise from his seat and address the Moderator by the words, "Brother Moderator."

SEC. 2. The person thus speaking shall not be interrupted unless he is out of order; the person speaking shall adhere strictly to the subject and in no wise reflect on the person who spoke before him, but fairly state the case so as to convey his ideals.

SEC. 3. No brother shall abruptly break off or absent himself without obtaining liberty from the Association and Moderator.

SEC. 4. No person shall speak more than twice on the same subject without obtaining liberty from the Moderator.

SEC. 5. No person shall be at liberty to whisper during the time that a brother is speaking; the Moderator shall not interrupt any member or prohibit his speaking, unless he gives advice on the subject, or unless he violates the rules of the Association.

SEC. 7. The Moderator may be entitled to give his advice on any subject before putting the vote, but is entitled to vote only in case of tie.

SEC. 8. Any member who knowingly breaks any of the above rules shall be reproved by the Association.

SEC. 9. When any member or church is recognized, the same shall be manifested by the moderator, extending the right hand of fellowship.

ORDER OF BUSINESS

1. Call to Order and remarks by the Moderator.
2. Address of welcome and response.
3. Invite visitors and members to seats. Introductory sermon.
4. Read Constitution and By-laws.
5. Enroll churches and delegates.

6. Report of churches failing to represent in last session. Appoint committees.
7. Report of President of Roanoke Institute.
8. Report of Treasurer.
9. Trustees of Institute Report.
10. Reports of various committees.
11. Miscellaneous business.

The Roanoke Missionary Baptist Association demonstrated self government and self rule among its community of churches from its inception by its Constitution, the By-Laws, the Order of Business and the Educational Resolutions. The Association also possessed the faculty of self-criticism and the ability to enforce discipline. The Founding Fathers of the Roanoke Missionary Baptist Association established Elder B. J. Lomax as State Missionary[36] and immediately formed an education Committee almost from the inception of the Association. The following resolutions wonderfully address the importance placed upon educating the populace of the Roanoke Missionary Baptist Association, and its serving communities.

1875 Resolution

We, your committee, beg leave to report that we have taken the subject of Education under consideration, and are glade to learn that the people are becoming more deeply interested in the important work. We deem it necessary to submit the following preamble and resolutions" WHEREAS, Education is the only lever by which any race or people can be raised to a high standard of citizenship civilization; and whereas, we greatly need men who are intellectually, morally, and religiously qualified to carry the gospel into the remote and destitute portions of the State; and whereas, this is the progressive age, and demands a higher standard of education: therefore be it **Resolved,** 1. That we, the ministers and delegates of the Convention, do all in our power to interest the masses in common school education. 2) That we discountenance all designing men who strive to occupy stations of importance and instill their errors in the minds of the people. 3) That we disapprove of everything that tends to create schism in our ranks or churches. 4) That we recommend to all of our young men who feel that God has called them to His gospel ministry, to attend Shaw University until they are fully equipped for the important work; and we also recommend all, both male and female, who are desirous of obtaining a higher education, to attend said University, which affords superior facilities, and has, during the last three years, supplied the public schools with 240 teachers. 5) That we tender our hearty thanks to the American Baptist Home Mission Society, and all Northern friends for their sacrifices and liberal giving for the education of our people in the South. 6) That each minister be required to read these preambles and resolutions to his congregations and impress upon them the importance of carrying out the same. Respectfully: N. F. Roberts, A. A. Powell, and C. Johnson Committee.[37]

1877 Resolution

We, your Committee, to who was referred the subject of Education, beg to report the following as our deliberations: Education is the strength of the nation and the handmaid of religion; it is the civilizer of the world; the great lever by which men and women are raised form degradation and sin to respectability in society. There is no position in life but that we need an education.

Are we to engage in agriculture, we need an Education? Are we to be mechanics, then we should require an education; are we lawyers or doctors, and then we need the most profound education? We are living in an age when education is needed in all walks of life. There is no position in life that it is so much needed need as the Minister of the Gospel. Oh, to see a minister of the Gospel, who, by his intelligence to take hold of the mind of his congregation, and lifts them up from ignorance like the wheelman that turns the steamship at pleasure. But if he is ignorant, unlearned and illiterate then his congregation cannot advance. We are glad to see the improvement of our ministers within the past year, in their public preaching as well as their private examination, therefore, **Resolved** That we return to our different fields of labor with a greater determination to labor, educate and to lift up the whole people. In the language of the Prophet Isaiah, we will lift up a standard for the people." We, take pleasure in recommending to our people the Shaw Collegiate Institute at Raleigh, N. C. A. Powell, M. Conway, & H. White. Committee.

1880 Resolution

We, your committee have taken the subject of education into consideration and find that our people are becoming more deeply interested in this important work. And whereas, education is the only power by which a race of people can rise to a higher plane of civilization and citizenship; **Resolved:** That we recommend to our people to secure educated ministers to fill our pulpits and competent teachers to train and instruct our young people. We believe that a minister of the gospel of Jesus Christ is or ought to be a successful educator, he being an educator, he being an educated man. These resolutions set forth the goals and the objectives of the Roanoke Missionary Baptist Association: the extension of the Gospel to their recently emancipated brethren, and the establishment and the fostering of an institution for Christian training of youth and adults.[38] Two years later, in 1869 the association had sufficiently increased in size to become a convention, and became known as the General State Convention. "Therefore, we rejoice to see the rapid advancement of our churches towards an educated, pious ministry. As our sole object is the diffusion of the Gospel of Light, we cannot be too careful of the intellectual and spiritual qualifications of our minister. Our people are becoming more intelligent, and therefore more critical. Witness the secular and theological institutions springing up throughout our beloved land. We are glad to record that the Baptist is not behind in this noble cause. This Convention has ever manifested a more earnest desire to build up denominational schools. We are proud of our Baptist Schools in Richmond, Va., Atlanta, Ga., Columbia, S. C., Selma, Ala., and Raleigh, N. C. Let us improve the present and see that our institutions of learning are fully equal to the great and growing demands made upon them. A denominational school gives strength to the denomination that supports it, supplies its ministers and professional men. Your committee would urge upon our denomination the importance of sustaining Shaw University, at Raleigh. N. C. We are grateful to God for what it has done in the past, and willing to trust it in the future, and recommend it to others. We further recommend to this Convention the necessity and duty of selecting and educating some young man for the ministry at Shaw University as soon as practicable. And thereby evince its appreciation of the noble work 'done by said University in training all young' men for the ministry. Respectfully submitted, G. W. Perry, G. W. Holland, and Wm. A. Green. Committee[39]

During the Twentieth Annual Session of the Roanoke Missionary Baptist Association Mr. J. W. Pope made the following educational resolution to the Roanoke Association: "That the Roanoke Association recommends the Plymouth State Normal School to all the teachers within her bounds."[40] The following Association year, The Committee on Education expanded the resolution to the 1885 assemblage of the Roanoke Missionary Baptist Association to include: "That the churches of this Association do recommend the following named Institutions of learning for the Christian education of the young people of the east, and use their influence in encouraging them to attend the same, viz: Shaw University; the Plymouth State and Normal School, and the Colored Academy, of Elizabeth City.[41] The motion passed. It was further recommended and passed that the Association churches and schools use lessons of the American Baptist Publication Society, our denominational organ.[42]

North Carolinians from the tobacco fields, the rice swamps, the cotton and sugar plantations and the pecan groves in northeastern North Carolina, for almost a century, sent up one long agonizing cry for help. They stood on their tip toes to catch the northern breeze of the first sound of hope, and they awaited its arrival with eyes and ears and souls expectant. While waiting Negroes heard a voice on every wave, a sound on every sea! The watch-word of the brave, the anthem of the free from Negro ministers like Reverend Lemuel Washington Boon who was better trained than their white counterparts. In places such as Hertford County, North Carolina and regions reaching to the mountains of Ashville, North Carolina, exhorters got the Spirit and preached the Word with exactness and precision. Reverend Lemuel Washington Boon was literate and this might indicate why he was the first temporary President of the Negro Baptist in the State and then is elected as the Recording Secretary and because of his ability to read and write, as well as his oratorical and leadership qualities the Chowan Association (white) approved the appointment of Lemuel Washington Boon, colored, as an evangelist in 1866.[43] Few preached without any training or guidance. Ex-slaves recall with pride particular accomplished preachers. Elizabeth Ross Hite remembers a local preacher in Louisiana who spoke five languages. Andrew Goodman, an ex slave from neighboring Virginia, recalled a preacher named Kenneth Lyons as a man of "good learnin" and the best preacher I ever heard. Feribe Rogers, an ex-slave spoke of a literate preacher who presided at weddings and taught others to read. W. L. Best, an ex-slave in our State of North Carolina, recalled a terrible smart young preacher who paid special attention to the plantation children. Throughout the South, North Carolina in particular, so many whites as well as African America commented on the literary and the sophistication of the African American preacher that we are left to wonder if these did not constitute a majority. [44]

Du Boise refers to this community of preachers (priest) in the shared community as the only "Intact" African institution to survive in America. ". . . The chief remaining institution was the priest or medicine man. He early appeared as the healer of the sick, the interpreter of the Unknown, the comforter of the sorrowing, the supernatural avenger of wrong, and the one who rudely but picturesquely expressed the longing, disappointment, and the resentment of a stolen and oppressed people. Thus, as bard, physician, judge, and priest, within the narrow limits allowed by the slave-system, raised this Negro Preacher." [45]

The actions that Lemuel Washington Boon and the other Founding Fathers (priest) of unquestionable abilities performed as they worked within the community context of the Roanoke Missionary Baptist Association has been defined by James H. Cone as Black Liberating Theology. "From his ordination till his death, no person in Eastern North Carolina exerted a wide and more lasting influence among his people than did Elder Boon." [46] Boon was recognized by Carter G. Woodson in his book, *The History of the Negro Church,* as a preacher of power.[47] Rev. Charles B. Williams, historian of the Baptist State Convention (white) writes of Negro Baptist minister pioneers: "These men appointed themselves to do missionary work throughout the State, and their work will never be fully known. Crude log churches, and not infrequently bush arbors, were tabernacles where they met and called people together to offer service to the Most High. These pioneers with the exception of Boon were unlettered men could scarcely read a single line intelligently, and were almost entirely dependent on the Holy Spirit for inspiration and mental illumination. And yet some of them were remarkable men. Those who had the good fortune to hear L. W. Boon preach, both black and white, testify that he possessed a "got" of oratory and mental ability seldom excelled by men of the best opportunity."[48] [49] Thus, they meet Cone's working definition of Black Theology that best describes the greater context of the Roanoke Missionary Baptist Association. "Black Theology is a theology of liberation. It seeks to plumb the black condition in light of God's revelation in Jesus Christ, so that the black community can see that the gospel is commensurate with the achievement of black humanity that emancipates black people from white racism, thus providing authentic freedom for both white and black people in that it says No to the encroachment of white oppression. The message of liberation is the revelation of God as revealed in the incarnation of Jesus Christ. Freedom is the gospel. Jesus is the liberator! "He hath sent me to preach the deliverance to the captives" (Luke 4:18). Thus the black patriarchs and we know this reality despite all attempts of he white church to obscure it and to utilize Christianity as a means of enslaving blacks. The demand that Christ the Liberator imposes on all men requires all blacks to affirm their full dignity as persons and all whites to surrender their presumptions of superiority and abuses of power." [50]

When considering the founding of the Haven Creek Missionary Baptist on Roanoke Island, North Carolina in 1865, the first thing that has to be kept in mind concerning the Haven Creek Missionary Baptist Church and thus the founding of the Roanoke Missionary Baptist Association in 1865 is that the Black church was the only institution which the Roanoke Missionary Baptist Association could call its own.

Sunshine In My Soul

There's sunshine in my soul today,
More glorious and bright
Than glows in any earthly skies,
For Jesus is my light.

There's sunshine in my soul today,
A carol to the king
And Jesus listening,
Can hear the songs I can not sing.

There's a springtime in my soul today,
For, when the Lord is near,
The dove of peace sings in my heart,
The flow'rs of grace appear.

There's gladness in my soul today,
And hope, and praise, and love,
For blessings which He gives me now,
For joys "laid up" above.

O there's sunshine, blessed sunshine
When the peaceful, happy moments roll;
When Jesus shows His smiling face,
There is sunshine in the soul.

O there's sunshine, blessed sunshine
When the peaceful, happy moments roll;
When Jesus shows His smiling face,
There is sunshine in the soul.

2

HAVEN CREEK MISSIONARY BAPTIST CHURCH

The Haven Creek Missionary Baptist Church founded on the Freedman Colony on Roanoke Island, North Carolina is the mother church of the Roanoke & West Missionary Baptist Association. Although, the Haven Creek Missionary Baptist Church is not the oldest church in the Roanoke Missionary Baptist Association, it holds the distinction of being the mother church because the Founding Father met at Haven Creek Missionary Baptist Church in 1865 to organize the Roanoke Missionary Baptist Association which occurred after numerous meeting in 1866.

The Freedman Colony on Roanoke Island was established following the 1862 capture of the Roanoke Island by the Union General Ambrose Burnside. The battle for Roanoke Island was important, historians say, because it gave federal troops control of North Carolina waterways.[51] Following the establishment of the colony, hundreds of freed blacks and runaway slaves began arriving on the island. Able-bodied men were offered rations and employment building a fort on the north end of the island. By late 1862, there were more than 1,000 Freedmen. By May 1863, the fort was completed, but the African American population was so large the military government ordered lands seized to construct homes for the new settlers. Later that year, freedmen were enlisted in the First and Second North Carolina Colored Regiments.[52]

The Haven Creek Missionary Baptist Church derives its name from the Roanoke Island Contraband and the Roanoke Freedmen sending word across the creek to the confederate held slaves that if they could come across the creek to Roanoke Island they would find a safe haven, thus the name "Haven Creek." The Haven Creek Baptist Church was organized in 1862 as soon as the slaves began having church services after their arrival on Roanoke Island. They held their services in the clearing in the woods. They made their benches and pulpit out of discarded quartermaster boxes near the site of Camp Foster on the north side of the island. Not much is known about this floorless and windowless one room building.[53] Another building was constructed in 1865 by Rev. Zion Hall Berry on the land of John B. Etheridge land on Burns Road. Unlike the previous building, this one room building had long windows and a wooden floor.[54] One year following the building of the church, the Roanoke Missionary Baptist Association was started at the Haven Creek Missionary Baptist Church. Arvilla Tillett Bowser states in her book *Roanoke Island: the Forgotten Colony,* that the early records of Haven Creek Missionary Baptist Church shows that the church's interest in the Roanoke Missionary Baptist Association has been long with standing. It record:

1897   T. H. Mackey was sent to the Union Meeting.

1900   The church sent in money.

1904   The Pastor represented the church at the State Convention.

1904   W. B. Ashley was sent to the Association.

1905   W. B. Bowser was sent to the State Convention in Durham.

1905   B. Baum was elected to the Association Committee.

1906   William S. Bowser and M. H. Pugh were elected delegates for the Association. J. W. 1907 McPherson & H. Mann was sent as delegates to the Union meeting.

1908   G. H. Midgett, C. Harrison, Mary Collins, H. H. Mann and I. R. Hopkins were collectors for the Union meeting.

1909   Brother Edward Bowser and G. E. Spencer were delegates for the Union meeting to be held at the Haven Creek Baptist Church.

1912   Brother John McPherson was appointed delegate to the Association.[55]

Since its inception in 1865 the Haven Creek Missionary Baptist Church has had the following 24 pastors and ministers: Zion Hall Berry, J. K. Lamb, J. A. Fleming, Ivy Boone Roach, George D. Griffin, Harry H. Norman, Benjamin D. Dance, Rubin R. Cartwright, Butler M. Mullen, Mr. Lamb, L. M. Lassiter, Samuel L. Lawrence, R. R. Cartwright, J. C. Owen, Raymond Griffin, B. C. Ellis, J. C. Simms, Horace Moore, Dallas T. Spruill, Rev. Burnan, Alfred Winslow, Lemuel Anderson, Calvin Whidbee, Lionel Griffin. Other ministers included: W. B. Ashby, W. H. Beasley, T. M. Collins, Daniel Hopkins, J. W. McPherson, Jonas Midgett, Calvin Moore, J. S. Westcott, C. W. Wise.

The funeral of Tony Ferrow, the oldest colored man on Roanoke Island, age 98 was preached on Sunday, July 18, 1898 at Haven Creek Baptist Church by Rev. H. H. Norman, of Elizabeth City.[56] On September 19, 1926 Rev. John W. McPherson preached a powerful sermon at the morning worship service. This sermon marked the beginning of the Fall Revival. He was assisted by Rev. George A. Wise until the pastor; Rev. S. L. Lawrence arrived on Tuesday night. He was accompanied by Rev. W. H. A. Stallings who rendered faithful service and preached wonderful sermons during the day time. The twelve candidates were baptized on Sunday, September 26, 1926 by the pastor in Croatan Sound near Burnside Beach.[57]

Rev. R. R. Cartwright, pastor of Haven Creek Baptist Church held a series of meetings in late November 1931 with Rev. H. H. Norman as speaker. On the fourth Sunday Rev. R. R. Cartwright preached the morning and night sermons. Collections for the day totaled $138.70. The Eighty-First Anniversary of the historic Haven Creek Missionary Baptist Church, and the first of the Rev. G. Raymond Griffin, pastor, was celebrated at the Roanoke High School of Manteo, Roanoke Island, North Carolina on November 3rd-10th, 1946. Special programs and sermons by neighboring pastors highlighted the pre-anniversary service. Rev. Joseph White of Free Grace Disciple Church delivered the message at the opening service. Music was provided by the choir of the church. The Sunday School and B. Y. P. U. had charged of the service on Monday night. They conducted a Community Night program with Marshall Collins, the Sunday School Superintendent, and Emma Mann, the president of the B.Y. P. U. conducting worship. Rev. James Gaskins of Elizabeth City, North Carolina preached the sermon. On Tuesday night the Sick Aid Committee under the direction of Haywood Wise, president and Rev. T. B. Hoyle, pastor of Weeping Mary Disciples Church, Silgo and Macedonia Disciple Church with the Popular Branch Baptist Church providing the music. The Pulpit Aid Club, Agatha Grey, president, sponsored the meeting Wednesday night. The Rev. O. L. Sherrill, Dean of Theology at the Roanoke Institute for Ministers delivered the sermon and the music was by the Haven Creek Church Choir. Thursday night was the Floral Club Night, headed by Emma Mann, president. Rev. B. C. Ellis was guest speaker. His choir of Corinth Baptist Church, Jarvisburg, and other members participated. Friday Night was the Dollar-A-Month Club's night. Alphonso Scarborough, president. The Rev. Waitman Jasper Moore, pastor of Mount Carmel Baptist Church, Newland, delivered the message. The Haven Creek Baptist Church Choir furnished the music. On Sunday, November 10th 1946 at 3: 30 P. M. the anniversary message was delivered by the Rev. A. W. Lamb, pastor of Pleasant Branch Church. The services were brought to a close by the Rev. Elijah Harrison Griffin, an uncle of the pastor, who attended with his choirs of St. Paul Missionary Baptist Church, Sunbury and congregation from the Blanchard Grove of Hobbsville, North Carolina. The total amount raised during the week was $455.81. During the year over $3,000 was raised by the membership of the church.

The Journal and Guide published the obituary of Rev. Ashby in its June 25, 1955, page B3: *"Rev. W. H. Ashbee, Pioneer Minister, Dies At Suffolk."* Reverend W. H. Ashby, the son of Jacob and Susan Ashby, a well known former pastor of Virginia Baptist congregations, namely: Palm Tree Baptist Church, and Pleasant Grove Baptist Church both in Nansemond County; First Baptist Saratoga Place and Saint Paul Baptist Church, Suffolk, Virginia for 27 years. He was the former president of the Suffolk Ministerial Alliance for 27 years; and former Moderator of the Sharon Baptist Association Church Union. He was eulogized on Saturday, June 11, 1955 at St. Paul. Rev. W. H. came to Suffolk in 1913 from the Haven Creek Missionary Baptist Church, Manteo, North Carolina were he had previously served as the superintendent of the Sunday school. After serving on the deacon board, he was called into the ministry at age 25.

Rev. Ashby's floral tributes were carried by Mrs. Ocie Mitchell, Mrs. Alberta Scott, Mrs. Mary Crocker, Mrs. Rena Lankford, and Mrs. Lottie Taylor. Active Pall-bears were the Reverends John Dillard, A. Whitaker, and J. King. Elder E. D. Dillard and M. D. Mitchell. He was survived by his wife, Rev. Mrs. Julia T. Ashby; a foster daughter, Mrs. Hazel Harrison Waller, of Danville, VA, a step-son, James Thomas, of Portsmouth; stepdaughter, Mrs. Mable T. Williams, Baltimore, Maryland; foster son-in-law, Harvey Waller, Danville; step-daughter-in-law, sister & brother-in-Law, Sally & Joe Robert Hill, Sedley, Virginia. Interment took place in Oak Lawn Cemetery with the graveside ceremonies conducted by St. Esther's Pilgrim Lodge.

I Never Knew A Night So Black

I never knew a night so black,
Light failed to follow on its track.
I never knew a storm so grey it failed to have a clearing day.
I never knew such black despair that there was not a rift, somewhere.
I never knew an hour do drear,
Love could not fill it full of cheer.

John Kendrick Bangs

3

THE RULES

In 1866 many of the Roanoke Missionary Baptist Association Founding Fathers were under-educated, and undisciplined to the Eurocentric organized church. However, their superb mental acuity was sufficient to allow them to deal proficiently with a variety of problems associated with the growing pains of the Association. In 1868 they were compelled to revolt the preaching license of Miles Harvey, who was suspended "until he has retrieved his former character and reputation in the church."[58] He was the founder of the Harvey Chapel Baptist Church in the Newland Section of Pasquotank County, North Carolina. After his expulsion from the Association, the Harvey's Chapel Church changed its name to the Mount Carmel Missionary Baptist Church. The Association appointed a council to investigate the difficult existing between two churches at Windsor. They made the following report: Report of the council appointed to investigate the difficulty existing between the churches at Windsor. "We met in Windsor on the first Tuesday in September in 1878, called a committee, of six, consisting of three members from each church; and, after the examination, found the two churches in Gospel order, and willing to abide the decision of the council. The following rules were suggested by which they might be recognized by the Association:" 1). To recognized each other in brotherly and Christian love. 2). Should the members of one church trespass upon the rights of those of the other, they shall be regularly dealt with by their own church. 3). And should the pastors or deacons depart from the rules of Christian brotherhood, the same shall receive the disapproval of their respective churches. 4). These two churches shall not recognize longer than the above rules are adhered to, nor shall they be members of this Association by our recommendations.

Elder L. W. Boon and Elder Zion H. Berry[59]

The fact that the Roanoke Association intervened and settled various disputes, suspended several licentiates and excommunicated numerous members from 1868-1885 verifies the fact that the Association had developed sufficiently to be able to enforce discipline as required by the Constitution, the By-laws, and the Order of Business. Listed are a variety of instances. The report of the Committee on Grievances in regard to Pleasant Plains was agreed to by the Association and the letter was returned to its church. On motion of M. W. Wynn, St. Matthew's Church has a letter of dismissal. On motion of Elder J. K. Lamb, Elder Marshall Land was granted a letter of dismissal.[60] At the May 30, 1878 Thursday Morning Session, the Association and its council members, recommended to the churches composing this body, "that when they have members having the ability and fail or refuse to make good their obligations in defraying the expenses of their church, be dealt with for covetousness and expelled."[61]

Augustus Hays, the Committee on Grievances investigated the cases between Brother H. Bradams and Providence Church, Edenton, North Carolina and found that the case drew out in such a character between the said brother and Providence Church that do not become Christian, therefore, the board recommended to the Association to recommend to the said church to call a Council of disinterested brethren to settle the difficulty.[62] On motion of I. B. Roach the case of Joseph Godwin was suspended until further understanding.[63] On motion of Elder Henry H. Hays the action taken by Antioch Church with Solomon Webb stand approved.[64] The Grievance Committee convened in council, and investigated the case of Bethany Church against Wilson Mullen, and endorsed the course of Bethany Church in turning the brother out; and recommended the Association to let it stand.[65] This committee consisting of Elders I. B. Roach, G. W. Lee, H. Hays, J. K. Lamb, J. H. Fleming and Thaddeus Wilson, next took up the case of Elder Moses W. Wynn. They agreed and found that the course he took to secure ordination was an improper one; we approved of it, and recommend to the churches composing this Association not to recognize him as an ordained minister of the Gospel.[66] Z. H. Berry motioned that the petition of Jerusalem Church, in regards to Kader Boon, be not granted, and that the names of Miles Rogers and Frank Smallwood be dropped from the list of Licentiates,[67] and on motion of W. M. Wynn, St. Matthew's Church at Windsor were dismissed from the Roanoke Missionary Baptist Association.[68]

The ministers of the Roanoke Association assembled in council at Zion Hill Church on May 22d, 1884. Elder H. Hays was elected Chairman, and Elder Luke Pierce Secretary. The Chairman announced the Council for business. On motion of Elder J. K. Lamb, the case of Elder J. W. Godwin was taken up for consideration. The Chair ruled that Elder Godwin absent himself from the Council. On motion of Elder Wm. Reid, ordered that the evidence in the case be presented. The evidence was presented and received, and that decision of the Council stands approved by striking out the limit of six months, which leaves Elder Godwin's credentials revoked. On motion of Elder Wm. Reid, the name of J. W. Godwin was ordered to be erased from the list of Roanoke Missionary Baptist Association Roster of Elders and Ministers. On motion, the case of Elder Solomon Webb is taken up. On motion of Elder G. W. Lee, the witness in the case of said Webb was ordered sent for. On motion, the name of Levi Postle was ordered to be erased from the minutes. On motion, the decision of the Church and Council at Elizabeth City stands approved. On motion, the Council decided to vacate the house and convene at some other convenient place. On motion, the Antioch Church was urged to call Bro. Solomon Webb to account for his conduct as a minister. All of which was submitted. H. H. Hayes, Chm'n.[69] On motion, the case of Elder I. B. Roach went into the hands of the Grievance Committee.[70] On motion, the case between Middle Swamp Church and Joppa Church was tabled.[71] On motion, letters of dismissal was granted to thirty-churches of this Association.[72]

On motion of T. M. Collins, the Clerk was empowered to grant a letter of dismissal to any church petitioning in Gospel Order,[73] and on motion the J. W. Godwin and Solomon Webb was declared to be no longer minister's of the Gospel of our Blessed Lord.[74] At the Wednesday morning, May 12, 1903 Roanoke Missionary Baptist Association Annual Session, the roll of ministers was called after the Moderator had announced that the names of those who do not pay their assessment will be dropped from the roll, which met the hearty approval of the house.[75] Moderator G. D. Griffin informed the 1910 Annual Session that Ministerial Misconduct existed among their ranks. Moderator Griffin stated that there was a growing complaint on the part of the lay men that the preachers are not truthful and reliable; and too often some of us verify the truth of the assertion. The preacher of the Gospel, above all men, should be eminently honest and straightforward in his dealings. He should be prompt in the fulfillment of his obligation of whatever nature. He should say what he means and do what he says. The good book says: "the preacher must be blameless-irreproachable. Moreover, he must have a good report of them which are without." As preachers, we are the recognized leaders of the people, so we should set examples worthy of their emulations. We want to keep a constant watch over our character, and see to it that it is kept clean and spotless. Dodging around in the dark and questionable places, living careless and immoral lives, etc., may do for the world, but not for the minister of Jesus Christ. Do not misunderstand me to allege any accusation against you, no, but simply to call your attention to these things by way of admonition.[76] On the Wednesday, May 20, 1925, Afternoon Session of the Association, on motion the Minister's Conference voted to withdraw the right hand of fellowship from Rev. Z. W. White for conduct unbecoming a minister, namely drunkenness.[77] Rev. R. A. Morrissey's name was dropped from the roll of ministers, he having left the denomination. Motion sustained. Motion was made and passed to strike from the roll of ministers and from the Associations the name of Samuel Price, he having joined another denomination. Rev. R. A. Morrissey was the pastor of New Chapel Missionary Baptist Church, Plymouth, North Carolina during the Forty-Ninth Session {1915} of the Roanoke Missionary Baptist Association.[78]

Higher Ground

I'm pressing on the upward way,
New heights I'm gaining ev'ry day;
Still praying as I onward bound,
"Lord, plant my feet on higher ground."

My haer has no desire to stay,
Where doubts arise and fears dismay;
Tho' some may dwell where these abound,
My pray'r, my aim is higher ground.

I want to live above this world,
Tho' Satan's darts at me are hurl'd;
For faith has caught the joyful sound,
The songs of saints on higher ground.

I want to scale the up most height,
And catch a gleam of glory bright;
But still I pray till heav'n I've found,
"Lord plant my feet on higher ground"

Lord Lift me up and let me stand,
By faith on heaven's table land;
A higher plan than I have found,
Lord, plant my feet on higher ground.

4

THE RIGHT HAND OF FELLOWSHIP

The Roanoke Missionary Baptist Association was a very thoughtful and welcoming organization to churches, pastors, ministers, and others. Rev. Lemuel Washington Boon made the following thoughtful resolution to the Roanoke Missionary Baptist Association during its Thursday Afternoon, May 30, 1878 session: *Resolved 1st.* That a vote of thanks is due and are hereby tendered to the white brethren and friends in this vicinity for assisting nobly in this association.[79] This spirit is reflected again by a motion on Thursday Afternoon, May 20th 1886 by J. D. Jones that the ministers and delegates of this Association are recommended upon returning home to take up a special collection for the benefit of Haven's Creek Church and forward the same to J. A. Fleming, Elizabeth City, N. C.[80] The Committee on Petitions read their report, which was adopted. It here follows: We, your Committee on petitions beg to report the following: "We have carefully considered the following petitions, viz: Center Hill Church (destroyed by fire), Rev. Harry Woodley (aged), John McPherson (aged), Sister Charity Gordon, (widow), and Rev. I. B. Roach, (aged). We recommend in the spirit of fellowship and love that an offering be taken for them at some convenient time."[81] This thoughtful and welcoming spirit is further seen in the 1878 Committee on Application of New Churches report: "Your committee to who was referred the 1878 petition of New Churches, beg leave to submit the following as their report: We recommend the reception of the churches at St. Matthews, Conoconary, and Zion Tabernacle's."[82] Additionally, the report on the committee on Chapel Hill and Pollock's Ferry, were received and the delegates invited to a seat.[83] This welcoming spirit was very pervasive throughout the length and breadth of the Roanoke Missionary Baptist Association. On motion, the report of the church at River Neck Salem was read and inserted into the minutes. On motion Elder Luke Pierce, the delegates from the newly constituted churches were invited to come forward and present their petitions.[84] On motion of Elder Luke Pierce, the delegation from the newly constituted churches was presented the Right Hand of Fellowship by the Association. [85]

On Wednesday, May 28, 1879, on the motion of Rev. G. A. Mebane the new church at St. John was presented the Right Hand of Fellowship. On Wednesday, May 21, 1884, on motion, a committee of three was appointed on Newly Constituted Churches, consisting of Elder A. Cowper, Benjamin Clark and William Reid.[86] The committee's report was received and the committee discharged. At the Thursday Afternoon Session, May 29th, 1879 on Motion of Elder J. H. Flemings, the report on Piney Grove and Oak Grove were read and adopted.[87] At the next annual session in 1885, the committee on Newly Constituted Churches reported that they found one church, according to their judgment, in gospel order, namely: Whites Branch, in Gates County, North Carolina, pastured by Brother A. Saunders, Jr.[88]

Rev. J. A. Faulk, speaking for the Committee on New Churches reported that the committee examined one new church and found her in gospel order. The committee recommended her to the Association for membership, viz: Bell Street Baptist, Elizabeth City, North Carolina.[89] By the motion of L. C. Newby at the Thursday Morning, May 20[th.] 1886 session the Woman's Home Mission Society of Elizabeth City was connected with the Association by paying the sum of one dollar.[90] The 1907 Committee of New Churches submitted the following report: We have examined one new church, Blanchard's Grove and found her in Gospel Order, and we, therefore, recommend her for membership. The Right Hand of Fellowship was given her.[91] The committee on New Churches reported and presented to the Association New Zion Baptist Church. She was received and given the Right Hand of Fellowship.[92] The Committee on New Churches reported one new church, Harrell's Grove, Suffolk, Virginia. The report was adopted. The 1912 Committee of New Churches found that Calvary Baptist Church of Elizabeth City, N. C., properly organized and duly recognized and in Gospel order, desiring to be united with us.[93]

The Committee on New Churches reported to the 1922 Association that "they had investigated the matter and found that the Saint Luke Baptist Church, South Norfolk, VA., is in Gospel Order, and desiring to become a member of this Association, we recommend her." J. F. Bryant of Number 7 Williams Street, Elizabeth City, Pastor.[94] The Right-Hand of Fellowship extended. The New Light Baptist Church of Grasfield, {Hickory} VA was organized properly and in accordance with the regular Baptist usage. She paid the membership fee of three dollars to this Association and received the Right Hand of Fellowship.[95] On Thursday Morning, May 24, 1923, two new church were reported to the Roanoke Missionary Baptist Association as having been organized according to Baptist standards and applied for membership, and the Right Hand of Fellowship. Those churches are Cornerstone, Greenville, N. C., Rev. W. H. Bryant, Pastor, E. R. Revier, Clerk, Greenville, N. C., and Bethlehem Missionary Baptist Church, Berkley, Virginia, A. M. Johnson, Pastor; J. Arterbridge, Clerk. These churches paid $3.00 each, joining fee.

The Committee on Ministerial Credentials reported that they had examined the credentials of B. D. Harrell, Miles Waugh, E. D. Nowell and William Reid, and the Right Hand of Fellowship was extended to those examined.[96] The names of E. G. Armistead, J. T. Doles, W. D. Johnson, R. W. Norman, Isaiah Williams, M. T. Riddick, S. A. Askew, W. E. Smith, J. W. Yeats, W. H. Bryant, F. M. Jones, Luke Pierce, H. H. White were added. The following named licentiates were also examined and found in gospel order to receive the Right Hand of Fellowship as ministers: M. Briggs, L. J. Staten, A. T. Wilson, A. T. Wilson, Butler M. Mullins, S. L. Newby, A. R. Valentine, H. A. W. Valentine, G. T. Skinner, W. H. Freeman, Julius Johnson, J. T. Jones, and Isaiah Brinkley.[97] Additionally, the Committee on Credentials stated that they had examined the following brethren and found them worthy to become members of the Association, as ordained ministers, VIZ: N. Sledge, W. H. Baker, J. J. McCleese, C. S. Jones and J. J. Tillett. The report was adopted and the Right Hand of Fellowship extended to them.[98] The Committee on Credentials submitted their reported to the Forty-Fourth {1909} Annual Session of the Roanoke Missionary Baptist Association that they had examined the credentials of the following named brethren and found them to be in Gospel order, viz-Rev. John M. Jones, Elizabeth City, Rev. J. J. Bing, Eure, N. C., Rev. Thomas A. Eure, Buell, Virginia, and Rev. James E. Felton, Winfall.[99] The Right Hand of Fellowship was extended to the brethren.[100] The Committee on Credentials reported on Thursday Afternoon, May 20, 1915 that Rev. R. L. Holly had been ordained to the Gospel Ministry and theRight Hand of Fellowship was given him.[101] The Committee on Credentials report was received and adopted; and the Right Hand of Fellowship was given to Rev. S. L. Lawrence of Route 1., Edenton, N. C., Rev. G. W. House, Elizabeth City, N. C., and Rev. J. J. Parker, Tyner, N. C.[102] The Moderator gave the Right-Hand-of-Fellowship to the following brethren: A. H. Robinson, A. W. Holfer, C. E. Skinner, D. C. Cobb, H. M. Bixby, D. E. Mullen and I. W. Penn.[103] The following ordained ministers paid the required 50 cents and joined the Roanoke Association on Tuesday Morning, May 22, 1923. D. W. Reid, Newbern, N. C; J. R. R. McRay, Elizabeth City, N.C., John Forbes, Elizabeth City, N. C., E. M. Lewis, Franklin, VA., Zion H. Lewis, (no city and state provided), W. S. Creecy (Old Member), Rich Square, N. C., S. A. Askew, Tyner, N. C., G. T. Hassell, Hertford, N. C., M. H. Beasley, Route 3, Box 18, Elizabeth City, N. C., J. W. Moore, Route 3, Hertford, N. C., and A. C. Tillery, 350 E. Bute St, Norfolk, VA. Rev. Tillery was the newly elected pastor of Gale Street Missionary Baptist Church, Edenton, North Carolina. The following licensed ministers joined the Roanoke Association on Tuesday, Morning, May 22nd, 1923: Richard Arrington Route 3, Box 85, Berkley, V. A., W. J. Elliott, Shiloh, N. C., W. R. Freeman 39 St. James Street, Berkley, VA, A. W. Holfer, Hertford, N. C., C. M. Jones, Columbia, N. C., C. H. Lamb, Route 3 Box 98 "(City & State Not Provided) The Committee on Credentials reported and the report was adopted and the Right Hand of Fellowship was extended to the following ministers during the Thursday Afternoon, May 22nd, 1918 Session of the Roanoke Missionary Baptist Association: Rev. G. W. House, Elizabeth City, N. C., Rev. S. L. Lawrence, Edenton, N. C., Rev. J. J. Parker, Tyner, N. C. The Credentials Committee reported to the Roanoke Missionary Baptist Association Annual Session on Thursday morning, May 20th, 1926 that they had examined the credentials of the following brethren and find them to be regular: G. C. Owens, Columbia, N. C.; E. H. Griffin, Corapeake, N. C.; and W. H. Davis, Jamesville, N. C. On motion the report was adopted and the Right Hand of Fellowship was given by the Moderator.[104] Signed: H. H. Hayes, J. J. Walker, E. W. Parker, W. M. Eason and W. N. Douglas.[105] Rev. A. C. Tillery, pastor of Gale Street Baptist Church was introduced to the Association.[106] Rev. Zion H. Lewis joined the Asso'n, paid 50c and was given the Right Hand of Fellowship. Rev. C. S. Lewis joined the Association, paid the fee of $2.50 and was given the Right Hand of Fellowship.[107]

The Elizabeth City Office of the Journal and Guide published the particulars of the May 25, 1925 session of the Roanoke Missionary Baptist Association held at Union Chapel. Union Chapel Missionary Baptist Church, Weeksville, North Carolina welcomed the 1925 Annual Session of the Roanoke Missionary Baptist Association when it convened for its session on Tuesday, May 22nd, 1925. Reverend R. R. Cartwright, Belcross, moderator; Rev. C. S. Mitchell, Gates County, secretary. The session continued for three days. Reverends H. H. Norman, Z. B. Wynn, F. S. Evans, J. A. Nimmo, W. S. Sharp, J. J. Armstrong, J. W. Ward, G. C. Lassiter, H. W. Ruffin, T. S. Cooper, Professor C. F. Graves, Messrs. J. H. Perkins, J. J. Slaughter, S. W. Harris, D. W. White, and Rev. R. McRay attended the Association.

The Right-Hand Of-Fellowship extended to the Communion Service: Brethren, I fear that some of us are becoming too lost and careless regarding the Doctrine of the Lord's Supper and other distinctive doctrines of the church. We seem to be gradually drifting away from the old land mark, which restricts the Lord's supper at most, to all of the same faith and order, and inviting all who wish to partake of it, whether they believe as we do or not. In other words we are cultivating a tendency to disregard the long standing and much honored practice of what is known in the Baptist ranks as "close Communion," which was so strictly adhered to by our fathers, and are gradually throwing open our doors, and welcoming any and all denominations to that table which we believe Christ has restricted to Baptized believers whose profession of faith is creditable, and who are voluntarily associated under special covenant for the maintenance of the worship, the truths, the ordinances, and the discipline of the Gospel. We have no right to invite any guest to the Lord's Table, other than those he has authorized us to invite. No well informed person of any other denomination would feel himself slighted in the lease to be present at a Baptist Church during the time of Communion and not be invited to partake; he would rather be surprised to be invited, knowing the rules of the church to forbid it. Let us come back to the old Land mark, and sustain the principals and doctrines of our church.[108]

Jesus for Me

Jesus, my Savior, is all things to me;
Oh, what a wonderful Savior is He,
Guiding, protecting, o'er life's rolling sea,
Mighty Deliv 'rer Jesus for me.

Jesus in sickness and Jesus in health,
Jesus in poverty, comfort or wealth,
Sunshine or tempest, whatever it be,
He is my Savior, Jesus for me.

He is my Refuge, my Rock and my Tower,
He is my Fortress, my Strength and my power;
Life everlasting,
My Daysman is he,
Blessed Redeemer Jesus for me.

Jesus in sorrow, in joy or pain,
Jesus my Treasure in loss or in gain;
Constant Companion, where-ever I may be,
Living or dying, Jesus for me.

He is my Prophet, my priest and my King,
He is my bread of life,
Fountain and Spring,
Bright sun of Righteousness,
Daystar to me,
Horn of Salvation, Jesus for me.

Jesus for me, Jesus for me,
All the time, everywhere,
Jesus for me.
Jesus for me, Jesus for me,
All the time, everywhere,
Jesus for me.

5

THE DIVIDING LINE

The Roanoke Association was divided geographically into three associational groups in 1883. *The Banner-Enterprise Newspaper* reported this anticipated action in its Thursday, June 7, 1883 paper. The article reads: "The Roanoke Missionary Association convened in its Sixteenth Annual Session with the Union Chapel Missionary Baptist Church, on the 22nd of May 1883 and continued three days. There was an immense gathering of people every day.

This is the largest association in the State, there being nearly fourteen thousand communicants. It has several able divines. From present indications there will be a division of the association a year hence. The Board will convene in Edenton in October to consider the feasibility of a division and recommend its action to the next session. In the event of a division, the Chowan River will probably be the dividing line."109 These groupings would accommodate all of the rural church populations of Northeastern North Carolina. The Northeast Bound, comprising Dare, Pasquotank, Currituck and Camden Counties, The Middle Ground Union, comprising Chowan, Gates and Perquimans, and the Albemarle Union, comprising Tyrell, Washington and Beaufort met at one of the churches along the Sound.[110] "The Community of Churches" concept was an instant winner! It was just what the doctor had ordered. In response to its success, The Association took an excursion from Elizabeth City to historic Roanoke. The Wednesday, September 25, 1883 records the event this way, "Quite a number went down to historic Roanoke on the excursion last Friday."[111]

Three things happened during the Nineteenth Annual Session in 1884 that points to dissention, differences and contempt among the ranks within the dividing line. Firstly, the Association decided by motion during its Thursday Morning session to reject the report and disband the Permanent Organization Committee.[112] Although there is no discussion as to the nature of the rejection and the nature of the dismissal, it is painfully clear that the decision by a 2/3 majority to reject this committee was due in part to its grievous nature. Secondly, the Association decided to elect the Moderator by the house. The names of brothers: A. Franks, Elder C. E. Hodges and Elder Luke Pierce were put in nomination. On motion of Brother C. M. Billups, the nominations were closed and the balloting proceeded with. There was no election. Thirdly, on motion, a new committee of five was appointed on Permanent Organization, which reported as follows: For Moderator, Elder G. W. Lee; Vice-Moderator-Elder Luke Pierce; Recording Secretary-Asbury Reid; Assistant Secretary, Bro Eli Jones; Corresponding Secretary, Brother J. O. Holloman; Treasurer Brother Moses Hardy. The report by the committee chairman Bro. J. A. Faulk was adopted.[113] In all probability these three events were symptomatic of a far great problem which would reach its apex at the Twentieth (1885) Annual Session held with the Church of Christ at Providence, Edenton, Chowan County, N. C., the Tuesday after the Third Lord's Day in May, 1885. Six events at this session were noteworthy. Firstly, following the Moderators announcement that the house was ready for business, he proceeds to extend an invitation to visiting brethren. Among the visiting friends from other Associations from various parts of the State were: Rev. C. S. Brown, Rev. Caesar Johnson, Rev. S. G. Newsome and Rev. H. Clemons. Those from our sister association (Virginia) were Rev. H. L. Barco, Rev. J. W. Dungee and Rev. Joseph Gregory. Secondly, "owing to some misunderstanding on the part of the chair during the first day's sessions, it was harmoniously settled by the Moderator begging to be excused."[114] Thirdly, the following ordained elders refused to accept the positions where to they were elected: Elder Luke Pierce, Eli Jones, J. O. Holloman and Hardy Jones. There are no explanations provided in the annual minutes for the decisions. Consequently, Elder J. K. Lamb was selected Vice-Moderator; A. S. Dunstan, Assistant Secretary; E. W. Felton Corresponding Secretary; and A. G. Reid, Treasurer. Fourthly, a committee of sixteen was appointed on Permanent organization, Viz: I. Bond, Augustus Reid, A. Cobb, S. P. Knight, L. L. Elliott, E. E. Randall, W. Arterbridge, C. B. Bonnett, D. C. Ricks, I. Tillett, B. J. Bowser, B. J. Hockard, Thomas Brickus, D. Harris, J. Close, and E. C. Wilson. Fifthly, during the afternoon session, the Committee on Permanent Organization with its sixteen members was reduced to a committee on nine, viz: S. P. Knight, I. Bond, Thomas Brickus, J. Close, W. Arterbridge, W. A. Cobb, L. L. Elliott, B. J. Bowser and D. Harris. Sixthly, however, without any explanation included in the minutes, this new Committee was rejected by the Association, and its report tabled, and subsequently lost. Sixth, on motion, Rev. C. S. Brown, the over plus fund of the Association was equally divided between the following schools: The one at Plymouth, the one to be established at Winton, and the one to be at Windsor.

When this session ended the Ex-Treasurer Moses Hardy was allowed five dollars, the widows, L. W. Boon and Lennie Wilson were given fifteen dollars, Mrs. Boon received 10 dollars and the widow Wilson received $5 dollars. The Committee on the Spread of the Gospel recommended that four annual sermons be preached rather than the two usual sermons. The first sermon, a Doctrinal Sermon to be preached by Rev. G. W. Lee, Missionary Sermon to be preached by Rev. J. K. Lamb, the Temperance Sermon to be preached by Rev. J. Fleming and the Sermon on Education to be preached by Rev. Charles Hodges. On motion of Rev. J. A. Faulk, the rules of the Association already adopted were sustained; the association endorsed the work of the Ministerial Council held in Greensboro, N. C., in April, on the 9th, 10th and 11th, 1885. The Council disapproved the actions of any church which receives a member who has been excommunicated from another church. Separately, it is unsubstantial if either of these incidents independently of the other eight would have been sufficient to cause a breakup of the Association. However, it is clear that any combination of any two or more of these incidents lead to, or brought about the dismissal of thirty-eight churches from the Roanoke Missionary Baptist Association.

When the association convened at Antioch Church, in Camden County, North Carolina in 1886 the Roanoke Missionary Baptist Association could no longer boast of having three-thousand five hundred people in regular attendance,[115] and many of its most stalwart members were absent, and their voices silent within the hollowed and sacred walls of the Antioch Church. Among them were: Rev. Lemuel Washington Boon and son, Rev. Clinton Boon, W. D. Cherry, W. A. Cobb and First Baptist Powellsville, Mount Sinai, Woodland Plains and Zoar, Moses Hardy, James Jenkins, J. B. Lenox, Andrew Parker, Luke Pierce at Mount Pleasant, Olive Branch, Sandy Branch, and Sandy Point, Asbury Reid, William Reid, Thomas Sharp at Bethany Baptist, D. L. Simmons, Claiborne Speller, Robert Valentine, M. W. Wynn. The Reverends C. M. Cartwright at First Baptist Severn, H. H. Norman at Second Baptist Colerain, M. W. D. Norman at Zion Hill, maintained their pastorate within the Roanoke Missionary Baptist Association, although their churches were members of the splinter group. J. B. Catus, formerly the clerk in the Roanoke Missionary Baptist Association, assumed the position of Recording Secretary in the West Roanoke Association. This appointment was followed by his Thursday Morning, October 10, 1888 appointment as one of nine people appointed to investigate the condition of Winton Academy and Richard Rankin's Institute, viz; W. H. Smith, J. O. Holloman, J. W. Ricks, Rev. H. Clements, Madison Brewer, W. H. Leath, Rev. W. H. Morris and L. D. Holly.[116] Consequently, when the association convened at Antioch Church, in Camden County, North Carolina and the splinter group known as the Western North Carolina Association concurrently convened at Zion's Grove Missionary Baptist Church, Colerain, North Carolina, Rev. J. A. Faulk and Rev. J. K. Lamb were appointed Messengers from the Roanoke Baptist Association to meet the Western N.C. Association next session. While the Association was convening, the following message arrived to the Roanoke Missionary Baptist Association from the Western North Carolina Baptist Association and its president, Rev. William Reid. The communication read in part: "WHEREAS, a strenuous effort has been made by our Brethren on the Westside of the Chowan to erect a school of respectable grade at Winton for the purpose of affording convenient accommodations to the youth among us to obtain an education, and whereas, they have so nobly succeeded in the erection of suitable building and propose to open school on the first Monday, and continue seven months therefore, BE IT RESOLVED: that, recognizing the importance of such school, we hearty endorse the enterprise and commend it to the patronage and sympathy of the lovers of humanity; and we will use our influence to make it a success and blessing to our race; and that, when the principal, Rev. C. S. Brown, or any agent of the School, desires to visit our community or churches in its interest, we will most heartily and gladly welcome him; and be it further RESOLVED, That we grant the Trustees of said Winton Academy, permission to print in our Minutes and advertisement of the school."

The division of the Western North Carolina Association from the Roanoke Missionary Baptist Association awakened new life in the ministry of the Roanoke Association to the extent that it developed an interest for a new State Convention in Northeastern North Carolina. A convention that would be more aligned with the wishes of the Roanoke Missionary Baptist Association. This new life and this new line of thought almost caused a fourth breakup of the Roanoke Missionary Baptist Association. During the 1903 Association, Rev. Ivy Boone Roach stated in his Moderator address that he was calling for a Ministerial Council on Wednesday night April 8, 1903, for the purpose of investigating some important matters in our work; I hope the same will be adopted by the Association. Brethren, seeing the great need of a Baptist State Convention being organized, we therefore ask that we set aside Wednesday, night for that purpose of organizing the same, which will better prepare us for officiating with the Convention which will meet in Philadelphia, September, 1903. By motion the address was referred to the Committee on Moderators address.[117] During the afternoon session, the Committee on the Moderator's Address reported favorably and a motion to adopt and spread the minutes was entertained, but Rev. C. S. Brown interposed an objection to that part of the address referring to the organization of a State Convention. Replies were made by Rev. G. W. Lee, D. D., of Washington, D. C., and by Rev. E. W. D. Isaac, D. D., of Nashville, Tenn. Rev. S. N. Vass, D. D., also made objection along the same line as Dr. Brown. Rev. Pegus, Ph. D., of Shaw University, spoke to discouraging the organizing of the Convention. Rev. M. W. D. Norman, D. D., Portsmouth, Virginia, thought that if the old convention would make satisfactory concessions it would be best not to organize. Mrs. Mebane was fervent and demanded that immediate action be taken. Rev. Dr. Isaac made a powerful and telling speech, afterwards the vote was taken. Carried in the affirmative.[118]

Truth, crushed to earth, shall rise again!
The eternal years of God are hers;
But Error wounded,
Writhes in pain,
And dies among his worshipers.

6

THE ROANOKE PREACHERS

The Roanoke Missionary Baptist Association ministers were second to none of the other ministers in the Baptist Convention of North Carolina. This was an unintended consequence of the geographical division, and the recovery from the splint in 1885. Attesting to this position are the frequent visits from some of the leading diviners in the State of North Carolina. At the 1912 association session, Moderator Griffin stated that he was honored with the presence of some men of distinction. He called the names of Rev. Dr. M. W. D. Norman, D. D., Pastor of Metropolitan Baptist Church Washington D. D., Rev. W. Bishop Johnson, D. D., L. L. D., Secretary and Treasurer Afro-American Correspondeua College, Washington, D. C., Rev. C. C. Somerville, D. D., editor of the *Vigil* and pastor of Ebenezer Baptist Church, Portsmouth, Virginia; Rev. C. S. Brown, A. M., D. D., pastor and President of Water's Normal Institute, Winton, North Carolina.; Rev. James A. White, pastor of Vermont Avenue Baptist Church, Washington, D. C.; and the Rev. A. B. Vincent, D. D., editor of the *Search Light*, Raleigh, North Carolina.[119] Rev. Vincent was later presented to the Association. He spoke in high praise of the men of the Association and then spoke briefly of the Search Light a magazine edited by him. They were made welcome.

The Roanoke Missionary Baptist Association pastors and ministers developed a strong forceful style of preaching, and teaching which assisted the Roanoke School in the constructing of stalwart churches. The geographical divisions and the Roanoke School soon awakened new life in the ministry throughout the State; many libraries were purchased, schools and institutes were better attended, even by the pastors; more attention was given to the preparation and delivery of sermons, and in many ways decided changes were realized as the direct result of these meetings held in the different and destitute sections of the State. Not only was there an awakening in the pulpit, but especially was it seen and felt in the pew; and as might be expected many changes were made in the pastorates throughout the State. Much of the sentimental and demonstrative worship gave way to intelligence and practical Christianity. As a natural consequence a change in the churches meant change in the associations and other religious organizations. At the end of the twelve years of cooperation in many respects the colored Baptists of North Carolina stood in the foremost ranks of Baptists, certainly in the management and deportment of their deliberative bodies. Such things as points of order and needless discussion, rows and confusions were things of the past said a gentleman visiting our State Convention, "When are you going to fuss?" The reply was, "We are not going to fuss." North Carolina Baptists had been taught that it was not dignified, it was not religious to "fuss," and this New Era Institute Training through which they had so recently passed had much to do with such a conclusion.

President O. S. Bullock's statement to the 1921 Baptist State Convention of North Carolina strongly supported this Herculean undertaking.

> "Understand me Brethren, I do not mean for our great denomination to slack its reins in Christian Education, but only to urge that we continue our effort so that we may be able to do more effective educational. I am praying and trusting that the men of this convention shall forget themselves and personal gains and plan for the best things our great and good people at home, if we do, unborn generations will rise up and call Shaw and its Feeder Schools blessed." When describing the advancement of Negro education, Rev. O. S. Bullock continued: "There has been an unusual awakening in the educational system of North Carolina, possibly more than any other state in the South. The long prayed for day had already dawned upon us, when the state is stepping in to do its part for Negro Education. We are continually praying that the day that has dawned will fully break. Yet as the state does this more efficient work, it shall be more encumbered upon Christian church to step in and do a certain class of educational work more effective than ever."[120]

These Feeder Schools were properly called secondary school of which the Roanoke School at Elizabeth City was one of several. President R. W. Underwood's presidential address at the Sixty-Second Annual Convention at First Baptist in Goldsboro, North Carolina clearly articulated that issue when he stated, "We note with pride a few Secondary schools at the following named places, viz: Thompson Institute {accredited}, Lumberton, North Carolina, Burgaw High School,{accredited} Burgaw N. C., Rich Square Academy {accredited}, Rich Square, N. C., Pee Dee Institute, Hamlet, N. C., Western Union Academy, Spindale, N. C.; Faison Normal and Industrial Institute, Faison, N. C., Higgs Roanoke Seminary, Parmele, N. C., Shiloh Institute, Norlina, N. C., and Roanoke Institute, Elizabeth City, N. C."[121] Rev. R. W. Underwood placed special emphasis on the fact that "the head of each of these institutions is a product of Shaw University, and they are looked upon as feeders to Shaw and the Baptist of the State and especially to their respective communities should their entire support in the preparation of the above named institutions"[122]

Na'Im Akbar states in the introduction of his book, *Breaking the Chains of Psychological Slavery* that it is absolutely important to remember; as the leaders of the North Carolina Convention of North Carolina did; the realities of slavery and to confront the impact of this historical trauma on our collective minds as African Americans. Item 4 of the 1875 Resolution stated: That we recommend to all of our young men who feel that God has called them to His gospel ministry, to attend Shaw University until they are fully equipped for the important work; and we also recommend all, both male and female, who are desirous of obtaining a higher education, to attend said University, which affords superior facilities, and has, during the last three years, supplied the public schools with 240 teachers. The 1877 *Resolved* "That we return to our different fields of labor with a greater determination to labor, educate and to lift up the whole people. In the language of the Prophet Isaiah, we will lift up a standard for the people." The 1880 Resolved: That we recommend to our people to secure educated ministers to fill our pulpits and competent teachers to train and instruct our young people. We believe that a minister of the gospel of Jesus Christ is or ought to be a successful educator, he being an educator, he being an educated man. James Cone and Gayraud S. Wilmore, agree with Na'Im Akbar, Cones says in his book, "Black Theology/A Documented History Volume one: 1966-19 79" that Black Theology is an affirmation of "Blackness" and, an affirmation of black humanity that emancipates black people from white racism, thus providing authentic freedom for both white and black people. It affirms the humanity of white people in that it says No to the encroachment of white oppression.

The June 1948 edition of the Baptist Informer characterized the effective work of the Roanoke Missionary Baptist Association this way: "Perhaps, of the 56 Associations in the State of North Carolina, Roanoke has the most challenging program and is as intensively organized." The article continues, "There are 75-80 churches. It operates a school—Roanoke Institute-for Ministers in service for seven months. It has a teacher on the level of Shaw University Extension Service, and the Roanoke Institute is the only school unit of Shaw doing Theological Training.[123]

The contemporary scholar Peter J. Paris has provided an illuminating analysis that is helpful for understanding the actions of the Roanoke Missionary Baptist Association and the theology of this period. He has argued that white theological ideals did a disservice to the black church, because these ideals did not parallel black church activities, especially in relation to racial justice. Consequently, the white Christians saw no contradictions between their theological thought and the ruthless treatment of blacks, because their theology was dynamic. On the other hand, Paris contends, blacks viewed this same theology as static and transcendent. Therefore, they have always seen a contradiction between white theological belief and practice. In this sense, white ecclesiastical theology was indigenous and met the particular needs and activities of the local white churches and the social status quo.[124] However, white theology was powerless to do for the Negro church the things that the Founding Fathers did for themselves.

The Church's One Foundation

The Church's one foundation is Jesus Christ Her Lord;
She is His new creation by water and the Word;
From heaven He came and sought her to be His holy bride;
With His own blood he brought her,
And for very own.

'Mid toil and tribulation and tumult and war,
She waits the consummation of peace forever more;
Till with the vision glorious her longing eyes are blest;
And the great Church victorious shall be the Church at rest.

Elect from every nation, yet one o'er all the earth,
Her charter of salvation one Lord, one faith, one birth;
One holy name she blesses,
Partakes one holy food
And to one hope she presses,
With every grace endued.

7

BIOGRAPHIES OF THE FOUNDERS

L. W. Boon

Reverend Lemuel Washington Boon was free-born about 1827 in Northampton County, North Carolina to Patsy Boone. Historical Records reveal that the name Boone was more commonly spelled Boon, without an 'e', (see the Dedication page of William A. Boon). The only known document known to exist with his signature appears to have been altered after he signed it with an 'e'. Beginning in 1867, the Meherrin Baptist Church Murfreesboro, North Carolina, clerk changed the spelling of Boon's name from Boon (no 'e') to Boone. Reverend Lemuel Washington Boon married the former Charlotte A. Chavis[125] born August 5, 1833, and to this union 13 children were born, two of whom, Reverend Dr. Clinton C. Boon and Rev. Philip L. Boon, would later distinguish themselves as ministers and leaders in their own rights. Boon was apprenticed as a brick mason and later employed, until the beginning of the Civil War, in that profession. He moved to Hertford County and operated a private school and engaged in teaching for a short time.[126] During the Civil War Boone moved to Pasquotank County, where he remained until its close. L. W. Boon was a member of the Trustee Board of the Shaw University, Raleigh, N. C. He is listed as such in its 1872-1873 General Catalogue of the Officers and Students of Shaw University. Boon returned to Gates County and finally returned to Hertford County where he purchased a farm and remained there until 1878.[127]

Boon was a self taught man! He used his education to the benefit of those under the sphere of his influence. Boon was literate and to the dismay of the detractors of freedom would write slave passes for those who wanted to leave a life of bondage and freedom. [128] No doubt, when Rev. Boon met on October 17, 1866 at Haven's Creek Baptist Church on Roanoke Island, North Carolina with Edwards Eagles, Joshua Flemings, H. Grimes, R. H. Harper, C. Johnson, Immanuel Reynolds, R. B. Spicer, and William Warrick and organized the East Roanoke Missionary Baptist Association [129] his literacy possibly led to Boon being asked to preside over the opening meeting, and his cousin Asbury Reid's appointment as the first secretary. These men set forth the goals and the objectives of the Association: the extension of the Gospel to their recently emancipated brethren, and the establishment and the fostering of an institution for Christian training of youth and adults.[130] Three years later, in 1869 the association had sufficiently increased in size to become a convention, and became known as the General State Convention.

This Baptist Association begun on Roanoke Island, North Carolina collectively decided to use "politics, pulpit and penitentiary, the three "P's" of the Freedman and their Bush Arbors churches as a guiding force for their work. The prime directive of this Roanoke endeavor was the education of the Negro Preacher. Most scholars are aware, as were the early founders of the Roanoke Missionary Baptist Association Ministers that in the beginning there were no thought by White Americans of educating the Negro, yet, the necessary to do so was always present. The Founding Fathers were also aware of the restrictions placed upon education during slavery which had only ended two years prior. Unlike many, Boon and these early founders did not think that these restrictions and prohibitions had ended with emancipation. Therefore, Boon and the Roanoke Missionary Baptist Association organized a *Committee on the Spread of the Gospel.* The 1878 report by Rev. Boon follows: "We, your committee on the Spread of the Gospel, beg leave to make the following report; We believe that the Gospel is God's good news to a dying world, and in every way suitable to man's lost condition, possessing in its pure and unmixed character a renewing influence which man cannot resist, Such being some of the merits of the Gospel of Christ, it should be handled by pure hearts and clean hands. Those having been called as vessels for the diffusion of the gospel should strive to cultivate themselves mentally, as well as morally, in order that they may explain the gospel in its purity and truth. Christ sent His Apostles two by two into every city where He would come. Therefore, we would advise school teachers who have in hand training of the child's mind to forget not the worth of daily prayer and moral teaching in their schools. Solomon says, "Train up a child in the way that he should go, and when he is old he will not depart from it." Knowing that it is hard to straighten a crooked tree when it is grown, and much more to train the mind of youth after it has been poisoned by evil influences at the fireside, we again urge the attention of teachers to this point, and ask them to aid in the diffusion of religious intelligence and truth. In this way the Gospel would spread like fire among dry stubbles, and God would add to our ranks daily. We call upon fathers, mothers, and the school committees everywhere, to do all in their power to employ only these who are morally qualified to take charge of the education of their children. Oh! May heaven's smile rest upon all who may read this, and may they all say we will do all in out power to aid this great and glorious work. All of which we humbly submit for your consideration."

Elder L. W. Boon, Chm'n.131

The Report of Committee on Permanent Organization of the Roanoke Missionary Baptist Association made the following report on Thursday Morning, May 30, 1878: We, your committee, beg leave to report, for Moderator, Elder L. W. Boon; Vice Moderator, Elder Wm. Reid; Secretary, Asbury Reid; Assistant Secretary G. A. Mebane; Corresponding, M. W. Wynn; Treasurer, Moses Hardy; to preach the Introductory Sermon, Elder D. L. Simmons; his alternate, Elder Luke Pierce. Respectfully submitted, H. Outlaw, Chm'n.[132] The Association paid Rev. Boon $10.00 for his services.[133]

Twenty-three years later, the Roanoke Association was divided geographically into three groups. *The Banner-Enterprise* next reported this anticipated action in its Thursday, June 7, 1883 paper. The article reads: "The Roanoke Missionary Association convened in its sixteenth annual session with the Union Chapel Missionary Baptist Church, on the 22nd of May 1883 and continued three days. There was an immense gathering of people every day. This is the largest association in the State, there being nearly fourteen thousand communicants. It has several able divines. From present indications there will be a division of the association a year hence. The Board will convene in Edenton in October to consider the feasibility of a division and recommend its action to the next session. In the event of a division, the Chowan River will probably be the dividing line." [134]

Boon organized twenty churches with over 3,000 members in the area. In that respect he had been compared with Harry Cowan, black Baptist preacher of Salisbury before the war, who organized numerous congregations. Records of the First Colored Baptist Church at Murfreesboro, North Carolina from 1867-1873 indicates Boon's involvements in the organization of the new independent Baptist Churches. Boon, who served as the fifth president of the group, sought a reconciliation between the white and black Baptists and opposed a rule requiring that white churches dismiss former slaves who ran away to join the Union army. Boon was regularly praised in the pages of the *Biblical Recorder* by white Baptists for his work. At his death in 1878, the minutes of his association recorded that "it is safe to say that from his ordination till his death, no person in eastern North Carolina exerted a wider and more lasting influence among his people than Elder Boon."[135]

Rare minutes of this period share the first letter of organization of the First Colored Baptist with Lemuel Washington Boon as pastor. [136] In his book *The History of the Negro Church,* the notable black historian Carter G. Woodson referred to Boon, well known for his oratorical skills, as a "preacher of power."[137] Boon's leadership abilities and influence were not confined only to formal religious associations, (although he was one of the founding persons of the following North Carolina Churches: New Hope Baptist Church, Gatesville, North Carolina, New Middle Swamp Missionary Baptist Church, Corapeake, North Carolina, and Mill Neck Missionary Baptist Church, Como, North Carolina.)[138] conventions, or trustee boards, but extended to the pulpit and politics arenas as well. Charles B. Williams stated that "Those who had the good fortune to hear L.W. Boon preach, both white and colored testified that he possessed a gift of oratory and mental ability seldom excelled by men of the best opportunities. Boon was highly regarded by his white contemporaries, S. J. Wheeler, a prominent white minister, singled Boon out as deserving "praise":

"On the first Lord's day in November last [1866], a colored Baptist church was organized in this place [Murfreesboro, NC] . . . [by] Elder L. W. Boon [sic] . . . The colored members have built for themselves a church edifice in town, for the erection of which our citizens of every class contributed cheerfully.

They have called Elder Boo [sic} to go in and out before them. He has a good report not only among his brethren, but among those that are without. Of his spirit and feelings you can doubtless form some ideal, as you were present last May, in the Chowan Association, and read the communication which he made to that body. His labors are in such great demand that he has laid aside all secular employment devoting him entirely to the ministry. His plans seems to be to divide his members into bands, each under an instructor, who looks diligently to the spiritual culture of those connected with him and when necessary calls in the aid of the minister at the monthly visit. The members here have kept up social religion meetings, and the Sunday school has contributed much to the life of religion among the Negroes.

Boon did not confine his oratorical abilities to religious issues only. He used them for political purposes as well. His report on the state of the county delivered in 1869 at the fourth annual session of the Roanoke Association provided an indication of his political interest: "Instead of men being deprived of their own wives and children, they now enjoy equal rights as American citizens. As soon as the Fifteenth Amendment [sic] is adopted by five other states, universal suffrage will be a part of the Constitution of the United States. It [US] is first in peace."

The Inscription on his tomb reads: "Sacred to the memory of Rev. L. W. Boon—Died September 18, 1878-In the 49 year of his age.

The Life That Counts

The life that counts must toil and fight; must hate the wrong and love the right; Must stand for the truth by day and night: This is the life that counts. The life that counts must aim to rise above the earth to sublime skies; Must fix its gaze on Paradise-This is the life that counts. The life that counts must helpful be; In darkest night make melody; Must wait the dawn on bended knee-This is the life that counts. The life that counts must helpful be; The cares and needs of others see; Must seek the slave of sin to free-That is the life that counts.

A. W. S.

Z. H. Berry

Reverend Zion Hall Berry was born about 1830 in Camden County Court House, North Carolina. In 1850, twenty year old Zion Hall Berry was living in Camden County, North Carolina with his mother, Lucrecia Berry, and his sisters Mary Berry, Nancy W. Berry Overton, and Francis Berry. When the Union Army attacked Roanoke Island in 1862, thirty-one year old Zion Berry possibly watched as General Burnside set up his command on the John Berry House on the Croatian Sound. Presumably, the Berry name was came from the John Berry lineage. In 1870, Rev. Zion Berry was living in Camden County with his wife, the former Nancy A. Harvey and Sedulous Thomas, Jane Gregory, Elizabeth Gregory, and Joseph Martin. In 1880 Zion Berry's Camden Courthouse household consists of his children" Catherine (18), Mary A. (16), Edward (7), Ida (6), Joseph E. (5), John T. Gregory {6 nephew) and six servants: Martha Barnes, Martha Lamb, Richard Grandy, Abram Snowden, John Snowden, and S. Thomas. In 1900, 70 year old Zion Berry was living in the Mount Herman Township of Pasquotank County with his wife Nancy A. Harvey Berry, his 80 year old sister, Nancy Berry Overton, his adopted daughter, Lillie Berry, and twenty-four year old grandson Joseph Berry. Several other people boarded at his residence.

Zion Berry was the founder and pastor of Corner Stone Missionary Baptist Church, Elizabeth City, Philadelphia Missionary Baptist Church, Camden,[139] and the Zion Bethlehem Missionary Baptist Church that once stood on the corner of Pitt and Queen Streets, in Windsor, North Carolina. The church was named for the Rev. Zion Hall Berry.[140] In 1890 Rev. Berry was called to the pastorate of the First Colored Baptist Hertford, North Carolina. In 1897 he remodeled the church and added six more deacons to the diaconate, namely: John Dail, Nathan Reid, Augustus Reid, L. H. Hall, Elijah Bryant and Isaac Wood. The first parsonage was constructed under his leadership.

Rev. Z. H. Berry was the Moderator of the Roanoke Missionary Baptist Association from 1881-1884.[141] He delivered the Annual Sermon when the Association convened at Bethel Baptist Church in 1871, and again when the Association convened at Cedar Landing Missionary Baptist Church in Windsor for its 1880. On Tuesday, May 28, 1878 at the Afternoon session, a Committee On Hours of Service was appointed, consisting of Elder Z. H. Berry, Thomas Gatling and Elder

Alfred Saunders, and by motion, Z. H. Berry, a Committee on Finance was appointed, consisting of Brothers Claiborne Speller, W. D. Cherry, and W. C. Jones.[142] The February 23, 1899 edition of *The Carolinian* stated that: "Rev. Z. H. Berry has been sick for several days at his residence in the country. His condition is but at this time is somewhat better."[143] Three months later, *The Carolinian* reported: Rev. Berry returned from Roper, North Carolina on Monday, where he spent Sunday." [144] Apparently, Rev. Berry's ailments and physical conditions were a great concern for the Corner Stone Missionary Baptist Church, where he pastured and for the surrounding community. *The Carolinian* reported "Rev. Berry was absent from his pulpit at Corner Stone Church on Sunday but it was filled by Rev. S. Hockaday of Berkley, Virginia."[145] Less than thirty days later, *The Carolinian* reported: Rev. Berry being absent at Roper did no occupy pulpit at Corner Stone as usual."[146] Rev. Berry conducted a revival at Cornerstone during the week of April 26, 1897[147] On Thursday, May 3, 1897 *The Carolinian* reported that "the revival services which had been in progress at Corner Stone for two weeks closed on the 4th Sunday in April with the baptism of twenty-eight persons." [148] During the month of April & May 1900, Rev. Berry's itinerary resumed at an alarming rate. "Rev. Z. H. Berry will baptize several candidates at the usual place tomorrow."[149] The following week, he delivered the Annual Odd Fellow Address to the Harrellsville North Carolina Chapter of the Odd Fellows on, Saturday, May 15, 1900.[150] Zion Hall Berry died before 1913. He was buried at the New Sawyer's Creek Missionary Baptist Church in Belcross, North Carolina.

J. A. Flemings

Reverend Joshua A. Fleming was born a slave in Virginia during May 1831, and his wife Judith Carey was born in Virginia about February 1832. Joshua and Judith were married in the year 1854 by a minister of the gospel. Joshua lived at Boiling Hall, owned by Colonel William Boiling at "Cobbs", in Chesterfield County, and then at "Boiling Hall", in Goochland County, Virginia, and Judith lived at Judge William Josiah Leake's plantation also in Goochland, a few miles away from Joshua at Boiling Hall. Passes were required for the slaves to visit each other on different plantations. Therefore, when Joshua wanted to see his wife Judith, he would have to get a pass from Colonel Boiling to go to see her Judge Leake's place. If he did not get a pass, and instead slipped out without the pass; the patty-rollers and their starved crazy dogs would chase after him until they caught him or until he eluded their chase. If he was caught by the patty-rollers, he would receive twenty-five licks on his naked back.

Rev. & Mrs. Flemings lived together as man and wife for two or more years. A daughter, Cora was born to this union before January 1, 1868. Joshua was later sold and moved to Edenton, North Carolina. Consequently, Judith Carey was later remarried again in Virginia. Cora Hall would later recall visiting her father Joshua A. Fleming in 1886 in Elizabeth City. During those visits, he treated her as his child, calling her daughter, and telling his children that she was his daughter by his first wife.

Rev. Joshua Fleming and a portion of the people of African descent and citizens of Elizabeth City, North Carolina, assembled in the African schoolhouse at Elizabeth City on March 15, 1871, and on motion, the Rev. Andrew Cartwright was appointed President, and Joshua Fleming, Vice-President; Henry Kale, Treasurer; and John James Secretary and the Elizabeth City North Carolina Freedmen's Emigrant Aid Society was organized.[151] At the 1879 Annual Session of the Roanoke Missionary Baptist Association the Reverend's Joshua Fleming, Ivy Boone Roach, Harry H. Hays, G. W. Lee, B. J. Lynox, J. K. Lamb, Thaddeus Wilson and were appointed to the Committee of Grievances. Later in the day on Tuesday, May 27th, 1879, Rev. J. A. Fleming in the absence of Elder D. L. Simmons and Elder Luke Pierce, preached the Introduction Sermon from Zachariah 11:17. Following the sermon, the alter prayer was delivered by Elder J. K. Lamb.[152] Rev. Flemings accepted the call to the pastorate of the "Will-You-Grow" Baptist Church, later known as the Willow Grove Baptist Church in the Pleasant Grove District of Old Norfolk County, now known as the City of Chesapeake, Virginia.[153] He was called to the pastorate of the Haven Creek Baptist Church on Roanoke Island, Manteo, North Carolina. In 1903 he was pasturing the Piney Grove Baptist Church, Creeds, Virginia.[154]

Mrs. Carrie E. Stallings Fleming was called to Gates County, N. C., on Thursday, August 16, 1923 on account of the serious illness of her mother.[155] Rev. J. R. Fleming, and daughter, Miss Mildred was called to Gates Co., on account of the death of Mrs. Fleming's mother, Mrs. Stallings.[156] Pasquotank County Rural School held their second annual county commencement at the State Normal School Friday Night May 2, 1925 with a variegated program of music, addresses and prizes contests. The day opened with a parade of the school children from Corner Stone Baptist Church to the State Normal School headed by the Cosmopolitan Band. The principal address was delivered by the Mrs. A. W. Holland, supervisor of the Colored Elementary School of North Carolina. She was introduced by Rev. J. R. Fleming.[157] Corner Stone Baptist Church celebrated its 40th Anniversary; and the fourth of the pastor, Reverend J. R. R. McRay during the week of March 20-27, 1927. Services were held the entire week with sermons by the different pastors of the city and the closing sermon on Sunday, March 27th, with the anniversary sermon being preached by Reverend E. M. Lassiter, pastor of Mount Zion Baptist Church, Berkley, Virginia. The history of the church was presented by Mr. J. R. Flemings. Beautiful solos were rendered by Mrs. Elizabeth Watson, Miss. Ethel Maloy, and Mildred Flemings.[158]

After the death of Joshua A. Flemings, Sr., Cora Hall's birth rights were called into question by her half-brother, Joshua A. Fleming, Jr., son of Joshua A. Flemings, Sr., second wife Elizabeth Norcum. In the Matter of *Hall-vs-Flemings*, the Pasquotank County Superior Court ruled in her favor, affirming the following: The children of colored parents, born at any time before the first day of January, 1868, of persons living together as man and wife, are hereby declared legitimate children of such parents or of either one of them, with all the rights of heirs at law and next of kin with respect to the estate or estates of any such parents, or either one of them," etc. Rev. Joshua A. and Elizabeth N. Flemings were the parents of eight children: Joshua A. Jr., Louisa V., Elizabeth, and Florence. The names of the other children remain lost to the author. [159]

H. H. Hays

Elder Henry Harry Hays was born about 1824 in the Eure section of Gates County, North Carolina. In 1866 he married the former Jane Wilder daughter of Cator Wilder and Jane Wilder[160] of Hertford County, North Carolina.[161], [162] On August 17, 1868 Elder Hays performed the wedding ceremony of Benjamin Duck and Martha Howell of Gates County. This was his first recorded marriage ceremony. Over the next fifteen years Elder Hays would perform more than 27 weddings. In 1869 Elder H. H. Hayes of Gatesville, North Carolina is named by the General Assembly of North Carolina along with Emanuel Reynolds of Winton, North Carolina, Bryant

Lee of Woodville, North Carolina, R. R. Creecy of Plymouth, North Carolina, and Charles E. Hodges, of Lake Drummond, Virginia as a body of corporate and policy, by the name of "the Society for the Relief of Preachers of the Roanoke Missionary Baptist Association.[163] In 1870 Elder Hays listed his occupation as Baptist Minister with a household that consisted of all literate members, his 46 year old wife Jane, his 15 year old son Augustus, his 12 year old domestic servant Amanda Riddick and his 19 year old cook and domestic servant Mary Lassiter.[164] Ten years later in 1880, Elder Hays lists his occupation as farmer. He lives alone with his 54 year old wife Jane. He was the second pastor of the New Middle Swamp Missionary Baptist Church, Corapeake, North Carolina.

Elder Hays was a committee member and a signor of the September 18, 1878, Roanoke Missionary Baptist Association Memorial Dedication for Elder Lemuel Washington Boone. He was selected on the Thursday, May 9, 1878 session of the Roanoke Missionary Baptist Association to serve on the Committees of Grievance, Printing, and Chairman of the Ministerial Council. At the Twentieth Annual Session {May 1885} Elder Hayes of Gatesville, North Carolina was one of five people appointed on Sabbath School Statistics, and he was subsequently appointed as an alternate to preach the Introductory Sermon when the Association convened at Antioch, Camden County, North Carolina in 1886. Elder Hayes was an active member of the Lebanon Grove Baptist Church, Gatesville, North Carolina. A huge monument on the church's burial ground marks the place where his remains are resting.

Blest Be The Tie.

Blest be the tie that binds our hearts in Christian love;
The fellowship of kindred minds is like to that above.
When we asunder part, It gives us inward pain;
But we shall still be joined in heart,
And hope to meet again.

C. E. Hodges

Reverend Charles E. Hodges was free born during the year of 1819 to Charles Augustus Hodges {whose mother being free women made her children free-born, although her husband was a slave} and Julia Nelson Willis in Princess Ann County, Virginia. He married Fannie E. Hodges in 1889. To this union Charles Jr. was born in 1842, and Sarah was born in 1854. Between 1831 and 1837 Rev. Hodges had successively purchased, and accumulated an estate of 253 acres. Charles A. Hodges was a successful Free Person of Color who lived in the Blackwater section of Princess Ann County. Hodges hired a white woman in his community to teach his children to read, write and comprehend the English language. This was the only rudimentary education available to the Hodges children. The Hodges children would later attend an unknown and unidentifiable Negro school in Norfolk. They return home to teach their siblings the wonderful things they had learned while in Norfolk attending school.

Between 1831 and 1837 Rev. Hodges had successively purchased, and accumulated an estate of 253 acres. In 1852 William Star acknowledged the difficulty some blacks were having selling their efforts and getting ready within a short period of time. After being subjected to visits from white vigilantes, Tommy Bogger, Ph. D., stated in his book, "*Free Blacks In Norfolk Virginia from 1790-1860* that "the Hodge family decided to sell off their land and livestock in Princess Ann County and move north." Others say that the Hodge family was driven out of Princess Ann, Virginia to the State of New York by the slave parole of the county, presumably due to his unwillingness to conform to the laws of Virginia restraining the movements of free Negro. He wrote a widely circulated anti-slavery pamphlet entitled *The Disunion Our Wisdom and Our Duty*, which expressed his feelings, attitudes and the vicissitudes of slavery. The following paragraph will show his spirit:

> "He is not a traitor to his country, but a true patriot, as well as a Christian, who labors for the dissolution of the Union. We do not expect to dissolve the Union alone; we simply as co-operation and for this appeal to the people. This is not the time to lay out the plan of a campaign, to open trenches, dispose of forces and besiege the citadel. The thing to be now done is to urge upon every man this question: Are You ready?[165]

Abolitionist like Rev. Charles E. Hodges often and rather cleverly covered up their call for violent warfare inside a call for peace. His tract *The Disunion Our Wisdom and Our Duty* conceded the claim of the pro-slavery forces that the Constitution itself protected the institution, Therefore explained, Christians were required to view the Constitution as immoral and, because: it is wrong to sustain sin," to work for the end of the Union-a result, as everyone knew but Rev. Hodges failed to mention, that could hardly be brought about peacefully. "Can you do otherwise," he demanded, "than commit yourself to the cause . . . ." It is very unlikely that Rev. Hodges had to point out to his readers that a commitment to the cause of abolishing slavery by abolishing the Constitution was, in the politics of the time, little different from a call for civil war. Understandingly, most of the abolitionist preachers were careful to avoid any talk of violence, and some of them spoke against it directly.

Rev. Charles E. Hodges, L. W. Boon, J. T. Reynolds, C. E. Hodges, J. A. Fleming, Asbury Reid, J. T. Reynolds, J. A. Fleming, J. K. Lamb, Zion H. Berry, A. Mebane, Wm. Reid and Emanuel Reynolds were present when the East Roanoke Missionary Baptist Association was organized in the Haven Creek Baptist Church, Roanoke Island, North Carolina in 1865. These founding fathers later founded the Roanoke Collegiate Institute, Elizabeth City, N. C.

Rev. Hodges was the first pastor called to the Divine Baptist Church, Princess Ann County, Virginia in 1863. The land for the first Divine Baptist Church was given by the Rev. E. G. Corprew a former slave and a prominent pre and post Black Reconstruction Politician in Virginia. Rev. E. G. Corprew family members Sgt. March Corprew, an old Civil War Veteran and his wife Martha Jane Miller Corprew were also members and contributors to Divine Baptist Church. In 1867 Rev. Hodges donated the land on which the "Will-You-Grow" Baptist Church, later known as the Willow Grove Baptist Church in the Pleasant Grove section of Norfolk County, (now (2011) known as Chesapeake, Virginia) was constructed. After the church's construction; he became its first pastor.

In 1869 Charles E. Hodges of Lake Drummond, Virginia was named by the General Assembly of North Carolina along with Armanuel Reynolds of Winton, Bryant Lee of Woodville, R. R. Creecy of Plymouth, and Elder H. H. Hayes of Gatesville, as a body of corporate and policy, by the name of "the Society for the Relief of Preachers of the Roanoke Missionary Baptist Association.[166] Rev. Hodges was elected to the Virginia House of Delegates representing Norfolk County and Portsmouth from 1869 to 1871. Rev. Hodges was the brother of Willis Augustus Hodges, a delegate to the 5th Virginia Constitutional Convention 1867 to 1868. In 1878, C. E. Hodges offered the prayer for the May 28, 1878 Afternoon Session[167]; the collection taken up during the Association amounted to $7. 04, of which amount 75 cents paid to Elder C. E. Hodges, $5.00 to Sister Julia John, and the remaining $1. 29 turned over to the church at New Bethany,[168] as Elder Hodges was the delegate from the Antioch Baptist Church at Camden Courthouse, and New Ramouth Gilead Church at South Mills. In 1879, on motion of H. H. Hays, C. E. Hodges was appointed Vice-Moderator, and he was appointed to the Committee on Time, Place and preachers For Next Association. It was the recommendation of this committee that the 1880 session of the Association convene at Cedar Landing, Bertie County, North Carolina on the Tuesday after the 4th Lord's Day in May, 1880 with Elder Zion Hall Berry preaching the Introductory Sermon and Elder C. H. Hodges his alternate.[169]

Tommy Bogger, Ph. D., the director of the Harrison B. Wilson Archives and Gallary at Norfolk State University, Norfolk Virginia stated in his book; *"Free Blacks In Norfolk Virginia 1790-1860."* that Willis A. Hodges responded to an advertisement for laborers on the Dismal Swamp Canal. He was one of only twelve free blacks among 500 black laborers. He was paid the same wages that the slave received, $12 a month, and he was treated just like them. They all slept in crude huts and rose at daybreak to the sound of a bell. After cooking their own meals, they toiled until sundown digging to deepen the canal. The slaves, As well as free blacks, were constantly wary of incurring the wraft of the cruel taskmasters who served as overseers.

A number of churches tendered a reception for Rev. Charles E. Hodges at Asbury African Methodist Episcopal church on Monday evening March 7, 1920. Pastor Hodges received a purse of $56.00. The Sunday morning Band gave him a leather hand bag and Mrs. Hodges $10.00. Musical selections were given to him by the Elite Singing Association and by the Toussaint L' Ouverture Circle. Mrs. Henrietta Johnson was the mistress of ceremonies.[170] Rev. Hodges, read the Second Scripture Lesson at the funeral of Reverend Alfred Young which was conducted at the Sharpe Street Church, Baltimore, Maryland. Rev. Young, the retired pastor was known throughout the A.M.E. Z. Church as the preacher of the "Railroad Sermon-" Don't Miss The Train For Heaven."[171] Reverend Charles E. Hodges died in 1900.

W. A. Hodges

Reverend Willis A. Hodges was born in Black Water, Princess Ann County, and Virginia in 1815 to Charles Augustus Hodges {whose mother being free women made her children free-born, although her husband was a slave} and Julia Nelson Willis. Tommy Bogger, Ph. D., the director of the Harrison B. Wilson Archives and Gallary at Norfolk State University, Norfolk Virginia stated in his book; *"Free Blacks In Norfolk Virginia 1790-1860."* that Willis A. Hodges responded to an advertisement for laborers on the Dismal Swamp Canal. He was one of only twelve free blacks among 500 black laborers. He was paid the same wages that the slave received, $12 a month, and he was treated just like them. They all slept in crude huts and rose at daybreak to the sound of a bell. After cooking their own meals, they toiled until sundown digging to deepen the canal. The slaves, As well as free blacks, were constantly wary of incurring the wraft of the cruel taskmasters who served as overseers.

Nearly one hundred seventy-one years ago, Willis A. Hodges, was a minister of the Roanoke Missionary Baptist Association and the brother of Charles Edward Hodges, one of the Charter founders of the Roanoke Missionary Baptist Association, complained when an article he paid to have inserted in the *New York Sun* was altered, then buried in the advertising column. *The New York Sun's* editor advised Mr. Hodges that "*The Sun*" shines for all white men and not for colored men, and that if he wished to advocate the cause of his people he would have to publish a paper himself for the purpose." Hodges founded *the Ram's Horn,* one of the first of a line of great New York Colored Papers, yet despite the flight of a hundred seventy-five years, if any paper shines for the colored people they are their own weeklies.[172] In 1847 Willis began publishing a weekly called *the Rams' Horn.*

Willis played a pivotal role in educating black youth. In 1847 Hodges helped to start an association of parents and community leaders in Williamsburg, New York. The association set out to open a private school for black youth that initially was supported by Hodges and other black leaders.[173] Hodges was proud of the fact that he had purchased three dozen books, materials, and alphabet cards out of his own pocket to help the children in his small but growing community. By 1848 this school could boast of having 80 males and females children in attendance and two teachers who were paid a salary of six hundred dollars each a year. The association's school grew so quickly that it was eventually granted public school funds by the white officials as a result of the work and prodding of Hodges and his brother William who worked diligently to educate both themselves and the black youth. [174]

From 1847 to 1867 Hodges headed a colony of black farmers called Blackville, this was one of the black communities in which he settled, and owned a grocery store. Hodges and family attended the Abyssinian Baptist Church. By the 1840s, Hodges functioned as one of the most outspoken advocates for abolition and equal rights in the State. His abolitionist newspaper caught the eye of Frederic Douglass and John Brown, both of whom contributed articles and funds. Brown published his essay entitled *"Sambo's Mistakes"* in Hodges' paper, castigating northern blacks for not doing more to end slavery. Because of such essays as Brown's, the paper reached a peak circulation of 2,500. Hodges also argued in favor of re-settling free blacks and escaped slaves on farms in up-state New York rather than in cities.

John Brown's communications with Willis A. Hodges expressed his deeply felt feelings about his responsibility towards his Negro neighbors and their well being is obvious in the following letters, two of many written to Willis A. Hodges, who was likewise active in settling Negroes on the South lands. A second letter written to Hodges on October 28, 1848 solidifies the mutual love, devotion and affections share between Brown and Hodges:

Springfield, Mass. January 22, 1849.

Friend Hodges—Dear Sir: Yours of the 22n January reached me a day or two since. We are all glad to hear from you again and that you were getting along well with the exception of your own ill health. We hope to hear better news from you in regard to that the next we get news from you . . . . Say to my colored friends with you that they will be no losers by keeping their patience a little about building lots. They can busy themselves in cutting plenty of hard wood and in getting any work they can find until spring, and they need not fear getting too much wood provided. Do not let anyone forget the vast importance of sustaining the very best character for honesty, truth, industry and faithfulness. I hope everyone will be determined to not merely conduct as well as the whites, but to set them an example in all things. I am much pleased that your nephew has concluded to hang on like a man. With my best wishes for everyone, I remain, yours in truth, JOHN BROWN[175]

After the paper ceased publication, Reverend Willis A. Hodges continued to support abolitionist causes, including John Brown. It is not known if Hodges was part of the Harpers Ferry planning, but when Brown was arrested in 1859, Hodges burned their correspondence. The editor may have helped the U.S. army as a scout in Virginia during the Civil War, but the evidence is uncertain.

Rev. Willis A. Hodges was active in Virginia politics during the Reconstruction Era. After the Democratic Party regained power in Virginia he returned to New York in 1876, and returned back to North Carolina, and became active in the Roanoke Missionary Baptist Association. Rev. Willis Augustus Hodges was listed as an Elder on the 1878 & 1884 Roanoke Missionary Baptist Association Elders list.[176] He was living in Princess Ann County, Virginia with a Post Office Box in Kempsville, Virginia.[177] After the dust had settled from the Civil War, Willis, and Charles Hodges returned to Princess Ann County Virginia, where they had been ran out of thirty years earlier. Willis A. Hodges and two other Negro men were appointed as Negro County Supervisors in 1870, Willis was appointed for Kempsville, Virginia M. Bonney for Pungo and James E. Land for Seaboard.[178] Willis returned back to New York where he lived until his death in 1890.[179]

G. W. Holland

Reverend G. W. Holland was born in Virginia about the year of 1833. He was ordained to the Gospel ministry by the High Street Baptist Church, Lynchburg, Virginia, and served in the capacity of a missionary to the churches in and about Danville. In this capacity he organized and set apart fifteen churches. He was a part of the generation immediately following the emancipation, the day of brush arbors and log churches, the day of excessive "heat and burden." He was a signor of the 1880 Resolution on Education to the State of North Carolina Baptist Convention.[180]

He came to Winston, Salem, North Carolina in 1878, and took charge of the First Baptist Church, which position he held until his death. He organized the Mount Zion Baptist Church in 1889. During his pastorate, Mount Zion worshipped at its Third Street location until fire destroyed the structure in 1904. Rev. Johnson orchestrated the congregation's move in 1907 to a new edifice built on Nineth Street. Although a pastor it was the calling of Rev. Holland, it seemed, to organize and set apart churches. It was said of him many times even at midnight he would rest himself by the wayside after long journeys through the Blue Ridge Mountains, and would sit down to pick the blisters on his worn and weary feet.

Rev. Holland did not have many of the advantages of the present day. However, he managed to acquire a liberal education through his library. He had one of the largest libraries of any Colored man in North Carolina, and he made good use of it. While Rev. Holland was uncompromising in questions of faith he had many friends in all the denominations through that kindness and generosity so characteristic of him. Three thousand persons were baptized in his ministry. Fifteen Baptist churches in Virginia and twenty-three in North Carolina organized. Sixty young men and women were sent to Shaw University through his influence. From his entrance into North Carolina until his death he was a faithful and true friend of the Educational and Missionary Convention. He passed into a well-earned rest in November 26, 1906. A memorial service of unusual interest was held in the First Baptist Church, Winston Salem, North Carolina on Sunday, December 2, 1906 to commemorate Rev. G. W. Holland's life and the work. By the request of the deceased Rev. H. B. Brown made the opening address at his funeral which was followed by addressed from other pastors and distinguished citizens. Howard Benjamin Grose's article, "*A Tribute to a Leader*" appeared in the latest edition of The Home Baptist Mission Monthly; Volume 29-30 where he described his Winston-Salem funeral where the Mayor of Winston Salem and other city officials were present, and they may kind and warm remarks about him. Rev. H. A. Brown, D. D., for so many years the beloved pastor of First Baptist Church, white. He paid a warm tribute to the deceased. Reverend Brown wrote the following news article which appeared in the *Biblical Recorder*, the white Baptist paper of North Carolina.

> "He was generally loved not only by his own race, but by the white race as well. He had served his denomination here about twenty none years. He succeeded in organizing six or seven Baptist churches in this vicinity. The church of which he was pastor was organized through his instrumentality. It has grown to be a strong church numerically and has a splendid house of worship which is a fitting memorial to his self sacrificing labor for Christ and his people. His character was stainless as drifted snow. He stood for peace, industry, honesty, purity and obedience to the powers that be; he preached the gospel and avoided all political agitations. He had a good library and kept himself abreast of the times. He has been an untold blessing to his race in this city.

His funeral was the most largely attended ever held in Winston-Salem and the surrounding area. It was estimated that five thousand persons were in attendance, and many of them were the most prominent white people. The largest funeral procession which has honored any colored man in the State of both races followed the remains of this hero to his last resting place where he quietly sleeps to await the resurrection of the dead in Christ.

Am I A Soldier of the Cross?

Am I a soldier of the cross, A follower of the Lamb,
And shall I fear to own His cause, or blush to speak His name?
Must I be carried to the skies on flow'ry beds of ease,
While others fought to win the prize, and sailed through bloody seas?
Are there no fears for me to face? Must I not stem the flood?
Is this vile world a friend of grace to help me on to God?
Sure I must fight, If I would reign; Increase my courage, Lord;
I'll bear the toil, endure the pain, Supported by thy word.
Thy saints in all this glorious war shall conquer, tho' they die:
They see the triumph from afar, by faith they bring it nigh.
When that illustrious day shall rise and all thy armies shine,
In robes of vic-t'ry thro' skies, thy glory shall be Thine.

Caesar Johnson

Reverend Caesar Johnson was born about 1833 in Warrenton, North Carolina, and until the Civil War was a slave of Mr. John V. Canthron. He was baptized by Rev. N. A. Purefoy in 1862. Rev. Johnson attended Shaw University, Raleigh, North Carolina for nine years. He served as a missionary of the Home Mission Board, New York, for eight years; Treasurer of the North Carolina State Convention in 1889; a member of the Foreign Missions Board located in Raleigh, North Carolina; a member of the Board of Ministerial Education; and an 1889 Fraternal Delegate to the North Carolina State Convention. He was employed as a colporteur by the American Foreign Bible Society.

Reverend Johnson was among the group of devote men who formed the Roanoke Missionary Baptist Association in 1866 on Roanoke Island, North Carolina. In 1867 he assisted in the formation of the Negro Baptist of North Carolina and the General Baptist State Convention. Rev. Edward Eagles, William Warwick, Lemuel Washington Boone, R. B. Spicer, H. Grimes, R. H. Harper, and others met in Goldsboro, North Carolina, and organized the Baptist Educational and Missionary

Convention.[181] Rev. Caesar Johnson was a member of the first Freedmen's Convention, held in the City of Raleigh, North Carolina on October 1-5 1866.[182] According to the Constitution of the Freedmen Bureau the object of this Convention was to: aid in the establishment of Schools from which none shall be excluded for color or poverty, and, to encourage nonsectarian education in this country, especially among the freedmen. Any adult who favors the above object may become a member by signing this Constitution and contributing one dollar or more at the beginning of each year.

Rev. Caesar Johnson endorsed the Constitution and twelve years later, {1878} he was among the first graduating class of the Shaw University. The other graduating class members were: Henry Clay Crosby-Plymouth, North Carolina; Nicholas F. Roberts-Raleigh, North Carolina; Ezekiel E. Smith-Fayetteville, North Carolina; and Louis H. Wyche-Williamsboro, North Carolina. Rev. Caesar Johnson of Raleigh, North Carolina offered Prayer at the 1878 Executive Board Meeting when it convened at the Spruce Street Baptist Church Nashville, Tennessee on Monday evening, September 24th. The following year, 1879, The Roanoke Missionary Baptist Association was entertained by Rev. C. Johnson, of Raleigh, N. C., who made some remarks in regard to the State Convention.[183]Later in the session, the Report of the Sabbath School made the following recommended as it pertained to Rev. Johnson:

> We, your committee on Sabbath Schools, beg leave to report: We believe the Sabbath School to be the best institution in existence for training the young and preparing them for future life. Therefore, we consider it the imperative duty of every pastor and deacon to see that a Sabbath School is maintained in every church in this Association; to see that suitable books are provided and used; that the study of the Bible be made paramount; and that a healthy Christian culture be promoted among the scholars; and that the scholars be not compelled to remain in school longer than three hours each day. We, further recommend Rev. C. Johnson of Raleigh, as a suitable person to apply to for necessary books. Respectfully submitted, Luke Pierce, Chairman.[184]

The February 6, 1897 edition of *The Gazette*, made a very interest observation about Rev. C. Johnson and others as it related to the newly President elect, McKinley. The article reads as follows: "Rev. Caesar Johnson, Honorable John H. Williamston and General Traveling Agent W. S. Mitchell, left last Thursday, March 31, 1897 for Washington D.C. to witness the inauguration of President-elect McKinley."[185] We hope these gentlemen will not expose the treachery of any of the President's so called invited guest-, or, in other words, disturb the equanimity of our friend(?) the _____.[186]

Rev. Johnson was the first pastor of the Oak City Missionary Baptist Church, Raleigh, North Carolina. He was also a supporter of the Roanoke Missionary Baptist Association and a publisher and printer of some of the earlier editions of annual reports for the Roanoke Missionary Baptist Association.

The Royal Telephone

Central's never "busy," Always on the line, You may hear from heaven almost anytime. 'Tis a royal services, free to one and all! When you get in trouble give this line a call.

There will be no charges, telephone is free: It was built for service, just for you and me. There will be no waiting on this royal line. The telephone to Glory is always on the line.

Fail to get the answer, Satan crossed your wire by some strong delusion, or some base desire. Take away obstructions God is on the throne and you will get an answer through this royal telephone.

If you line is "grounded" and connections true has been lost with Jesus, tell you what to do: Prayer and faith and promise mend the broken wire, Till your soul is burning with the Pentecostal fire.

Carnal combinations and you cannot get control of this line to glory, Anchored in the soul. Storm and trial cannot disconnect the line held in constant keeping by the father's hand divine.

Telephone to glory, O what joy divine! I can feel the current moving on the line; Built by God the Father for His loved and own-We may talk to Jesus thro' this royal telephone. O, Telephone to glory, O what joy divine! I can feel the current moving on the line; Built by God the Father for His loved and own-We may talk to Jesus thro' this royal telephone.

MINUTES

OF THE

NINETEENTH ANNUAL SESSION

OF THE

ROANOKE

MISSIONARY BAPTIST ASSOCIATION,

HELD WITH THE CHURCH OF CHRIST AT

ZION HILL, BERTIE COUNTY, N. C.,

Tuesday after the third Lord's Day in May, 1884.

REV. Z. H. BERRY.....Camden C. H., N. C.,..........MODERATOR.
REV. LUKE PIERCE....Windsor, Bertie Co., N. C.,...VICE-MODERATOR.
ASBURY REID.........Gatesville, N. C.,..............SECRETARY.
ELI JONES...........Windsor, N. C.,......ASSISTANT SECRETARY.
J. O. HOLLOMAN......Winton, N. C.,..........COR. SECRETARY.
MOSES HARDY.........Coleraine, N. C.,..............TREASURER.

RALEIGH, N. C.:
PRINTED BY REV. CÆSAR JOHNSON.
1884.

Asbury Reid

Reverend Asbury Reid (1827-1901) was born to Micajah Reid, (a free person of color and head of a Free Family of Color in Gates County, North Carolina in 1820); and the former Judith Rooks (Free People of Color) of Gates, North Carolina. He married Clary A. Green of Gates, North Carolina. The Reid family consisted of William M., Scott S. W., George E., Elizabeth M., Nora A., Grant L., Edward, Ophelia, Luvenia A., Charles, Albert O., Washington A., and Charles W. Price. Asbury Reid's father Micajah Reed was head of a Gates County household of 4 "other free" in 1790 [NC:24], 8 in 1800 [NC:277], 10 in 1810 [NC:853], and 11 "free colored" in 1820 [NC:155]. In August 1817 he proved to the Gates County Court that he was the lawful heir of Nathaniel Hall, who died in Revolutionary War service. Nathaniel may have been the father of Nathaniel Hall, a "Molatto Boy," born about 1786, bound an apprentice cooper in Gates County in May 1806 [Fouts, *Minutes of Gates County*, IV:1001; III:499].

Rev. Asbury Reid was active in the community relations of the New Hope Missionary Baptist Church and the New Hope Community of Gatesville. He and his maternal relatives William Rooks, Wesley Rooks, James Rooks of Elisha and James Rooks of David; Zachariah Boon a relative of Lemuel Washington Boon, the first pastor, John W. Knight, Willis Duck, Benjamin T. Knight, Charles Townsend Knight were assigned trustees with the primary responsibility of purchasing land from Thomas Riddick. Asbury Reed's paternal relatives the Cuff's, were another founding family of the New Hope Missionary Baptist Church. Rev. Reid served as an associate minister under the pastorate of his brother, Reverend William Reid. During his ministerial time, membership at the New Hope church was based upon the fact that No slaves were admitted, and membership qualifications was based upon the fact that a perspective member was born free and not shot free. Admittedly, the first and second generations of members prominently displayed their blue veins as a badge of courage.

Rev. Asbury was present during the formation of the Roanoke Missionary Baptist Church on Roanoke Island, North Carolina in 1866. He was the first secretary of the association. At the Friday June 2, 1870 session of the Roanoke Missionary Baptist Association; Rev. Reid was selected to the position of secretary of the Committee on Organization, and Rev. Charles Hodges, the Moderator. Asbury Reid's Friday Evening, June 2, 1871 Report of Committee on Ministry reads: "Whereas, the Lord has instituted the means of the ministry, called the gospel ministry, and through the gospel the Lord has intended to such as believe. Therefore, we think the ministry is the only means through which the Lord has intended to convey his truth to the hungry Saints. Let him who hears, says come, and whosoever will, let him come and take of the water of life freely; and again we hear St. Paul say, how can we hear without a preacher, and how can he preach without he is sent? Hence, you will see that a minister must be sent. The gospel has a clearing quality, and should always be preached by men who practice what they preach. This seems to have been the intention of Christ, the great institutor of the gospel ministry. Oh! May our heavenly father attend His ministry and accomplish the same by the energy of His spirit to the hearts of His dear hearers everywhere." ASBURY REID.

Early in his life Asbury Reid was an elected justice of the peace and a Republican politician. In 1872 he filed a claim with the Southern Claims Commission as a pro-Union Southerners for reimbursement of their losses during the Civil War. His claim for his loses in Gates County, North Carolina was approved in the amount he sought.

Reverend Asbury Reid was victimized by the 1885-1886 split of the Roanoke Missionary Baptist Association. He became an active member of the West Roanoke Missionary Baptist Association. However, he remained closely associated with the Roanoke Missionary Baptist Association and with the lives and legacies of the Roanoke Missionary Baptist Association members. His labors and the labors of those that left to form the West Roanoke Missionary Baptist Association due to the split cannot say that their former deeds and actions in the Roanoke Association were over looked, unnoticed, ignored or forgotten.

Nothing Between

Nothing between my soul and the Savior,
Naught of this world's illusive dreams;
I have renounced all sinful pleasure,
Jesus is mine;
There's nothing between.

Nothing between like worldly pleasures;
Habits of life, tho' harmless they seem;
Must not my heart from Him sever,
He is my all,
There's nothing between.

Nothing between my soul and the Savior,
So that His blessed face maybe seen,
Nothing preventing the lease of His favor,
Keep the way clear,
Let nothing between!

W. Reid

Reverend William Reid was born November 16, 1836 in Gates County, North Carolina to Micajah Reid[187] of Nansemond County, Virginia and the former Judith Rooks, daughter Jacob Brady a slave, and Sally Rooks, a white woman. Jacob Brady was the slave of Sally Rook's father. Sally Rooks and Jacob Brady's children Polly Rooks, Judith Rooks, Sally and Peggy Rooks were Free People of Color.[188][189] The Rooks descendants including, Rev. William Reid are usually identified as Mulattos. Rev. Reid was an 1889 graduate of Hampton Institute, Hampton, Virginia. In 1916 he was awarded the degree of Doctor of Divinity by the West Roanoke Missionary Baptist Association for the great service he had rendered the church and community.[190]

When the lists of the Founding Fathers of the East Roanoke Association are enumerated, Rev. William Reid's name is always affixed to the list. During the infancy years of the East Roanoke Association at the Haven Creek Baptist Church, located on Roanoke Island, North Carolina, Reid demonstrated a supporting role as the Reverend's Lemuel Washington Boon, J. T. Reynolds, Charles E. Hodges, J. A. Fleming, Asbury Reid, Zion Hall Berry, Emmanuel Reynolds, and George Abram Mebane and others took the lead in this paramount endeavor. Reid actively participated in the Sister's Union connected with the General Baptist Convention of North Carolina. He accepted his call to Christian Ministry in 1863 and began his pastorate.

Rev. William Reid, Elder A. Cowper, and Benjamin Clarke were appointed at the May 1884 Association Session to the committee on Newly Constituted Churches.[191] He was appointed to the committee On Time, Place and Preachers of Next Association.[192] During the same session Rev. Reid was a voting member of the Report of Ministerial Council whose responsibility was to either affirm or deny the sanctions and or disciplines of individual or members churches.

He arrived at the Hampton Institute on September 29, 1885 to attend Hampton Institute, Hampton, Virginia. He immediately became employed as a waiter. Rev. Reid attended the December 1, 1913 Hampton Institute Farmer's Conference for High Schools and gave an account of his work. The farmers in North Carolina have organized various co-operatives societies to buy and sell for them. In this fertilizer worth sixteen dollars is brought for $12.00 dollars. The farmers mix their own ingredients. The majority of their business transactions are maintained with cash. In a letter dated February 24, 1893, Reid wrote, "Mrs. Bellows, a teacher at Hampton Institute, and said, I am employed as an assistant book-keeper with one of the largest real-estate firms located at 703 Nicollet Avenue in Minneapolis, Minnesota." Since graduating from Hampton Institute, Reverend Reid stated: "My first experience as a teacher was a three month school in Gatlington, (Reynoldson District) Gates County, North Carolina., during summer vocation, when I was a junior at Hampton. The next two summers, I taught in the same county, different schools; also three months at Wardsville, Chowan County, North Carolina. He was on the employment roll of the Gates County Schools for the school years ending June 1885, and December 3, 1888. He earned $50.00 for the 1896-1897 School years.[193] On March 21, 1899 William Reid of Gatesville, North Carolina "wrote under date March 21, 1899 "A term of busy work and hard study has just closed and I am at home for a few days rest." [194]

Rev. Reid was the second pastor of the New Hope Missionary Baptist Church in Gatesville, North Carolina. This church was purported to have been constructed in 1859 by a very prominent citizen, at his own expense for the free Negroes. [195] Only the free born was admitted for membership; even after the war it would not for a long time admit any negro who had been a slave, the line always being drawn between those "born free and those shot free."[196] In North Carolina and Virginia, most free Negro families were the descendants of white servant women who had children by slaves or free African Americans. Very few free families, perhaps as low as 1 percent of the total, descended from white slave owners who had children by their slaves. Under the law of *partus, male* slave-owners were not required to free their children by their slaves. Many free African American families in colonial North Carolina and Virginia were landowners.

The principal members of the New Hope Missionary Baptist Church were the relatives of Rev. William Reid, namely: the Boon's, Copeland's, Cuffs, and Rooks. These were all prominent mulatto free families. The New Hope Missionary Baptist Church Congregation was literate. Although there are no records of there being any schools for his congregants, the census of 1850 records over half of the male free Negroes as being able to read and write. There are no records of them voting but every tax list carries a number of free black polls. It was the custom to make the mulattoes and the Negroes pay all the tax that could be extracted from them.

An 1869 Hertford County North Carolina Deed shows Eley Carter selling a lot on the north side of Broad Street in Murfreesboro to William Reid, Phillip Weaver and Andrew Reynolds as a place for a Negro school house and church. The church became known as The First Baptist Church Murfreesboro, and the school was known as the Lincoln Institute, later known as the Oliver O. Howard School. Rev. Reid began his pastorate at First Baptist Murfreesboro Church in 1869. The church was located at Broad Street. *"The Elizabeth City North Carolinian"* for August 12, 1869 has an article about the commencement exercises at Murfreesboro for Lincoln Institute. Rev. William Reid and Rev. Lemuel Washington Boone gave orations following the speech by Mr. J. T. Reynolds.

In 1860 William Reed was living with his 26 year old wife Elizabeth, and their children: Samuel C., (1) and William T (3). His personal property was valued at $300.00. In the 1880 Census Records of Murfreesboro Township, in the County of Hertford, on June 29, 1880, forty two year old William Reid, a minister of the Gospel was living with his 34 year old wife the former Mary E. Reynolds, and their children: Willie, (13), Lorenzo C., (11), James E. (9), George C. (6), and Jessie C. (3) Twenty years later, {1900} Rev. Reid was living in Murfreesboro, North Carolina with his new thirty year old wife, the former Nancy E. Hall (Born May 1870) and their children: Floyd L., 12, born July 1887, Josephus June 1891, Claudia L. June 1892, Robert R May 1894, and Dewey M. August 1898. In 1920, 84 year old William Reid was still living in Murfreesboro with his 47 year old wife Nancy E. Hall Reid, 21 year old son, Dewey, 14 year old son, Theodore, and seven year old daughter Nellie Ruth. In the later 1890's Rev. Reid and Booker T. Washington commenced private law study in Virginia under J. A. M. Johns, a scholarly West Indian, "J. Clay Smith, Jr. Dr. Reid lived to see his son Thomas Harrison Reid become an active practicing lawyer in Portsmouth, Virginia after his graduation.[198] Rev. Reid filled the pulpit at Cool Spring Baptist Church, Franklin, Virginia on the 4th Sunday 1923. His sermons were enjoyed by all who heard him. Rev. Sanderlin was out of town.

At the time of his death on July 17, 1925, Reverend William Reid was pastor emeritus of First Baptist Murfreesboro, New Haven Missionary Baptist Church, and Bethany Baptist Church, Harrellsville, North Carolina; three of the largest churches in Hertford County. He had held the pastorate of one of these churches for 52 years. The others he had held for 40 years. He was one of the oldest Baptist Ministers in Hertford County. Rev. Reid's funeral was preached by Dr. Calvin Scott Brown at First Baptist Murfreesboro. Dr. Brown's sermon was a masterpiece. He related in simple language Rev. Reid's merits and worth. Dr. Brown stated that Rev. Reid lived in the spirit expressed in "Thanatopsis" and with a life filled with faithful service, wrapped the drapery of his epoch about him and lay down to pleasant dreams.

Jesus Put the Seal of Heaven on My Soul

I was lost in sin and darkness on the mountain bleak and cold.
I ask'd the blessed Lord to take control;
And He plac'd His arms around me;
And lead me to the fold.
Then He put the seal of heaven on my soul.

One day when the Lord calls you,
You must leave this earthly shore.
I can almost hear the Jordan billows roll.
He will calm the ragging tempest as He did in the days of old
If you have the seal of heaven on your soul.

Jesus Put the Seal of Heaven on My Soul
Yes, He put the seal of heaven when He made me whole.
No, I will never forget that Day when my Lord made me whole.
He Put the Seal of Heaven on My Soul.

E. Reynolds

Reverend Emanuel Reynolds was born February 1815 in Hertford County, North Carolina. In 1860 the mulatto household of Emmanuel Reynolds consisted of his wife, Sarah 46, and his seven sons: Henry 20, James 18, Dempsey 16, Joseph 13, Lemuel 11, George 4, and Samfron 1. In 1865, after the Civil War ended in the total defeat for the South in her efforts to maintain slavery as a norm for the southern aristocracy and freedom became a matter of law by President Abraham Lincoln's signing of the Declaration of Independence, Rev. Reynolds religious and social fervor along with his professional demeanor made him a much sought out member of the clergy. When the Old Eastern Missionary Baptist Association was organized at James City, North Carolina in the fall of 1865 in the church then known as "Slab Chapel," but since the name has been changed to Pilgrim Chapel. Rev. Emanuel Reynolds was present when the organization took place. Its first Moderator was Rev. Samuel Peterson, with Fred Long as Secretary, Hull Grimes, Nat Benton, Elias Brown, Henry Simmons, Thad Wilson, Thomas Erkett and John Washington. Although Rev. Reynolds was not present when the organization of the East Roanoke Association took place in the Haven Creek Baptist Church on Roanoke Island, 1886, According to their records, he and other notables led the forces for many years.[199]

Rev. Reynolds was licensed to preach the Gospel by the Pleasant Plains Missionary Baptist Church, Winton, North Carolina. Throughout his life he remained a faithful member of this church. Between 1865 and 1870 Rev. Reynolds is credited with the founding of the following North Carolina Churches: Jordan Grove, Winton; New Ahoskie Baptist Church, Ahoskie; Philippi Baptist Church, Cofield; New Bethany Baptist Church and Mount Pleasant Baptist Church in Harrellsville; First Baptist Church Colerain; Ashland Baptist Church, Bertie; and New Pineywood Chapel Baptist Church in Powellsville.[200]

In 1869 "Armanuel Reynolds of Winton, North Carolina was named by the General Assembly of North Carolina along with H. H. Hays of Gatesville, Bryant Lee of Woodville, R. R. Creecy of Plymouth, North Carolina, and Charles E. Hodges of Lake Drummond, Virginia as a body of corporate and policy, by the name of "The Society for the Relief of Preachers of the Roanoke Missionary Baptist Association.[201] By 1870, Rev. Reynolds signed all of his official documents with "D. D" "Doctor of Divinity." In the early days following slavery and during the Eve of Reconstruction Dr. Reynolds singularly performed more marriages in Hertford County North Carolina than any other minister, Black or White. The following list compiled from the marriage records in Hertford County Court House attest to the same.

Date	Groom's Name	Bride's Name	Groom's Father	Groom's Mother	Brides Father	Brides Mother
9/29/1868	Richard Jordan	Harriett Futrell	_____	Katie Jordan	Pete Futrell	Millie Futrell
1/17/1869	Abram Dildy	Rosetta Reddick	Drew Mitchell	Priscilla Dildy	Frazier Reddick	Sally Reddick
3/11/1869	Richard Britt	Ann E. Nickens	David Boon	Lavina Britt	William Nickens	Sally Nickens
5/14/1869	Preston Cumbo	Amanda F. Hall	David Cumbo	_____	Manuel Hall	Francis Hall
1/23/1870	Watson Hoggard	Eoline Chamblee	Minor Hoggard	Sadie Hoggard	Washington Chambee	Louiza Chambee
2/3/1870	Henry Flood	Martha Butler	Isaiah Flood	Abby Flood	Thos. Hall	Sally Butler
7/6/1870	Lewis H. Haughton	Anna Sessoms	Richard Houghton	Clairsey Houghton	Jenkins Sessoms	Lucretia Sessoms
7/23/1870	Nelson Harrell	Margaret Bazemore	Alan Harrell	Jenny Harrell	Simon Bazemore	Richard Bazemore
11/16/1870	Delphius Chavers	Eliza Hall	Henry Chavers	Patsy Chavers	Thomas Robbins	_____
12/10/1870	Henry Jerigan	Roseanna Cooper	Dossey Jernigan	Mary Jernigan	John Cooper	Elvira Cooper
12/31/1870	Daniel P. Askew	P. Perry	Harry Montgomery	Liddie Montgomery	David Perry	Mary Perry
6/27/1871	Umphery Flood	Cency Sessoms	James Manning	Martha Flood	Samuel Sessoms	Hannah Sessoms
11/26/1871	Turner Downing	Robecca Harrell	_____	_____	Moses Harrell	Hannah Harrell
10/17/1871	Washington Chamblee	Annie Wynns	_____	_____	_____	_____
12/26/1871	Peter Harrell	Harriett Skull	Tony Harrell	Lucy Harrell	Munroe Skull	Melia Skull
12/28/1871	Thomas Gerigan	Mary Eley	Wright Gernigan	Winnie Gernigan	Daniel Eley	Harriett Eley
10/29/1871	Boone Downing	Celia Beasley	_____	_____	Thomas White	Viley White

Elder Emmanuel Reynolds led the Roanoke Missionary Baptist Association in prayer during its Tuesday Morning, May 20, 1884 session.[202] The following year, Elder Reynolds was one of nine people appointed on the Committee on Grievances.[203] The Committee on Obituary reported on May 22, 1906 since the 1905 meeting of the Association it has pleased Almighty God to take out of our midst Rev. Emmanuel Reynolds, one of the fathers of and founders of this Association.[204] Rev. Reynolds was described "as a powerful speaker of God, a poor reader but of unusual force and common sense as a preacher."[205] The following ministers paid the following tributes to the character of Rev. Emanuel Reynolds. Rev. M. W. D. Norman, A. M., D. D., of Washington, D. C., paid a high tribute to the life of Rev. Reynolds as a pastor, whom he succeeded as pastor and said he was a light to him. As a revivalist he called him wonderful and said, he possessed unusual power of the unsaved. Rev. W. A. Taylor followed with tender recollections. Rev. Luke Pierce told of his great earnestness, his tears and loving heart. Rev. Father Hodges added his testimony to that of others, speaking especially of his excellent character. [206]

If Jesus Goes With Me

It may be in the valley, where countless dangers hide;
It may be in the sunshine that I, in peace, abide.
But this one thing I know,
It may be dark or fair,
But if Jesus goes with me, I'll go anywhere.

It may be I must carry the blessed word of life
Across the burning deserts to those in sinful strife;
And tho' it be my lot to bear my colors there,
If Jesus goes with me, I'll go anywhere.

It is not mine to question the judgment of my Lord,
It is but mine to follow the leading of His word.
But if I go or stay,
Or, whether here or there,
I'll be, with my Savior, content anywhere.

If Jesus goes with me, I'll go anywhere!
Tis heaven to me,
Wherever I may be, If He is there!
I count it a privilege here
His cross to bear
If Jesus goes with me, I'll go anywhere.

J. T. Reynolds

Reverend J. T. Reynolds was the Secretary of the Roanoke Missionary Baptist Association from its inception at Haven's Creek on Roanoke Island in 1866 until 1873 when the Roanoke Association met at Antioch Missionary Baptist Church in South Mills, North Carolina. He was also the Corresponding Secretary of the North Carolina Baptist State School Convention from 1877-1888. *"The Elizabeth City North Carolinian News"* for August 12, 1869 published an article on the Lincoln Institute formerly known as O. O. Howard School. The news article reported that the student population included 60 or more students. The student body orations were delivered by Master James J. Reynolds and Master George Reynolds, both current students. Additional remarks were made by Rev. Lemuel Washington Boon, Joseph P. Weaver, Simon Collins, Esquire and the Honorable J. T. Reynolds. The August 19, 1869 issue contains a column-length address delivered on above occasion by J. T. Reynolds of Northampton."

Send The Power Again

There was pow'r, O Lord, in the days of old,
To kindle a fire in hearts grown old.
That we on thy word may now lay hold,
Lord, send thy pow'r again.

There was pow'r by which ev'ry tongue could speak,
New life-giving powr' unto the weak,
That sent them the wandering to seek,
Lord, sent that pow'r again.

There was pow'r, O Lord, in the old-time pray'r,
It thrilled ev'ry heart and lingered there,
To speak and to pray and to work with thee,
Lord send the pow'r again.

8

GENERATION 1

Willis Arterbridge

Elder Willis Arterbridge (alternately spelled as Outterbridge in many of the records of the Annual Minutes of the Roanoke Missionary Baptist Association), was born during January 1839 in Plymouth, (Washington County), North Carolina. He married Emma Arterbridge in 1866 and this union was blessed with the following children: Joseph, Leah, Lizzy, July Ann., and, Joseph Arterbridge. Elder. Arterbridge was listed on the 1871, 1878, 1884, & 1885 Roanoke Missionary Baptist Association List of Elders. He was one of nine people appointed to the Committee of Permanent Organization for those years. He listed a Martin County Post Office Box in Hamilton, North Carolina for mailing purposes. Elder Arterbridge was the delegate from Sycamore Baptist Church, Hamilton, N. C., to the 1878 Annual Session. He was one of seven men appointed to the Committee on Time, Place and Preacher for the 1885 Annual Session. On the Third Day Afternoon Session of the 1884 Annual Session at Zion Hill, Bertie County, N. C., the Committee on Pulpit Supply reported that Elder W. Arterbridge (Elder H. H. Norman alternate) would preach at the stand in "The Grove" at 3 O 'Clock P. M. When the Annual Session convened at Providence Missionary Baptist Church, Chowan County, N. C., on Tuesday Morning, May 19, 1885 Elder Willis Arterbridge was one of nine men appointed to the Committee on Grievances. The other men were: Elder Thaddeus Wilson, S. Cherry, C. J. White, A. Cowper, Emanuel Reynolds, N. Hyman, M. Taylor and B. J. Lennox.[207] He was reappointed to the Committee on Permanent Organization in 1885. Elder Willis Arterbridge remained active in the Roanoke Missionary Baptist Association following the split to form the West Roanoke Missionary Baptist Association. He was reappointed to the Committee on Permanent Organization during the Twenty-First Annual Session held with the Church of Christ at Antioch, Camden County, N. C., on the Tuesday after the 3rd Lord's Day in May 1886, and was also selected as the Vice-Moderator. Reverend Willis Arterbridge, of Hamilton, organized a new church on the north side of Elizabeth City during February 1896.[208]

Nelson Beamon

Nelson Beamon was born in Gatesville, North Carolina about 1831 to unknown parents. On March 31, 1867, he married the former Mary Holfer of Gates, North Carolina. To this union seven children were born: James E. Beamon, Cora L., Catherine, William A., Harriet Ann, Peter G., Berneda, and Arosia P. Beamon. Mr. Beamon served as the Treasurer of the Roanoke

Missionary Baptist Association from 1900 to 1920. On Thursday, May 24th 1922 during the Fifty-Sixth Annual Session of the Roanoke Missionary Baptist Association held with Corinth Baptist Church, Jarvisburg, North Carolina, the Treasurer's bag brought for Brother Nelson Beamon while Treasurer was passed over to Brother L. S. Westcott, Treasurer.[209]

Harry Beasley

Reverend Harry Beasley was born about 1845. He was a resident of the Newland section of Pasquotank County, North Carolina. He was a member of the Ramoth Gilead Missionary Baptist Church, Newland. He was the president of the Northeast Bound Sunday School Convention. He presided over the 1927 Sunday School Convention when it convened at the Haven Creek Missionary Baptist Church, Manteo, N. C., on Friday, November 18th-20th, 1927. The church was beautifully decorated for the occasion. The Welcome Address was given by Mr. J. W. Woodley of Manteo. Remarks were made by the Reverends S. H. Jenkins of Elizabeth City, N. C.

The meeting was largely attended by scores and scores of visitors, friends and delegates in the midst of then were Professor Solomon Butts of Gatesville, N. C.; Mrs. H. H. Wilson of Bell—cross, N. C.; Mr. J. W. Forbes of Shiloh, N. C.; Rev. S. H. Jenkins, Mr. W. S. Westcott, J. H. Perkins, Mrs. Francis Beasley, and Mss Sarah Beasley from Elizabeth City, N. C., Rev. W. J. Elliott of old Trap, N. C., who preached the Introductory Sermon, which was a soul stirring sermon. After which an offering was taken and Mss Etheridge the chairperson of the Committee on Arrangement for the homes of the delegates made her report. The convention was then dismissed. The session was opened on Saturday morning by Scripture reading and Prayer by the Reverend S. H. Jenkins and Reverend D. H. Hopkins. After remarks by President W. Harry Beasley, Professor Solomon Butts discussed No. 1, *"The Duty of Every Sunday School, and B. Y. U. to the Roanoke Collegiate Institute."* He talked with power and eloquence. A Saturday Free for All Program was rendered. Music was furnished by the choir, with Mss Vann Lee Staton at the piano followed by an address by Rev. J. W. Forbes. Papers were read by Mss Sarah Beasley and Mss Elsie Etheridge, and Solo by sung by Mrs. H. H. Wilson. The services adjourned until Sunday. The delegates and Mr. Marshall Collins conducted Sunday school. Mr. J. H. Perkins made a forceful address to the children. The next sermon was the Northeast Bound Sunday School Convention Annual Sermon by Reverend M. H. Beasley. He chose his text from Exodus 3: 2, "Behold the bush burned with fire and the bush was not consumed." The president spoke with power! The B. Y. P. U. opened at 5:30 P. M. with Mrs. Emma Mann in her chair. Addresses were made by Rev. J. W. McPherson and Professor J. W. Staton. Papers were read by Ida M. Madjett, Ms Elsie Daniels, Mss Sarah Beasley, V. L. Staton and Elsie Etheridge. Duets by the following: Daisy Ashbey, Elizabeth Golden, Lillie M. Ashbey and Manava Golden, Ruby Louise Madjett, and Letha Collins, Almeda Dozier and Mable Wescutt, Mr. J. H. Perkins and V. L. Staten, Jessie B. Madjett, and P. O. Scarbough. Remarks were made by Mrs. Mary Mann and Mrs. Laura S. Wood. A solo was rendered by Mrs. H. H. Wilson. The Closing sermon was delivered by Rev. S. H. Jenkins. He preached as one sent from God. The total collection for the 1927 Northeast Bound Sunday School Convention was $106.00. The officers were: Rev. W. H. Beasley, President; Mr. J. J. Bearnard, Vice President, and J. H. Perkins, Clerk.

Reverend W. Henry Beasley died at home on Saturday, October 6, 1928. He was 81 years old. Funeral services were conducted on Sunday, October 7, 1928 at Ramoth Gilead by Reverend Edward Lamb. Mrs. Sarah Jane Beasley died January 10, 1933. She was held in high esteem by both Colored and white. She was survived by three sons: Rev. M. H. Beasley, Matt Beasley and Charles Beasley, all of Newland.

C. M. Billups

Reverend C. M. Billups, one of the pioneers of the Roanoke Baptist Association was on the sick list during May 1921. He died at his home on Bank Street on Sunday, July 27, 1925 at 75 years of age. Funeral services were held at St. Steven Church on Tuesday, July 29. Rev. H. H. Norman delivered the principal eulogy. He was also eulogized by Rev. C. M. Cartwright. Rev. T. James and several other ministers. He was a member of the Whitnut Lodge, 426 Prince Hall Masons. He was buried with Masonic honors. Rev. C. C. Drew, District Grand Deputy Master officiated in the ceremonies. Son and daughter, Mr. & Mrs. Charles Billups, of Hertford, were present for the funeral, also daughter, Mrs. Martha P. Turner, of Norfolk. He was a leading minister in the association for more than forty years.

Benjamin J. Bowser

Benjamin J. Bowser married Mary Susan Thomas, the daughter of James and Edna Thomas of Powell's Point, Currituck, North Carolina on June 22, 1892. There were several children born to this union. While serving at Pea Island, North Carolina Benjamin Bowser and the other surf men had a wonderful opportunity to become literate. The 1877 Annual Report thanked an anonymous donator for the books that were anonymous donated to the station. The books were "well adapted to the reading abilities and the interest of these brave men who constituted our crews," including adventure, travel, and shipwreck stories as well as religious works. Other Pea Island crewmembers also learned to read and write during their career on Pea Island. The 1880 Census listed Benjamin J. Bowser as a "fisherman" and "CRW" meaning cannot read or write.[210] He was hired by Etheridge in December 1881. In 1886, Etheridge appointed Bowser as the number one surf man when Lewis Westcott failed his physical examination.[211] From this point forward, when Etheridge was absent or ill, B. J. Bowser was the Captain of the Pea Island Lighthouse and recorded daily activities in the same log book and wrote very well.[212]

On Wednesday Morning, May 29th 1885.[213] Benjamin Bowser was appointed to the Roanoke Missionary Baptist Association Committee on Permanent Organization. On motion of H. H. Norman a Committee of nine was appointed to "*Time, Place and Preachers*" for the 1887 Roanoke Missionary Baptist Association, Viz: B. J. Bowser, B. Thomas, S. S. Norman, J. D. Jones, Walter Sweat, E. Perkins, Charles Barnett, J. H. Johnson, and E. E. Randolph.[214] Bowser was elected as Chairman of this group. He made the following report:

> We, your Committee on Time, Place and Preachers of the next Association, beg leave to report as follows: The proper place is Sycamore Chapel, Martin County, N. C.; the proper time is Tuesday after the 3d Lord's Day in May, 1887; to preach the Introductory Sermon, Elder Z. H. Berry, alternate, Elder I. B. Roach; all of which humbly submit.
>
> B. J. Bowser, Chm'n.[215]

Benjamin Bowser was buried in the Bowser family plot on the premises of the Corinth Missionary Baptist Church, 7300 Jarvisburg, North Carolina. One hundred years following his burial a committee made up of several Bowser descendants, along with a local historian and two ministers at Corinth Missionary Baptist Church secured the support and assistance of Currituck County and the Coast Guard to renovate his grave in anticipation of a memorial and tomb dedication on June 11, 2012. The dedication ceremony commenced promptly at 6:30 P. M. with remarks being made by the Coast Guard Small Boat Station Elizabeth City Chief Robert Riemer, North Carolina Secretary of State Elaine Marshall and Currituck County Commissioner Paul O'Neal. Retired Coast Guard Rear Admiral Stephen Rochon was the keynote speaker. The Coast Guard provided the honor guard and a Lyle Gun salute. Bowser's great grandson, William Forbes, Jr. of Newport News, Virginia, said that he and his family were very proud. What these men accomplished under very adverse conditions was quite remarkable. They love their country. A month earlier, William Aldred Boon, a free born mulatto of the Reynoldson District of Gates County, North Carolina received similar recognition by the Sons of the Union for his love of God and country.

J B. Catus

Joseph "Jeb" B. Catus was born January 1854 in Hertford County, North Carolina. He married Mary "Mollie" Cherry Hall, daughter of Albert Vann and Sally Hall of Hertford County on September 07, 1876 in Hertford County. The Catus' were the parents of William D. Catus, born Aug 1877, Aurora Mamie Catus, born June 15, 1880, James Catus born August 09, 1883, Joseph Catus born September 25, 1925, Lizzie Washburn Catus born October 16, 1885, and Seward Eugene Catus born April 24, 1898, all children born in Hertford County. Joseph had three brothers: Richard Eli Catus (1861-1927) who married Mary Lou Leonard and William Gaston Catus (1853-1932) who married Ella Moore, and James Catus, born about 1855 who married Mary E. Bizzell. Joseph Catus first appeared on the 1870 census in Winton living with a Walden family. Joseph B. Catus was the Postmaster in Winton from 1897 until his death in 1913. Booker T. Washington wrote to Charles D. Norton on November 21, 1910 that J. B. Catus, black postmaster at Winton, North Carolina., did not have tuberculosis as reported. Booker T. Washington had received a favorable report of his examination for tuberculosis by the president of the country medical society.[216] He graduated from the Hampton Institute, Hampton Virginia.

Rev. J. B. Catus was one of five people appointed to the Committee on Sabbath School Statistics by motion, on Tuesday morning, May 19, 1885 at the Twentieth Annual Session of the Roanoke Missionary Baptist Association held with the Church of Christ at Providence Baptist Church, Edenton, Chowan County, North Carolina. Other members were: A. Cobb, Elder Hayes, I. Pinder and J. A. White. Joseph B. Catus was a member of the 1886 faculty of the Water's Institute in Winton, North Carolina. Other faculty members included Miss Seabyrd Williamston, Matron; Dr. Manassas Pope and Dr. C. S. Brown, principal. In 1908 Mr. Catus of Nashville, North Carolina was the founder, president and member of the Endowment Department of the D. B. L. Number 7., of the Grand United Order of the Odd Fellows. He was also a member of the Jefferson Standard Life Insurance Company, Raleigh, North Carolina.[217] Mr. Joseph Catus died May 16, 1913 in Hertford Co., North Carolina.

Charles Capps

Reverend Charles Capps was born about 1825 in Belvidere, Perquimans, North Carolina. During 1870 the Capps family was living in the South Mills District of Camden County, North Carolina. The family consisted of his wife Ann Capps[218] (28), Georgiana (12) and Gideon Capps (1). In 1880 the Capps family included Charles's wife Harriett Anna (36), George A. (17), Gideon (11), and James A. Capps (7) was living in Belvedere Township of Perquimans' County, North Carolina. By 1910 sixty-four year old Harriett Anna is widowed and living with Charles' 40 year old single daughter Georgia Anna. Charles Capps name appeared on the Roster of Ordained Elders of the Roanoke Missionary Baptist Association from 1878-1885. He was the third pastor of the New Middle Swamp Missionary Baptist Church. He was the pastor of Mount Carmel Missionary Baptist Church in the New Land section of Pasquotank County, North Carolina. Rev. Capps died before 1900.

Benjamin Clark

Benjamin Clark born about 1815 in the Woodville section of Bertie County, North Carolina. He married Annie Unknown. He was listed on the 1878 Roanoke Missionary Baptist Association Roster of Ordained Elders living in the Woodville, section of Bertie County, North Carolina. He is one of the signatory's of the Elder Lemuel Washington Boon's Memorial. In 1880 censuses he listed his occupation as a Minister of the Gospel.

Rev. W. A. Cobb

Reverend Dr. William Alexander Cobb of 318 Spruce Street, Suffolk, Virginia was born in Bertie County, North Carolina about 1856 to the marriage of William Alexander, Sr., and Allie B. Cobb. His first marriage was to Ms. Pleasant Cobb and to this union, a daughter Mildred Cobb was born. His second marriage was to Mrs. Mary Alberta B. Cobb in 1897 and to this union four children were born: W. A. Cobb, Jr., Frank, Lula "Tency" and Lillie Cobb. Lillie's May 12, 1910 marriage to Thomas Dildy, son of Thomas and Susan Dildy of Nansemond County, Virginia marked the second time that the Cobb household had been in transition. Lula had moved out into the countryside to take a teaching position earlier. The Cobb's made their permanent residence in the City of Suffolk, Virginia after Lula's marriage. On the 1910 census record Rev. Cobb listed his occupation as minister of a Baptist Church. He was awarded the honorary Doctor of Divinity degree by the Rev. Doctor W. Bishop Johnson, D. D., L. L. D., of Washington D.C., during the Wednesday Night Service of the Forty-Seven Annual Session {1912)[219] Rev. Cobb was known as the "dean" of local ministry in Nansemond County and in Northeastern North Carolina. He was very active in the civic and the religious enterprises of both.

Rev. W. A. Cobb was an active member of the Roanoke Missionary Baptist Association. He was one of sixteen people appointed in 1885 as members of the Permanent Organization of the Roanoke Missionary Baptist Association. On Wednesday, May 22nd, 1907 during the Forty-Second Annual Session Convention at the Corner Stone Baptist Church, Elizabeth City, Rev. Cobb preached at the Olive Branch Missionary Baptist Church for the Pulpit Committee. At the Thursday Morning May 23, 1912 Session of the Roanoke Baptist Association Moderator Griffin presented Rev. W. A. Cobb, the pastor of St. John Baptist Church, Creswell, North Carolina. In his address, Rev. Cobb named many of the principals for which Baptist stand, complimented the brothers for the good work done in uplifting the people and building the moral character and spiritual strength. He entered a most hearty and pleasing welcome to the Association.[220] The following year, Dr. Cobb stated to the Forty-eight Annual Session of the Roanoke Missionary Baptist Association held with the Welch's Chapel Baptist Church, Tyner, North Carolina that "If a man is right the people will follow and the results will be good."[221] He was subsequently appointed to the Committee of Petitions. [222] At the Wednesday Afternoon Session of the Forty-Ninth Annual Session (1914) held with Saint Steven Baptist Church, Elizabeth City, North Carolina, the Moderator announced that the meeting was open and called the proceeding. A telegram was read from Rev. Dr. W. A. Cobb. By motion the Association expressed her sympathy for Rev. Cobb's bereavement and ordered the telegram be spread on the minutes. The May 20, 1914 Telegram, read: Rev. G. D. Griffin, Moderator R. M. B. Association: Advise Association that death of sister prevents me from coming. W. A. Cobb.[223] The following year (1915), Rev. Cobb gave expressions on the moderators address and delivered the Thursday 3: 30 P. M., afternoon sermon at the Gale Street Missionary Baptist Church, Edenton, North Carolina.

Reverend W. A. Cobb was the pastor of the First Baptist Powellsville, Norh Carolina during the 1885 split of the Roanoke Missionary Baptist Association. Rev. Alexander Cobb was elected to the pastorate of the Oak Grove Baptist Church, Nansemond County, (Suffolk), Virginia in 1900. He served this congregation until 1904. He pastured Mt. Eprew, St. Paul, and St. Stephen Missionary Baptist Church. He was called to the pastorate of the St. John Baptist Church, Creswell, North Carolina. Reverend Cobb accepted the second call to the pastorate of the Mount Sinai Baptist Church, Como, North Carolina in March 1917.[224] He had formerly pastured this church 1896. Reverend Cobb left Mount Sinai Church in 1913 to accept a church in Virginia. Rev. Cobb was concurrently pasturing the Mount Carmel Missionary Baptist Church (formerly the Harvey's Chapel Missionary Baptist Church) in New Land (Pasquotank County), North Carolina in 1920.

He pastured both churches for 10 years. Rev. Cobb is listed on the 1920 Roanoke Missionary Baptist Association Finance Report as the Pastor of Antioch Church, South Mills, Mt. Delane, Tyrell County, and St. John, Washington County, North Carolina. During 1929 he was the pastor of First Baptist Aulander Missionary Baptist Church where he delivered a powerful sermon to a full congregation.

Mr. W. H. Crocker of Suffolk, Virginia gave a reception at his spacious home on Wednesday, January 5, 1924 at 2:30. P. M. for Rev. W. A. Cobb. He was joined by several other ministers of Suffolk, Virginia, namely: Rev. T. J. Johnson, Rev. W. T. Faulk, Rev. J. W. Bridgeforth, Rev. James A. Harrell, Rev. B. F. Gaines, Rev. R. J. Butts, and Rev. J. E. Jordan. The menu consisted of fruit punch, tomato soup, Bouliean and saltine crackers, Smithfield ham and cheese, sweet potatoes, cream peas, corn cake, creamed potatoes, roasted turkey, sweet pickles, cranberry sauce, hot parker house rolls, pine apple salad served with lettuce and cherries, nut cake, fruit cake, pound cake, cocoanut cake, and coffee and cream. After this scrumptious dinner the guest spent a very pleasant afternoon visiting together. Mr. W. H. Crocker acted as toastmaster. The following questions were discussed by the ministers. 1). Is there sufficient harmony between the schools and the churches, if not why? 2). In what year did Suffolk have its greatest revival? 3). Why is Suffolk a desirable place in which to live? 4)What can local ministers do to assist the educational system to bring it up to other neighboring cities and what can they do to create a better cultural spirit? 5). The need of a nondenominational ministerial Union to advise along lines of business, civic and religion was discussed. Dr. James A. Herrel was selected to extend words of congratulations to the hostess. All agree that its equal had not been matched in Suffolk before.

Reverend W. A. Cobb's schedule was a very active one. On Friday night, December 2, 1916, Rev. Cobb and his choir and congregation were the guest for Rev. P. L. Boone's second Pastoral Anniversary at the Pine Street Baptist Church, Suffolk, VA. Miss Annie Webb and Mr. L. W. Spruell were married at Saint Mark's A. M. E. Zion Church by Rev. W. A. Cobb, on Sunday December 30, 1917. A large number of friends witnessed the ceremony. Rev. Cobb accepted the pastoral call of the Pleasant Hill Baptist Church, Suffolk, Virginia before 1916. He concurrently pastured the Balm of Gilead Missionary Baptist Church, Suffolk, Virginia. Rev. Cobb preached a powerful sermon at Pleasant Union Baptist Church, Suffolk, Virginia for the Woman Home Missions Day on Sunday, February 6, 1921. A collection of $36.84 was raised for Home & Foreign Missions. The service was well attended. On the First Sunday in January 1924 the Nansemond and Isle of Wight Sunday School Union held a very successful service on first Saturday and first Sunday at Pleasant Union Baptist Church. Rev. W. A. Cobb delivered the sermon to an appreciative crowd. On the 4th of July, 1924, Rev. W. A. Cobb, D. D., and his congregation, the Pleasant Union Baptist Church participated with a ground-breaking service for the Rev. J. T. Johnson and the Pine Street Baptist Church, Suffolk, Virginia. The Pine Street Baptist choir sent out appeals for members of the choirs of sister churches in the city to come from one great choir. Rev. Johnson erected a huge tent on the property purchased by Pine Street Church and after an inspiring sermon preached by Rev. C. P. Madison, broke ground for the new church edifice.[225] Immediately following that service Rev. Cobb motored to Travis, North Carolina to conduct the funeral service of Mrs. Winnie Rowsome, wife of Mr. Vann Rowsome. Mrs. Rowsome died July 18th 1924 at age 46. Rev. Cobb officiated at the funeral. In his eulogy he stated that the deceased had been a member of the St. John Church for 30 years and always responded to every call for service made upon her. The Second Baptist Church, Murfreesboro,

N. C. was crowded on the first Sunday in May 1925 to hear a sermon delivered by Rev. Cobb, who preached the funeral of Mrs. Porter, wife of Mr. Richard Porter. The town of Murfreesboro looked forward for the arrival of Rev. W. A. Cobb on the 5th Sunday in May 1925 to preach the Annual Odd Fellow sermon. On the 3rd Sunday in July 1925 Rev. Cobb and the Pleasant Union Baptist Church family baptized several new converts. A large number was immersed. At Eleven o'clock he preached to the delight of his hears, and Holy Communion was administered.[226] Mr. W. T. Goodman and family motored to Balm of Gilead Church on the 3rd Sunday afternoon where they worshipped with Dr. W. A. Cobb. Reverend Moore addressed the Sunday school at Pleasant Union on the second Sunday in August 1925. One member joined the Sunday school. At 11:00 A. M. he preached a spirited sermon. The pastor, Dr. Cobb was out of the city. Rev. W. A. Cobb, Rev. Anderson Boone, Dr. James Harrell, Rev. W. M. Brinkley, Rev. W. E. Spratley and Dr. C. L. Alexander were listed in the *Suffolk Journal and Guide* on October 17, 1925 as able and strong pastors who had risen far above the usual quarrellings of their contemporaries and had gone on to saving sinners from their sin. Rev. Cobb, D. D., and the congregation of the Pleasant Hill hosted the Sharon Baptist Association in September 1927. All churches, delegates and friends attending the body were instructed to get off the train at the Norfolk and Western Seaboard Coastline at Virginia Stations. Rev. Cobb and the Pleasant Union Baptist Church Congregation hosted a very successful meeting for the deputy's council of the Knights of Pythons on Thanksgiving Day 1927. A large number of deputies were present. The money raised totaled $31.37. Reverend Cobb and the congregation entertained the Minister's and Deacon's Union Rally. Rev. Cobb and the congregation were planning to build a new church, as he was known as a great church builder. The congregation had completed extensive repairs on the church. They were in the process to wiping out several other debts. The three hundred dollars was collected during this service.

Rev. Dr. & Mrs. W. A. Cobb and family returned from an extensive motor trip to the church, of which he was the beloved pastor, at Creswell, N. C. They had the experience of crossing the Albemarle Sound which they enjoyed very much. The Rev. Dr. Cobb was a great fisherman, but did not have the time to catch any of them while crossing. Rev. & Mrs. Cobb was the guest of his sister, Mrs. Ethel Brown of Columbus, Ohio. They motored to Rich Square, North Carolina. They were joined by Mrs. Cobb's sister, Mrs. Lula Keene. Rev. W. A. Cobb, Rev. W. S. Creecy, of Rich Square, Rev. D. L. Simmons, of Windsor, N. C. Rev. G. T. Rousen, of Murfreesboro, and Rev. P. A. Bishop, of Rich Square, left Norfolk, Virginia, Monday night, August 30th 1926 for Brooklyn, New York., where the Lott Carey Foreign Mission Convention met August 31 to September 3, with Holy Trinity Baptist Church, Rev. T. S. Harden, pastor. The party reportedly remained together throughout the journey. The trip was very much enjoyed by all.[227] The group went on a sightseeing trip in New York City and to Columbia University, Zoological Gardens and many other places of interest. On their return trip to Norfolk they stopped at the Sesqui-Centennial at Philadelphia. There they saw an art exhibition from all nations, the Negro included. They saw an exhibit of Negro newspapers, among them the Journal and Guide, the home town paper. Rev. William Allen Cobb stated that he returned home with a greater desire to do foreign missionary work.[228]

Rev. W. A. Cobb conducted the 1930 funeral services for Charlie Parker, Veteran of World War I from the Tyne's Street Baptist Church, Suffolk, Virginia. Mr. Parker was a native of Gates County, N. C., having moved to Suffolk several years ago. Left to mourn his loss were several family members including his wife, Mrs. Pinkie Parker, several children, and his mother, Mrs.

Annie Parker. Mr. Parker's casket was covered with an American flag and encircled with many floral tributes.[229] On the first Sunday in August 1930 Rev. Cobb conducted the Sunday afternoon funeral of Mr. John Newby at the Balm of Gideon Church, Suffolk, Virginia. Mr. Newby was buried in the church cemetery. He was survived by a wife, Mrs. Dina Newby, four sisters, Mrs. Jeaneete Pierce, Pearl Newby of New York, Mrs. Livia Lassiter of Nansemond County, Virginia; fourteen grandchildren and sixteen great grandchildren. Mr. Newby was an old resident of Nansemond County and died at his home near Nurneyville Friday, August 1, 1930 following an illness of a few days. The death of Mrs. Louise Jordan on April 23, 1932 at Cypress Chapel was a surprise to her friends. The funeral was held last Friday from the Balm of Gilliam Church, Suffolk, Virginia. Rev. W. A. Cobb, the pastor officiated.

Reverend Cobb was a teacher of the Nansemond County and City Minister's Conference which met each 4th Wednesday of the month. The fact that the conference was comprised of all such broad-minded theologically liberal, co-operative and well prepared men as the Rev. Dr. J. A. Harrell, the president; the Rev. J. H. Ricks, secretary; the Rev. Anderson Boone, Dean of Common-sense Theology; Rev. W. A. Cobb, Dean of Practical Theology; the Rev. P. L. Boone, Critique, and several others who were liberally endowed with natural and acquired ability was very amazing. [230] The Ministers Conference of Suffolk, and vicinity, met on time Tuesday at 1 o'clock, at Tynes Street Baptist Church with the newly elected president, Rev. W. M. Turner, in the chair. Rev. W. E. Tyler was appointed critic for the conference after which the president asked Rev. W. A. Cobb, who was present to lead in prayer service about thirty minutes which consisted of songs and experiences from those present.[231]

Mrs. Allie Cobb, the wife of Rev. W. A. Cobb was sick throughout much of January 1926. She returned home from the hospital in January and convalesced at home throughout the year. She suffered a nervous break-down after the death of her mother. She began to improve during the month of June 1931. Rev. W. A. Cobb died Sunday morning, January 17, 1934. The Pleasant Hill Baptist Church which he pastured for many years, and remained a member thereafter, was filled to an overflowing crowd for his funeral. Thousands were unable to gain entry to the sanctuary to pay their final respects to their fallen leader. Over 50 ministers were present and several made remarks on the great life and ministry of Rev. W. A. Cobb. The funeral service was in charge of the Rev. J. A. Lewis, pastor of the Tynes Street Baptist Church, Suffolk, Virginia, Dr. C. S. Brown, president of the Waters Training School; Winton, North Carolina was the main eulogist and delivered a masterful and impressive sermon. Among the out of town ministers present were the Reverend's: W. G. Privott, Edenton, N. C., and S. H. Jenkins. Rev. Cobb was survived by his wife, Mary Alberta Cobb and children. Interment followed in the Rosemont Cemetery, Suffolk, Virginia.

Closer Still

Savior, draw me to Thy side,
Near still, near still!
There would I in peace abide,
Near still, Near still!
Songs of praises I would sing,
Louder still, lounder still!
Praise to glorify my King,
Louder still, louder still.

May Thy love within me shine,
Brighter still, brighter still!
As a beacon light of Thine,
Brighter still, Brighter still.

Draw me closer, Lord to Thee, Let me now Thy beauty see;
Help me, Lord, to know thy will,
Draw me closer, closer still.

T. M. Collins

Reverend Thomas M. Collins was born January 1838 to William & Jane Collins of Hertford County, North Carolina. He married Christiana Collins. He did not followed his father's trade and become a painter, instead he became a brick mason, and logger. During 1850 nine year old Thomas was living in the Northern District of Hertford County, North Carolina with his siblings: Elizabeth (9), John (7), Simon (4) and Harrison Collins (1). In 1860 twenty-two year old mulatto Thomas M. Collins was living with Joshua Will (22 and overseer), and Roscious Gatling. They were earning their living as common field labors. In 1900 Thomas M. Collins was living with his 84 year old mother in Hertford County. Other household members included: his sister, Elizabeth Collins, and Sabra Lee his 82 year old maternal aunt. He listed his employment as a minister of the Gospel. He declared that he had been married for 24 years.

On May 19, 1863, Thomas M. Collins goes to Fort Monroe, Virginia and enlisted as a Private in Company B, 188 Pennsylvania Inf. He was discharged at the end of the Civil War on December 14, 1865. He suffered from a Gun Shot Wound to the Foot. He returned home and laid the underpinnings for the Philippi Missionary Baptist Church, Cofield, N. C.

Rev. Thomas Collins' contributions to the Roanoke Missionary Baptist Association were many. He held many positions in the Association prior to the split. He was called to the pastorate of the Pleasant Plains Church in 1884. He was the first mulatto to serve this church. He was a member of the church and filled the pulpit until an ordained minister could be appointed.

George Dyer

George Dyer, the Lord of the Great Dismal, died in the arms of his wife in the heart of the Great Dismal Swamp Thursday morning, October 23, 1924. He was buried at Elizabeth City on October 30, 1924. In a new grave in the Negro cemetery on the outskirts of the town a black woman and colored friends deposited the silent clay of one who suffered much by reason of a white man's lust, but who found himself and acquired a philosophy of life that enabled him to live happily to the end of his days.

George Dyer was born in Elizabeth City 68 (1849) years ago. His mother was a colored woman; his father was a white man. The mother abandoned him on the steps of the county jail the night he was born. When the puny infant was found there the next morning, everybody thought it was a white child. He was adopted by George Dyer, the village tailor of the day and Mr. & Mrs. Dyer raised him as their own until he was 14 years old. Some say that the tailor George Dyer was his father.

The child that had appeared so white at birth grew darker with the years and Mrs. Dyer, the tailor's wife, raised so many objections to keeping the colored child, that George was turned out when he was 14 years old. Out of the white world into which he had been taken without question he was thrown into the black world with a stigma upon his name. He might have resented what appeared to him as the inhumanity of man, and, in his bitterness and shame have developed into an enemy of society. But he did not do that. He says he tried for a long time to be a white man, but he made no progress. Finally, good naturedly, he said to himself" "there's no use trying to be what you aint." This was his philosophy of life.

For many years George lived in the heart of the Great Dismal Swamp. He was the keeper of the sluice gates that feed the waters of Lake Drummond in the Dismal Swamp Canal. He was also fire warden for Arbuckle Brothers., the sugar refiners who have big timber holdings in the heart of the Great Dismal Swamp. He liked to be called the Lord of the Great Dismal. He married a black woman and raised a family of six children by her there. In the arms of this black woman whom he loved devotedly, he fell and breathed his last when death laid a painful hand upon his heart.

Dyer Street in Elizabeth City was named for the tailor who in reputed to have been his father of George. Dyer the tailor lived on the corner of Main and Dyer streets, on the very lot where the home of W. J. Woodley once stood. George Dyer inherited property when his father died and sold the property to Mr. Woodley for what would be regarded today as an inconsiderable sum. George Dyer's church affiliations are unknown. He was included in this book just because his story is worth sharing. It mirror's the life of the mulatto throughout the South.

E. W. Early

Reverend E. W. Early was born about 1847. His Funeral Services were conducted on the first Sunday in December 1933. Rev. Early was eighty years old, and a pioneer member of the West Roanoke Missionary Baptist Association. Rev. A. W. Lamb officiated. The funeral was attended by many church representatives. His death Notice appeared in the December 9, 1933 edition of the Elizabeth City News edition of the Journal and Guide.

George Edward Freeman

Reverend George Edward Freeman was born during March 1845 in Bertie County, North Carolina. He married Catherine Unknown in 1865 and to this union, William was born about 1865, Penelope was born about 1867, Cora A., was born about 1868. In 1870, Reverend Freeman's household consisted of Anderson Freeman born 1862, 8, Penelope 5, Mitchell Lilly, 25, Jordan Lilly, 2 and Moriah Lilly 1 year old. Ten years later, in 1880 his household included John, born about 1871, Peter, born about 1873, Edward, born about 1875, Rosetta, born about 1875, and Gracey, born November 1870. In 1890 additional children have been added to the household William A., born about January 1882, Moses A, born during March 1886 and Lang E. Freeman born during July 1889. Most of the earlier household members are no longer members of the Freeman household.

Reverend Freeman was a very active member of the Roanoke Missionary Baptist Association. He was listed on the 1879 Minister's Roll as an ordain Elder. When the West Roanoke Association convened in its Third Annual Session with Swamp Chapel Church, Northampton County, N. C., on Tuesday before the second Sunday in October 1888, Rev. G. E. Freeman conducted the devotional services. He preached in "the Grove at 11:00 A. M., on Tuesday-Morning October 10th, 1888.

He was the first pastor called to the Saint Elmo Baptist Church, Windsor, North Carolina. Judge F. D. Winston of Bertie County North Carolina sold the land of the late Mrs. Hannah Burden, who died without leaving a written will or without having a next of kin, to the Rev. George Edward Freeman for the purpose of building the Saint Elmo Baptist Church. Therefore, Reverend Freeman and the congregation chose the name Saint Elmo after the phenomenon known as St. Elmo's fire. St. Elmo's fire is seen during thunderstorms when the ground below the storm is electrically charged, and there is high voltage in the air between the cloud and the ground. The voltage tears apart the air molecules and the gas begins to glow. It takes about 30,000 volts per centimeter of space to start a St. Elmo's fire is a type of continuous electric spark called a "glow discharge." The color of the glow depends on the type of gas involved. Thus the Saint Elmo Fire in Windsor, North Carolina appeared blue and violent on the tips of light on the extremities of pointed objects such as church towers. Additional pastorates include the Pineywood Chapel Baptist Church in Bertie County, North Carolina. Reverend Freeman was a farmer and a land owner in Bertie County.

Since Jesus Came Into My Heart

What a wonderful change in my life has been brought,
Since Jesus Came Into My Heart!
I have light in my soul for which long I have sought,
Since Jesus Came Into My Heart!
I have ceased from my wandering and going astray,
Since Jesus Came Into My Heart!
And my sins which were many are all washed away,
Since Jesus Came Into My Heart!
I'm possessed of a hope that is stead fast and sure,
Since Jesus Came Into My Heart!
I shall go there to dwell in that City I know,
Since Jesus Came Into My Heart!
And I'm happy, so happy as onward I go,
Since Jesus Came into my heart.

Rev. E. H. Griffin

Reverend Elijah Harris Griffin was born about 1835 in Pasquotank County, North Carolina. He married the former Emily Whitehurst of Newland. The Griffin family consisted of ten boys and three girls: Elijah Griffin (about 1850), Benjamin Griffin (about 1852); Isaac Griffin (about 1853); Elizabeth Griffin (about 1856); Clarisey Griffin (about 1856) and Amos Griffin (born about 1859).[232] In the 1880 Federal Census Report, Rev. Griffin listed his occupation as a Missionary Baptist Minister.[233] In the 1910 Census Report, the 67 year old Griffin stated that his mother was born in England.[234]

Rev. E. H. Griffin was appointed to the three member committee on Pulpit Supplies and Hours of Service on Tuesday Afternoon, May 27, 1879. Other members included: Elders Charles Capps and Z. H. Berry. It was later announced at the Afternoon Session of the Roanoke Missionary Baptist Association that Elder D. L. Simmons, and Elder E. H. Griffin his alternate, would fill the stand in "The Grove" at 11 o'clock.[235] Rev. Griffin was listed on the 1884 roll as an Elder.[236] On motion a committee of three was appointed on Pulpit Supplies, viz: E. Griffin, I. B. Roach and M. Spears,[237] and on motion of J. A. Fleming there was a Committee of seven appointed on Permanent Organization consisting of Elijah Griffin, M. Phelps, J. A. Garress, S. P. Knight, L. L. Elliott, Joseph Saunders, and W. D. Crude.[238] He served as the Moderator of the Roanoke Association for one year 1891. In 1892, when the Roanoke Missionary Baptist Association convened at the New Chapel Missionary Baptist Church in Plymouth, North Carolina, Rev. Griffin preached the Annual Sermon. Two years later 1894, when the Roanoke Association convened with the Welch's Chapel Missionary Baptist Church, Tyner, North Carolina his son, George Daniel Griffin preached the annual sermon.[239] Thirty years later, in 1913, He was subsequently appointed to the Committee of Petitions and [240] he delivered the closing Benedictions this ending the 1913 Annual Session of the Roanoke Missionary Baptist Association.

Reverend's Elijah Griffin, Samuel Booth, and J. M. Bray, Deacons C.E. Jones, and Henry Parker started the Baptist Sunday School Union of Hampton and adjoining cities.[241] The Union sprang from the need for some united effort to bring together the church schools of the area, adjoining area, and surrounding areas in an attempt to keep the attendance of youth in the church schools and to make older members of the churches more aware of the church school needs. For many years, the effort of these men reached from the Hampton Virginia vicinity back to Roanoke Missionary Baptist Association, as many of the churches closed on the fifth Sunday during the year and gives their members and opportunity to attend these sessions.

The services were largely attended at Saint James Missionary Baptist Church, Elizabeth City, N. C on Sunday, August 9, 1930. Several visitors were present to hear the new pastor, Rev. Elijah Harrison Griffin. By 1967 Rev. Griffin descendents had increased to more than 200 for the Griffin reunion held at Central Junior High School, Gatesville, North Carolina.[242] By 1970, there were more than 300 descendents including one grandson, Hollis F. Creecy, principal of the Central Junior High School, Gatesville, North Carolina.[243]

When The Roll Is Called Up Yonder

When the trumpet of the Lord shall sound, and time shall be no more,
And the morning break eternal bright and fair;
When the saved on earth shall gather over on the other shore,
And the roll is called up yonder, I'll be there.

On that bright and cloudless morning when the dead in Christ shall rise,
And the glory of His resurrection share,
When His chosen ones shall gather to their home beyond the skies,
And the roll is called up yonder, I'll be there.

Let us labor for the Master from the dawn till the setting sun,
Let us talk of all His wondrous love and care,
Then when all of life is over and our work is done, And when the roll is called up yonder, I'll be there.

When the roll is called up yonder,
When the roll is called up yonder,
When the roll is called up yonder,
When the roll is called up yonder,
I'll be there!

James M. Black

P. A. Hinton

Reverend Prince Albert Hinton was born on November 15, 1847. He married Mary Roach of Pasquotank County, North Carolina. He was one of three colored men who served Pasquotank County in the State Legislature during Reconstruction days, being elected to the General Assembly in 1887 and serving one term. For several years after the Civil War ended and before the disfranchisement he was a recognized leader in the Republican Party. [244] He taught himself to read and write while serving his master and rose to serve the county of Pasquotank as its representative. Although he had other means of transportation, Rev. Hinton walked everywhere he went; even to the New Land School located on Mill Pond Road. He taught there for several years.[245] `He would walk from Newland to the nearest store to get his wife sugar, then go back and open the school," Like his 100 year old granddaughter, Ada Kee, he was known for turning down offers for rides. Ada Kee said that her grandfather, Rev. Prince Albert Hinton was part of the turn-of-the-century committee that proposed the all-black state normal school that later became Elizabeth City State University. The proposal had to go before the General Assembly in Raleigh, but the committee couldn't afford the trip there and back. Therefore, Prince Albert Hinton left on foot, carrying train fare for his return, He walked all the way there. It took him a week.[246]

It is perhaps reasonable to assume that when former slave Prince Albert Hinton stood at the steps of the Camden County courthouse and purchased the freedom of his Mary and five children, he never once consider that one day his granddaughter would be campaigning for the first African American president. Ada Kee is that granddaughter. Her grandfather, a man she remembers well, had bought his freedom first, then his family's second. His granddaughter, who turned 100 last Saturday, is elated that she has lived to see this historical turn of events.

He was the father of nine children, twenty grandchildren. Two sons and a daughter, Mr. S. D. L. Hinton a letter carrier in Norfolk Post Office, Mr. Wellington Hinton and Mrs. Cleo Scott survived him. Rev. Hinton was a very industrious person. He reported to Benjamin F. Stafford, the 1900 census taker for the State of North Carolina, Pasquotank County, Township of Newland that he owned 181 acres of land in that county. Rev. Hinton died on April 17, 1922 as a result of being stricken with apoplexy. He was 75.

Rev. M. Hyter

Reverend Matthew Hyter was born about 1869 in Pasquotank County, North Carolina. He married Mary Louise Winslow and they began their mulatto family of six sons, John, Ernest, Roosevelt, Samuel, Richard and Lonnie. The Hyter families were members of Union Branch Baptist Church, Weeksville, North Carolina. Rev. Hyter began his ministry in 1895 and was held in esteem by all who knew him. He was one of the Founders of the St. James Baptist Church, Elizabeth City, N. C.Funeral services for Mrs. Mary Louise Winslow Hyter were held in Weeksville, N. C. She was survived by six sons: Ernest, John, Richard, Roosevelt and Lonnie Hyter.[517] Rev. Hyter died September 17, 1941, 17 days after the death of his wife, Mrs. Louise Hyter. He had been in failing health for several years.[518]

Sometime, Somewhere

Angels are always singing, Somewhere, somewhere,
Joy bells are ever ringing, Somewhere, somewhere;
Somewhere the sun is shining, even in darkest night.
Cease then your soul repining, Soon will your sky be bright.
Peace like a river is flowing, Somewhere, somewhere,
God His full pardon restoring, Somewhere, somewhere;
Over the hill tops of glory, shines the fair streets of gold;
Wonderful, wonderful story, Never has half been told.
Homeis waiting God's children, Somewhere, somewhere,
Bright golden crowns be given, Somewhere, somewhere;
Then the glade harps will be sounding, Round the white throne on high;
Heaven with praises resounding; Never more pain or sigh.
Somewhere, somewhere,
God will make all come right,
Somewhere, somewhere,
Skies will be always bright.

James Jenkins

Reverend James Jenkins, a 6 feet and 2 inches man with a black complexion, black hair and eyes was born about 1840 in Gates North Carolina, although he listed Nashville, North Carolina as his hometown on his 1863 enlistment papers. He married the former Melinda Hoskins, daughter of Richard Hoskins and the former Jennie Baker both of Gates, North Carolina. James and Melinda were the parents of six children born: Sarah E., Catherine, Dilcie E., Claudia M., James (1869-1952), and Charles A. Jenkins (June 1883). He earned his living and supported his family by farming. He was a member and an ordained minister of the Lebanon Grove Missionary Baptist Church, Gatesville, North Carolina. He is listed on the 1878 Roanoke Missionary Baptist Association Minister's Roll with a Gatesville, address.

The Civil War began on April 12, 1861 with the firing on Fort Sumter, and ended on April 18, 1865 with the surrender of the Confederate Army. While the Civil War is always covered, African American participation as soldiers in the Union army are not. President Lincoln feared offending the Border States and northern whites, he did not allow blacks to enlist legally in the Union army until the issuance of the Emancipation Proclamation on January 1, 1863. Though allowed to fight, they were placed in their own units, often headed up by white officers. Frederick Douglas' words in 1861 seem to ignite the flames and passions for freedom in James Jenkins, "He who would be free must strike the blow. This is your golden opportunity." In order to smite to death the power that would bury the Government and bury his liberty in the same hopeless grave James Jenkins mustered into the US Colored on October 23, 1863 at Portsmouth, Virginia. "After Private James Jenkins had gotten the brass letter, U.S., an eagle on his button, a musket on his shoulder and bullets in his pocket, there is no power on earth that could deny that he had earned the right to citizenship." He mustered out of the 36th U. S. Colored Regiment on June 5, 1865 by the Secretary of War by the State of Virginia at Norfolk, Virginia. The 36th U. S. Colored was organized February 8, 1864, from 2nd North Carolina Colored Infantry. It was attached to U.S. Forces, Norfolk and Portsmouth, Department of Virginia and North Carolina, to April, 1864 District of St. Mary's Department of Virginia and North Carolina to June, 1864. Unattached, Army of the James, to August, 1864. 2nd Brigade, 3rd Division, 18th Corps, to December, 1864. 1st Brigade, 3rd Division, 25th Corps, December, 1864. 1st Brigade, 1st Division, 25th Corps, and Dept. of Texas, to October, 1866. On June 1881 James Jenkins applied for and received a $2.00 pension from the government for a wound he sustained. He was one of eight people in Gates County, North Carolina to receive such a pension.

Rev. Jenkins was an active member of the Roanoke Missionary Baptist Association. In 1885 and 1886 he served as a delegate to the Roanoke Missionary Baptist Association from the Lebanon Grove Missionary Baptist Church. The following year, he was appointed to the Committee on the Spread of the Gospel. When the Roanoke Missionary Baptist Association convened at the Welch's Chapel Baptist Church, Tyner, North Carolina during the week of May 20-23, 1913 the Moderator mentioned Rev. James Jenkins during his Tuesday Afternoon address. He stated: "Since our last session (1912) the most dreaded enemy, death has stolen into our midst, wrecked many houses, left bereaved families, and robed the communities of noble and worthy citizens. Among those whom he severed warrant were the venerable and sagacious father in Israel, Rev. James Jenkins, who he summoned on the 24th day of last November, (1912)."[247] Reverend James Jenkins is interned in a very impressive plot at the Lebanon Grove Missionary Baptist Church Cemetery, Gatesville, North Carolina. The grave marker reads: *James Jenkins G.O.D. 36th U. S. C. L.*

M. N. Land

Reverend Marshall N. Land was born March 1848 in the Washington District (Berkley Township) Norfolk, Virginia. Following the Civil War, a number of Negro Baptist Churches sprang up in Norfolk and North Carolina under the evangelistic labors of such men as Marshall Land, Lewis Tucker, Richard Speller, Z. Hughes, David King and others. Among the more prominent survivals of their labors are First Calvary, Second Calvary, Queen Street, and Jerusalem Baptist Churches in Norfolk, Virginia. [248] Rev. Marshall N. Land married Sophia A. Harris[249] in 1868 (six years after the Confederate South felled to the Union North) and to this union six children were born namely: Walter A. (1869), Alenora E.,[250] (1871), Lemuel (1873), Lester Leroy (1876), and Luther (1879), and Russell Land, (1880. In 1870 Rev. Marshall Land entered the Maryland Seminary and studied for the ministry.[251] He was a member of the Roanoke Missionary Baptist Association. In 1878 he was the alternate to preach the Introductory Sermon, and at the Tuesday afternoon session, motioned that a committee of five be appointed for Letters, namely: Noah Simons, Benjamin Gray, A. W. Simons, Jackson Portor, and Jackson Mitchell. Brother Claiborne Speller.[252] Elder Marshall Land was granted a letter of dismissal from the Roanoke Missionary Baptist Association. Elder J. K. Lamb motioned the dismissal. [253]

Rev. Marshall Land served as Moderator in the church meeting of the First Baptist Church in December 1889, when the present pastor's father Richard H. Bowling, Sr. was elected as pastor of the church.[254] Among the founders of the Baptist Ministers Conference of Norfolk, Portsmouth and Vicinity, later known as the Tidewater Metro Ministers Alliance on March 1, 1882 were Rev. Marshall Land, Dr. James M. Armistead, Dr. Richard Speller, Rev. Zachariah Hughes, Rev. David King and Rev. Holland Powell. Rev. J. M. Armistead of Zion Baptist Church, Portsmouth was the first president of the conference. Dr. Richard Speller of Bank Street Baptist Church was the first secretary, and the Rev. Holland Powell the first treasurer.[255] Rev. M. Land was one of Norfolk's most prominent and influential citizens. He served on the Board of Supervisors of Norfolk County. [256]He retired from active ministry in 1917 due to declining health and the recommendations of his physician on account of a throat infection.

Rev. Land for forty years previous to that time had been a power in the Baptist Ministry and held enviable influence in the Roanoke Missionary Baptist Association until the day of his death. He founded a number of churches in Norfolk County, Virginia. He built a church in Bowser's Hill, Va., and Ebenezer Baptist Church in Portsmouth, Virginia and Union Baptist Church, Shoulder's Hill, Virginia; He pastured the Union Baptist Church Shoulder's Hill, Virginia from 1879-1890.[257] Rev. Land had been a member of Norfolk's First Baptist Church Bute Street for 49 years and would have celebrated his 50th year membership there in September. The congregation under the leadership of Pastor R. H. Bowling was a time of his sudden death planning to give him a grand surprise celebration as a member of the church.

Rev. Land was very instrumental in the setting of the Barbourville section of Norfolk. He was one of the first residents in the section. His home was opened for visitations from all. Mrs. Ethel Burke and Miss Edna Cuffee was the guest of Rev. & Mrs. Marshall Land on Christmas Eve.[258] It was through the great respect that the most influential white citizens of Norfolk City and County held for him, as he was able to assist a large number of them to become home owners. On Friday night September 7, 1917 at the Queen Street Baptist Church, Rev. Marshall Land, the Officials, Teachers and Parents of the Norfolk Colored Schools conducted a monster Mass Meeting under the auspices of the President's Council of Patrons League. The Superintendent delivered the main address and presented the subjects that were discussed and he outlined the work proposed for the ensuing year. Other people appearing on the program included Rev. R. J. Langston, A. B., pastor of Bank Street Baptist Church; Rev. Jas. Hatcher, B. D., pastor John Brown A. M. E. Church; and Mr. C. A. Palmer. Mr. Hatcher, president and Mr. Palmer secretary.[259]

Rev. Land was a member of the ranks of the Grand Army of the Republic, and an old mason. Rev. Land's funeral was held Tuesday at the First Baptist Church. Rev. J. M. Armistead, dean of the Baptist Ministry in Tidewater, and pastor of Zion Baptist Church, Portsmouth, delivered the eulogy. Dr. Armistead stated that when he came to this section in 1885 Rev. Marshall Land was one of the first Baptist ministers he met here. A large crowd attended the funeral. Rev. Armistead was assisted by Dr. Bowling, pastor First Baptist. Eulogies were read by Rev. C. C. Somerville, on behalf of the Tidewater Ministerial Alliance; Rev. Saunders, Princess Ann County.

On July 26, 1923 the following statement appeared in the *Norfolk Journal and Guide Newspaper,* "In Loving Remembrance of our dear husband and father, Rev. Marshall Land, who departed this life, June 30, 1923. Gone but not forgotten. From his wife and children: Sophia A. Land, Walter H. Land, Russell N. Land, Ella L. Faulcon, L. Marcella Paige."[260] Four years following the death of Rev. Marshall N. Land his daughter Mrs. Ella Land Faulcon of 1292 Bolton Street, Norfolk, Virginia assembled the family to pay homage to him as a husband, father, grandfather and village pioneer. His favorite hymns were sung, bringing back reminiscences of past days. Attorney R. G. L. Paige, son-in-law was the master of ceremonies. Rev. Charles H. Hodges, brother-in-law, eulogized the sire, the late Rev. Land. Rev. D. W. Harris, brother of Mrs. Land, eloquently spoke of the wonderful accomplishment and sacrifices of the father in whose honor the service was held. His words touched those who were present. Rev. Land's brother and son Russell Land from New York was present. This was an added joy to the assemblage. Mrs. Marcella Land Paige was soloist. Attorney W. H. Land, Mrs. Ella Land Faulcon, Mr. Russell N. Land and Mrs. Marcella and Paige formed a quartet and led in all the singing. They were assisted by Mrs. Cordelin Hodges Coleman. Rev. D. W. Harris, Mrs. Corine Johnson and other old members present. Mrs.

Corine Johnson accompanied at the piano, assisted by Mss Marcella Paige, Dr. A. N. Land and W. H. Land. During the evening, all retired to the spacious dining room where a delicious menu of Smithfield ham sandwiches, pickles, stuffed olives, potatoes chips, creamed chicken, saltines, French rolls, crackers, salted almonds, after dinner mints, chocolate almonds, punch, ice cream and cake were served. The affair closed with singing. All present expressed them as having one of the most delightful evenings in many years.[261]

M. L. Lane

Reverend Monroe Ramsey Lane was born about 1856 to Whitmel and Mary Saunders Lane of Elizabeth City. He married Amy A. Dance, [264] the daughter John and the former Ester Windslow on April 7, 1907 in Elizabeth City, North Carolina. There were no children born to this union. He was a life time member of the Olive Branch Missionary Baptist Church. He attended the first public school established in Elizabeth City for colored. After graduating from the Elizabeth City School System, he taught school and worked as a waiter in several local eateries. He was the first rural colored mail carriers in the State of Massachusetts, having moved north several years ago.[265] Mrs. Amy Dance-Lane was a teacher in the Parmalee School System. Rev. Lane was a former pastor and minister of the Roanoke Missionary Baptist Association and his name was listed on the 1914 Roanoke Missionary Baptist Association Ordained Minister's Directory.[266] Moderator R. R. Cartwright mentioned Rev. Lane in his Thursday Evening sermon at the Fifty-Third Annual Session at the Philadelphia Baptist Church, Shiloh, North Carolina. Rev. Lane was the pastor of the Antioch Presbyterian Church, Elizabeth City, North Carolina. He pastured several Presbyterian churches in Virginia[267] prior to returning to the Baptist faith of his youth.

Rev. M. R. Lane was a former president of a shoe retail company and a supporter of his wife, Mrs. Amy Lane's teaching career. On April 1, 1921 Mrs. Amy Dance-Lane, the assistant to Professor J. H. Barco, principal of the graded school at Manteo, N. C., closed a very successful term on Friday. Rev. Lane accompanied his wife back to Elizabeth City. During the first Sunday in May 1921 Rev. Lane preached the Installation Sermon of Rev. Trotman at Zion Hill Baptist Church.

Mrs. Louvenia Portlock, one of the eldest and most respected residents of Elizabeth City, died Wednesday, August 3, 1921 at her home on Edge Street, after several weeks' illness. Her funeral was held on Sunday, afternoon, August 7, 1921 from the Mount Lebanon A. M. E. Z. church, of which she was a loyal member. Services were conducted by Rev. M. R. Lane. He was assisted by Rev. H. R. Hawkins and Mr. S. J. Walson, the undertaker.[268] The Masonic Lodges of Elizabeth City celebrated St. John's Day, Wednesday night, June 28, 1922 with a Lodge of Sorrow at Mount Lebanon A. M. E. Zion Church. Rev. C. C. Drew, D. D., Grand Master officiated and Rev. M. R. Lane delivered the address.[269] Rev. Lane arranged for a sacred concert at Antioch Presbyterian Church on Sunday January 14, 1923, many were out and enjoyed the same.[270] Rev. Lane delivered the Invocation at the January 1,1924 Emancipation service held in Elizabeth City, North Carolina.[271] Mr. Jacob Spellman, an aged respected resident of Elizabeth City died at the home of his daughter Mrs. W. O. Carden, Monday, November 3, 1926. Funeral services were conducted the following Wednesday at 2 o'clock p. m. with Dr. C. M. Cartwright and Rev. M. R. Lane, officiating. Rev. Lane's wife Mrs. Amy Dance Lane left Wednesday for Portsmouth, VA., to spend some time with her brother, Rev. B. W. Dance.[272] Dr. Dance was in Elizabeth City, North Carolina on July 20th 1925 visiting his sister, Mrs. M. R. Lane.[273] Mr. Harry Lane of Morristown, New Jersey visited his uncle Rev. Monroe Lane on Martin Street, and his aunt Mrs. Overton corner of Speed and South Road Streets. Mr. Harry Lane was born in Elizabeth City to the late Calvin Lane. After reaching manhood he migrated to New Jersey and started their family.[274] Rev. M. R. Lane delivered the main eulogy for the funeral service of Mrs. Maggie Reid, a former resident of Elizabeth City, who died in Philadelphia, Pennsylvania during the week of November 6, 1927. Her body was brought to Elizabeth City for interment. She was accompanied by her son, Mr. Lee. Services were held Sunday afternoon from Mount Lebanon A. M. E. Z. church of which Mrs. Reid was a member. Resolutions on her life were given by Dr. C. M. Cartwright, and Rev. J. H. Case.[275] Rev. & Mrs. Lane returned from Portsmouth, Virginia on August 10, 1930 where they visited Mrs. Lane's mother, Mrs. Ester Winslow, and brother, Rev. B. W. Dance.

Rev. Lane was an active committee member of the 1937 Emancipation Committee. He was responsible for lining up soldiers of the Civil, Spanish and World Wars; he also line up the churches for participation in the exercises, as he had distinguished himself with the City ministry. Mr. W. S. Bowser associated with the superintendents lined up the Sunday Schools and other auxiliaries in Elizabeth City, and Pasquotank County.[276] During June 1938 Rev. Lane attended the Sunday School Convention at Carver Memorial Church, Newport News, Virginia and preached the opening sermon.[277] Rev. Monroe & Mrs. Amy Lane was called to New Burn, N. C. on account of the death of her brother the Reverend Daniel W. Dance.

Reverend Monroe Ramsey Lane departed this life suddenly on June 1, 1943, following several months of declining health. His June 4, 1943 Funeral Services were held at Olive Branch Baptist Church with the pastor, the Rev. C. M. Cartwright officiating. The Revs., S. L. Lawrence, J. R. R. McRay, R. Reece, T. J. Raynor, and the Rev. Mr. Ruffin participating. Obituary and condolences were read by J. R. Fleming. He was survived by his widow, Mrs. Amy Dance Lane, a school teacher; two sisters, Mrs. Jennie Overton of Elizabeth City and Mrs. Fannie Reid of Boston, Mass; a brother, Sumner Lane of Washington, D. C.; one half sister, Mrs. Ethel Lane, a half brother, both of New York, and several other relatives. Reverend Monroe Ramsey Lane's remains rest in the family plot on Perry Street, in front of Mount Lebanon A. M. E. Zion Church, Elizabeth City, North Carolina.

E. M. Lassiter

Reverend E. M. Lassiter was born August 22, 1851 in Hertford County, North Carolina to Charles and Annie Lassiter. At the age of twenty-five, he was called into the ministry and was licensed by the Galatia Missionary Baptist Church, New Hope, North Carolina, by Rev. Zion H. Berry. He experienced forty-four years as a successful pastor. During this time he pastured in Mount Zion Baptist Church for thirty-eight years, Christian Advocate, Popular Branch, North Carolina; Holly Grove, Shiloh Missionary Baptist Church, Belcross, {Camden County}North Carolina; New Sawyers Creek Missionary Baptist Church, Belcross (Camden County}, North Carolina; Ready Branch and New Haven's Creek, Manteo, North Carolina. Prayer was freely offered by Rev. Lassiter at the Wednesday Evening Session of the 1916 Association.

Rev. E. M. Lassiter's March 1926 funeral was one of the largest and most impressive ever held in that section of the state. The Rev. C. M Cartwright officiated, and the Rev. R. R. Cartwright, Moderator of the Roanoke Missionary Baptist Association of which Rev. Lassiter was the vice-moderator for eleven years delivered the eulogy. The Roanoke Association of which Mount Zion was a member was well represented by a large delegation of prominent ministers from the state of North Carolina. Rev. C. M. Cartwright officiated and touching eulogies were given by Rev. W. S. Creecy, Rev. B. W. Dance Rev. C. H. D. Griffin, formerly pastor of Central Baptist Church, also Rev. S. A. Howell, Rev. H. H. Norman, Rev. J. A. Nimmo, and the Rev. Z. B. Wynn. The local pastors were represented by Rev. J. C. Diamond. While the Baptist Ministers Conference of Tidewater sent its president, Dr. C. P. Madison to represent it at the service.

God Rode In A Wind Storm

God sent Jonah to Ninevah land to preach the gospel to sinful man.
Jonah got angry; he didn't want to go.
He hailed the ship and got on board.

The ship began to rock form side to side; Everybody was troubled in mind.
They searched the ship down in the deep;
And found Jonah fast to sleep.

Wake up sleeper and tell me your name. My name is Jonah.
I read in my claim,
If all of this trouble is for me,
Throw me overboard and your ship will sail free

Jonah was in the whale three days and three nights;
Obey God's will and you will be alright!
When the waves and billows rolled,
He cried out to the Lord,
Have mercy on my soul.

God Rode In A Wind Storm
God Rode In A Wind Storm, God Rode In A Wind Storm
And He troubled everybody's mind.

G. W. Lee

Reverend Dr. George Wellington Lee was born about 1851 to the Rev. Bryant Lee of Bertie County, North Carolina. He was often referred to as "The Daddy of Negro Preachers." Rev. Lee was among a group of North Carolina Ministers that effectuated positives changes for the tone of ministry in Northeastern North Carolina. In the absence of Elder Elijah Griffin and Elder C. M. Billups his alternate, Elder G. W. Lee preached the Introductory Sermon. On the motion of Elder G. W. Lee, the pastor and deacons of Zion Hill Baptist Church were appointed to the Committee on Arrangements. The Roanoke Missionary Baptist Association met promptly in its Twentieth Annual Session {1884} at 10:00 A. M. with Elder G. W. Lee in the chair. He was one of five people appointed to the Obituary Committee, and he was one of five people appointed to the Committee on the State and of the County, and he was one of seven people appointed to Committee on Credentials. He was elected moderator doing the same session. He was a leading member of the Ministers Council. He formerly served as the Moderator of the Roanoke Association from 1884-1885.[262] Rev. Ira Boone Roach completed his unexpired term.

Rev. George W. Lee pastured the New Middle Swamp Missionary Baptist Church, Corapeake, North Carolina for five years,[263] and the First Colored Baptist, Hertford, North Carolina form 1883-1885. [264] He left the Roanoke Missionary Baptist Association in 1885 to assume the pastorate of the Vernon Avenue Baptist Church, Washington D.C. He was installed as pastor of the Vernon Avenue Baptist Church in 1885 and served a quarter of a century. Rev. G. W. Lee was noted especially for three significant elements in his character. Near to his heart was the promotion of African missions in keeping with his deep sense of charity. He was always a friend of the poor and, being such, emphasized more than any other duty of the church that of supporting missionary work in Africa. As a result the Vermont Avenue Baptist Church did more for this purpose than many other churches of the District of Columbia combined. He was always disposed, moreover, to help the under man in the struggle with his uncharitable accusers and traducers. When a minister was under fire, he usually stood by the unfortunate, if there was any possible chance to save him for the good of the service. He made himself, too, a patron of young men aspiring to the ministry, raising money for their support by impressing upon the people the importance of educating them. In this connection he trained and helped to support Dr. James E.

Willis, who was baptized, licensed and ordained to preach under Rev. Dr. George Wellington Lee. In 1906, Rev. Dr. George Lee attended the Roanoke Missionary Baptist Association and was called upon to give remarks on his recent Europe to attend the World's Congress. He amused and instructed the body, ending with tender fatherly advice to the ministers and laymen of the Association. He stated that the Southern white man is our best friend, and concluded by giving the Association $20.00 for Roanoke Institute, $5.00 for Albemarle Association and $5.00 for age ministers or their widows. [265] Dr. Lee passed away on February 6, 1910.

B. J. Lenox

Reverend Birkley J. Lennox was born in Plymouth, North Carolina about 1843 and was living in Plymouth, North Carolina from 1886-1891[266] with his wife Matilda and daughter. Mary Lenox was born about 1867. He listed his address as such in the American Baptist Year Book. [267] On Tuesday Morning, May 28th, 1878, Rev. J. B. Lenox was paid $20.00 by the Roanoke Missionary Baptist Association in part by the Association for services as a missionary.[268] At the Afternoon session, he and Elder Alfred Sanders, his alternate, filled the stand in *"The Grove"* at 3:00 P. M.[269] He was the delegate from Mount Shiloh Baptist Church, Williamston, North Carolina,[270] and the Mount Eprew Church at Lee's Mill, North Carolina during the annual session in 1879.[271] In 1886 Rev. Lenox was the delegate from Mt. Eprew, and Mt. Pleasant Church, Gum Neck, and Saunders Grove Baptist Church, Perquimans County, North Carolina.[272] He was listed on the same reports as an ordained Elder living in Plymouth, North Carolina.

On February 12th, 1880 B. J. Lynox stated on the marriage certificate of 25 year old Albert Thatch of the Plymouth Township and, 18 year old Kate Maben that he was the pastor of the Colored Baptist Church. Rev. B. J. Lenox a Baptist Minister of the State of North Carolina united in Matrimony George Bennett and Martha Johnston the parties licensed above, on the 9th day of January, 1883, at the residence of Peter Johnston in Plymouth Township, in said County, according to law. Witnesses present at Marriage: Julia King of Martin County and Tempy Spruill of Washington Co.[273] In 1884 J. B. Lenox, Elder and Missionary for the North Carolina State Baptist General Convention used a Post Office Box in Plymouth for his mailing address. Rev. B. J. Lenox was appointed to the Committee of Grievances at the Tuesday Afternoon, May 27th 1879 session. At the Afternoon session, the Association approved the following resolution: "That the Treasurer be, and is hereby, ordered to pay Elder B. J. Lynox, former State Missionary, twenty dollars due for missionary services; balance due the Missionary, $12.31.[274] At the Thursday Evening, May 20th, 1886 session, The Investigating Committee consisting of Rev. J. B. Lennox and the following members: I. B. Roach, C. M. Billups, A. S. Dunstan, J. A. Fleming, W. S. Reid, S. P. Knight, were appointed by the Roanoke Missionary Baptist Association to investigate certain school property situated in the town of Elizabeth City and known as the Turner's Normal School, met in the above named city on the 22nd, of June, 1886, to confer with Mr. Turner in regard to the aforesaid property. [275]

On December 30th, 1886, B. J. Lynox, a Baptist minister united in Matrimony Joseph H. Toodle and Charlotte Lee, at the Baptist Church in Plymouth Township, in Washington County, according to law. Witnesses present at Marriage were: Dawson Lee of Plymouth N. C., Margaret Tow of Plymouth N. C., and M. M. Lynox of Plymouth N. C. At the Tuesday Morning, May 21st, 1907 session, Rev. C. M. Cartwright, the chairman of the Obituary Committee made the following report which forever immortalized Rev. B. J. Lenox in the annuals of history of the Roanoke Missionary Baptist Church: "We the committee on Obituary reports as follows: Since the last meeting of our Association, it has pleased Almighty God to take out of our midst Rev. B. J. Lomax, Plymouth, North Carolina. He was a strong Gospel Preacher and loyal to the interest of our Association. We humbly bow to the will of Him who loves us supremely and commend all whom they held so dear. [276] The following evening the Moderator said of Rev. Lenox. "Rev. B. Lennox another bright star of this Association has answered the summon call to death and has gone to the city of which the inspired apostle said, "I saw no temple therein: for the Lord God Almighty and the Lamb are the temple of it." The death of Rev. Lynox leaves a vacancy in the ranks of Baptist Ministry. Though our hearts are filled with sadness at the early demise of this inspired gospel minister, and at the thought that we will not see him naturally again, still we must bow in submission to the Divine will and strive to meet our departed friend in that land where sickness and sorrow never enter. He was the pastor of Mount Ararat Missionary Baptist Church, Windsor, North Carolina in 1882-1893.

I'll Tell It Wherever I Go

I'll tell of the Savior, I tell of His favor, I'll tell it wherever I go.
I count every blessing, I'll go on confessing
I'll Tell it wherever I go.
Though life is uncertain; I cannot understand
But thank Him and praise Him while I can
I'll just tell it, excel it, let all voices swell it,
I'll tell it wherever I go!

G. A. Mebane

Reverend George Abraham Mebane was born July 4, 1850, at Hermitage, in Bertie County, North Carolina to slave parents, of which nothing is known. By the late latter half of 1864 Mebane was a mess boy in Company a, 85th New York Regiment of Volunteers. After the Civil War ended Mebane returned to North Carolina and taught school for forty years.

He was authorized to perform marriages in Bertie County, North Carolina prior to June 15, 1867. The following entry was extracted from the marriage bonds of Bertie County Marriage Records: "You are hereby authorized to solemnize the rites of matrimony between Elleck Bond and Winny Bond. Witness William P. Gurley, Clerk "I, Abram Mebane, a Minister of the gospel do hereby certify that I solemnized the rites of matrimony between Elleck Bond and Winny Bond on the 15th June 1867." On July 25, 1870, Rev. Mebane performed the marriage of Bertie County natives Ben Pool (colored) and Winney Mebane at Merry Hill, North Carolina.[277] On the 27th day of December 1870, Rev. Mebane performed the marriage of Windsor colored residents George Bond, the son of Solomon Carter, and Celia Ryom the daughter of David Ryom and Mary A. Ryom.[278] Rev. Mebane would perform April 1, 1872 marriage of George Cook and Notice Bond in Colerain; and the June 18, 1871 marriage of Davis Speller and Jane Speller in Windsor.[279] On December 29, 1877, Rev. Abram Mebane performed the wedding ceremony of 21 year old David Bryant of Windsor, North Carolina and 21 year old colored Rosetta Shields, also of Windsor, at the Indian Woods Baptist Church. Eli Jones, Joseph Smallwood, E. Smallwood were the witnesses.

In 1867 Rev. Abraham Mebane entered into a lease agreement with the Lowell Colored School Society, giving New Chapel Baptist Church, Plymouth, North Carolina the right to erect a church on lot no. 41 in the town of Plymouth. Prior to this time the Prayer and Bible Band that composed the New Chapel Baptist Church were worshipping under a bush arbor. The following year, on Thursday before the 2nd Sunday in October 1868 Rev. Abram Mebane and Rev. J. T. Bailey of Edenton, North Carolina organized the Providence Missionary Baptist Church, Edenton, North Carolina.

The Roanoke Missionary Baptist Association met in its Thirteenth Annual Session with the Church of Christ at New Bethany, Hertford County, N. C. On Tuesday, May 28, 1878 Elder Abram Mebane preached the Introductory Sermon from Matthew 24: 4. Later in the session, he motioned that the new church at St. John be set aside until Wednesday. Rev. C. E. Hodges delivered the prayer for the Afternoon session. Following the sermon the Association took a recess for one hour and a half.[280] It was announced at the Wednesday, May 28th Afternoon Session that Elder Abram Mebane and Luke Pierce would fill the stand in "The Grove" at 3.00 P. M.[281] Elder T. M. Collins motioned that a committee of five be appointed on the Spread of the Gospel. Elders Abram Mebane, Willis Melton, Amanuel Reynolds, and Brothers Aaron Morris and John Boone were appointed on this committee.[282]

On March 19, 1867 Abram Maben a minister in Washington County, North Carolina performed the Freedmen Marriages of Gabriel Joiner, and Delitha Perry; and Richmond Moore, son of Washington Williams & Jenette Moore to Anna Johnson, daughter of Levin Johnson and wife. On December 7, 1867 Abram Maben performed the marriage of John Gibson, son of Robert Gibson & wife Harriett to Milla Boston, daughter of Newbern Ash & Nancy Boston.[283] He performed the July 30, 1868 Freedmen marriage of Martin Ruffin and Annie Jones.[284] On October 10, 1868 he married Daniel Pugh and Amanda Smallwood. On May 17, 1869 he married David Buston and Sylvia Saunders. On November 24th, 1869 he married Moses W. Wynne and Harriett Ann Bell. He married Seth Jeanette and Mary E. Armistead on December 23, 1869. On January 6, 1870 he married Cainion Jeanette and Harriett Johnston. He married Isaac Beasley to Gazelle Norman on February 24, 1870. On December 11, 1870 he married Samuel Pool (colored) and Martha Gaylord (colored). On May 27, 1871 he performed the marriage of Ebenezer Garrett Jr., of color and Adeline Holley, colored as J. M. Bateman witnessed. Thomas Crawford, colored and son of Amos Crawford & Lydia Crawford and Ann Rebecca Harris of color daughter of Dempsey Miller and wife married on December 7, 1871. He performed the April 18, 1872 marriage of Jerry Reddick of color, son of Thomas Reddick & wife Rosa Reddick and Ester White, colored, daughter of Ga . . . . y Tucker, and wife Nancy White.

Three memorable things happened in Rev. Mebane's life in 1876. First, he was called as the first pastor of the newly organized Indian Woods Missionary Baptist Church, Windsor, North Carolina and the Weeping Mary Baptist Church, Jamesville, North Carolina; and second, he was elected as a Republican state senator from Bertie and Northampton County, North Carolina.[285] He represented the third Senatorial District.[286] He would be re-elected to serve again in 1883. Three years later, Rev. Mebane on motion of Elder T. M. Collins, was one of four was appointed to the Committee on the Spread of the Gospel. The other members were: Amanuel Reynolds, Aaron Morris and John Boone were appointed on this committee.[287] In addition to this responsibility, Rev. Mebane was the editor of the black owned Carolina Enterprise.

Rev. George A. Mebane used his early popularity at the district convention to run against the native born Henry Plummer Cheatham from Henderson, North Carolina. Mebane claimed that he had the backing of the Republican executive committee.[288] Cheatham declined Mebane's invitation to debate, refusing to recognize any other party candidate for the seat, and each candidate spent the summer of 1888 blaming the other for sustained Republican divisions. The rivalry continued unabated until October, when Mebane suddenly withdrew and asked his supporters to back Cheatham. Though Republicans praised him for acting for the sake of party unity, Democrats spread rumors that Cheatham supporters had bought off Mebane.

In additional to owning a farm in Windsor, North Carolina, Rev. Mebane maintained a provisional store, and acted as an incorporation, financial agent, and general superintendent of the Elizabeth City Colored Normal School. *The Baltimore-Afro-American Newspaper* reported his October 12, 1901 death in the local paper with the following sentences: Honorable George E Mebane of North Carolina, who for the past few years has spent his time traveling for an educational institution, died at his home in Elizabeth City this week.[289,290]

I Want To Be Ready

I want to be ready,
I want to be ready,
I want to be ready to walk in Jerusalem just like John.

O John, O John didn't you say?"
Walking in Jerusalem just like John.
That I'll be there at that great day,
Walking in Jerusalem just like John.

John said the city was just four square,
Walking in Jerusalem just like John.
He declared that he would meet me there,
Walking in Jerusalem just like John.

When Peter was preaching at Pentecost,
Walking in Jerusalem just like John.
He was endowed with the Holy Ghost,
Walking in Jerusalem just like John.

I want to be ready,
I want to be ready,
I want to be ready to walk in Jerusalem just like John.

P. W. Moore

Peter W. Moore was born June 1859 to Reddick & Alecy Lexie Thompson Moore, both slaves. His father allegedly was killed by the Ku Klux Klan during Reconstruction, and the task of rearing the five children fell to his mother. The Moore family lived on a little plantation farm about three miles northeast of Turkey in Sampson County, North Carolina. The names of two of Reddick & Lexie Moore's children; George Moore, & Winnie Moore survived the records. The Moore families were members of the Six Runs Baptist Church near Turkey. In 1889 Moore married Symera T. Raynor of Windsor, and they later became the parents of two daughters: Ruth Lawrence and Bessie. In 1892 he joined the Olive Branch Missionary Baptist Church and remained a very active member for 47 years. He was an active member of the Roanoke Missionary Baptist Association.

Peter Moore took advantage of the little education that the public schools of rural Sampson County offered. It was not much! However, he attended a school operated by the Freeman's Bureau north of Turkey. He was not a brilliant student; he had to dig laboriously for his learning. Fortunately, he was endowed with a long term memory, and he retained every good lesson learned; and with divine inspiration and intuitiveness rejected those things that made not for character. He furthered his studies at the Philosophian Academy, in nearby Sampson County, under the leadership of Burke Marable, who would become an important mentor. In 1876 he entered Shaw University, Raleigh, N. C., and labored for eight years to obtain that higher education that qualified him for teaching. He graduated in 1887. Professor Moore received an honorary degree of L. L. D. from Shaw University. In recognition of this fact the Roanoke Missionary Baptist Association made the following resolution during its Fiftieth Annual Session held with the Providence Baptist Church, Edenton, N. C., during the week of May 23-25th A. D. 1916: "Whereas Shaw University has seen in her son and brother and one of our strong educational leaders, real worth as a true educator and recognized the same by conferring upon him, our Professor P. W. Moore, degree of L. L. D., be it RESOLVED: That a vote of thanks be given to Shaw University, and that our heavenward sent wish that her shadow may never grow less but lengthen and that we may learn to love her more and, be it also RESOLVED: that our means and influence shall contributes to make our wish a reality.[1]

When Dr. Moore first came to State Normal School, North Carolina had only begun to make an effort to train Negro teachers. With an appropriation of $900 the work was this started, and Dr. Moore was given a salary of $50.00 a month. For several years later the annual appropriation for maintenance of the school remained at the $900 figure and the salary of the principal remained stationary. His first teaching experience was in 1886 at the Holy Grove School in Gates County, North Carolina. During the academic year of 1888 he taught in Bertie County, North Carolina. He taught in other one and two room school house throughout Northeastern North Carolina for several years. Dr. Moore believed that improving the ability to think would improve one's own standard of living & that the improving of the standards of living would improve the black race. On the recommendation of Major S. M. Finger, state superintendent of public instruction, Moore was made principal of the new State Normal School for the Colored Race (now Elizabeth City State University) in 1861. The sole purpose of the State Normal was limited to preparing young people to teach. He started off with two members of the faculty & 23 students. When he retired in 1928, there were 15 faculty members & 355 students. Dr. Moore's daughter Ruth Moore Bethea followed him into an educational career that spanned from 1920-1973 in the Winston-Salem public school system. She was active in her sororities: Sigma Gamma Rho and the National Association of College Women.

On Commencement night, Friday, May 25, 1928, in recognition of his services on behalf of Negro education and in the promotional of wholesome racial relations in this city and state P. W. Moore retired and after 37 years as principal of State Normal School and was made principal emeritus with a home and a salary for life by the board of trustees. Principal Moore retired with the school's annual appropriation totaling $38, 000 which was augmented by fees paid by the students, while his own salary reached $2, 500 annually. The school was started in a little rented shack on Roanoke Avenue and Dr. Moore was allowed an assistant whose salary was the pricy sum of $30.00 to $40.00 a month. This was the highest honor that the state of North Carolina had ever conferred upon its educators. Throughout the 37 years he served the State Normal School faithfully, his race and his state with unswerying devotion, loftiness of purpose and meekness of character. He was known throughout Negro educational circles of America, and was respected for his high devotion to the cause wherever known.

Dr. Moore remained ill for much of 1932-1934. He made few appearances doing this time. However, On March 1, 1933 he attended the Matron's Social, Literary and Art Club with Mrs. Bessie Moore-Watt as hostess. The club opened with the club song *"Lifting As We Climb"* Dr. Moore offered prayer. He died April 4th 1934. Excerpts from his funeral sermon best described Dr. P. W. Moore's life:

In speech, gentle: in demeanor, quiet and refined: in devotion to duty, thoroughly consecrated and in personal integrity, he lived above reproach. He was a man of even temper, and sane: He loved truth and fair play, and was an apostle of good-will between races. However, the best of all, he was pre-eminently pious, a faithful believer in Jesus, the Savior of Men. He possessed of magnetism which could not be explained, he lived a useful life. He enshrined himself in the hearts of thousands who came under his influence.

W. O. Sanders, owner and editor of the *Elizabeth City Independent* printed Mayor Flora's Memorial Tribute in Volume XXV; No. 1,376 of its April 6, 1934 local pager. The tribute follows: "I consider the death of Dr. P. W. Moore, President Emeritus of the Elizabeth City State Normal School, is one of the greatest losses sustained by the community in many years. Elizabeth City has very little racial tension and has an unusually high type of Negro citizenship and I attribute this to the leadership of Dr. Moore. He did more for the up-building of his race here than any other man. Few men, since the days of the late Booker T. Washington, have done so much to further the cause of education of the Negro as Professor Moore has done. In his death Elizabeth City State and North Carolina, and the Negro race have sustained a distinct and great loss. But I feel that the good he has done will live for a long time to come, and I trust that his life will serve as an inspiration and a model for future generation of Negroes, here and elsewhere. If there were more men of the Professor Moore type among the Negro race, racial strife would be a thing of the past.

The Rev. Dr. C. M. Cartwright officiated at the obsequies, and delivered the funeral sermon. Dr. C. S. Brown, of Winton, N. C., and principal of the Waters Training School, and the Most Worshipful Grand Master of North Carolina Mason, served in the same capacity at the Memorial Services. He was buried in a small, shaded plot in Oak Grove Cemetery near the roadside, and within a half-mile of the State Normal School where he labored for nearly a half century.

The Dunbar High School located at 606 Roanoke Avenue was built in 1923 as the first high school for blacks in Pasquotank County. Following Dr. Moore's death the school was renamed to honor him and his notable contributions. After desegregation in 1970 and opening of Northeastern High School, P.W. Moore became a junior high school until it was vacated and eventually demolished in 1988.

R. A. Morrissey

Reverend Richard Albertus Morrissey was born in 1858 in the Magnolia Township of Dauplin County, North Carolina to Thomas & Priscilla Morrissey. He and his siblings: Robert, Laura, Willis, Emma and David Morrissey attended the local schools in Dauplin County. Rev. Morrissey came to the Baptist faith following years of toil and successful labor within the Western North Carolina Conference of the African Methodist Episcopal Zion Church, 630th Western Alabama Conference, the Tennessee and Philadelphia Conference. Rev. Morrissey is listed among the 114 preachers attending the West Alabama A. M. E. Zion Conference in Tuscaloosa, Alabama on December 14, 1881.[631] He remained in Alabama and became the first efficacious principal of the Zion Institute known as the Josephine Allen Institute from 1900 to 1904. He was also the first president of the Greenville College in the large and progressive Tennessee Conference of the A. M. E. Zion conference. From 1908-1912 he was the General Secretary of the Foreign Mission Department, served as editor of the *Missionary Seer.* [632] In 1908 he was also elected corresponding secretary of the Missionary Department with an office at the headquarters, Philadelphia. He was a keen educator and pastor for some of the largest and most influential churches, including Big Wesley, Philadelphia. He entered upon the work in regular order and did well for a while. He took some unreasonable obligations (which he thought was right), and increased the obligations of an overburdened and handicapped department, which made it impossible to meet the claims of the department. "Finding that the department would not be able to make any show towards satisfying the claimants unless some retrenchment was made to relieve the situation, Rev. Richard Albertus Morrissey agreed to serve without salary until the meeting of the General Conference. This method made it possible to greatly relieve the embarrassment of the situation.[633] This unfortunate overreach concluded his administration by the Board of Bishops just before the 1912 General Conference.[634]

Rev. Morrissey, the newly called pastor of the New Chapel Missionary Baptist Church, Creswell, North Carolina made a statement to the Roanoke Missionary Baptist Association during its 1914 Annual Session informing them for his reason for coming to the Baptist Church, and stating the principals for which he stood.[635] He was introduced at the Thursday Evening session by Rev. C. M. Cartwright to preach the Missionary Sermon. He chose the subject: "*The Great Commission as God's Command,*" based upon the Matthew 28:19-20 Text. He was appointed to the committee on Sabbath School during the 1913 annual session. A fourteen day Revival Service at New Chapel Baptist Church netted sixty souls for the church. The revival closed on the 3rd Sunday in February 1922. The services were a great success in every way. Dr. Morrissey resigned on the second Sunday in September 1922 to assume a position in Elizabeth City, North Carolina as a Superintendent of the Grade School. [636] Rev. Morrissey accepted the pastorate of the Saint James Missionary Baptist Church, Elizabeth City, North Carolina during the early part of 1922.

Rev. Morrissey went to Camden, N. C., on the third Sunday in January 1922 to preach the Fifth Anniversary sermon of Dr. R. R. Cartwright of the Philadelphia Missionary Baptist Church.[637] He delivered a very practical and inspiring sermon at Zion Baptist Church, Portsmouth, Virginia on June 14, 1922, at 8:00 P. M. Dr. Morrissey pointed out as the greater needs of the race today as: 1.) A Man's chance in Life; 2) Equal Justice and Protection of the Laws; 3) Education; 4) Wealth; 5) Practical Christian Living; 6) Greater Attendance at church service and engagement in Church activities. Without these the pastor urged that it would be impossible for the race to attain permanent prosperity as well as the protection and blessings of God.[638] Rev. Morrissey was the principal of the Elizabeth City Colored Graded School during the same time frame. Rev. Morrissey left Elizabeth City, North Carolina on Tuesday, August 25, 1922 for South Mills, North Carolina where he conducted revival for Rev. Sharpe.[639]

Reverend R. A. Morrissey's name was dropped from the roll of ministers of the Roanoke Missionary Baptist Association during the Tuesday Morning, May 22, 1923 session; he having left the denomination. Motion sustained.[640] On Thursday evening December 14th 1922 a reception was tendered for R. A. Morrissey by the Negro Business League, the affair was held in the assembly room of the Roanoke Collegiate Institute. Rev. Morrissey had been assigned to take charge of the A. M. E. Zion Church at Ashville, North Carolina.[641] Dr. Morrissey maintained a positive working relationship with the Baptist churches of the Roanoke Missionary Baptist Church, even after his departure from the Association. Rev. Brooks, Rev. W. H. A. Stallings, Rev. S. D. Morton, Rev. W. M. Brinkley and Rev. Hannibal Badham attended the 1927 Roanoke Association that convened in Elizabeth City the week of May 22, 1927.[642]

Dr. Morrissey returned back to the A. M. E. Z. Church and accepted the pastorate of Hopkins Chapel A. M. E. Z. Church, Ashville, N. C. [643] in 1929 Dr. Morrissey was serving as presiding elder of the Knoxville District in the Tennessee Conference.[644] The following news article appeared in the Norfolk Journal and Guide about Dr. Morrissey on September 7, 1929: "Mrs. Hattie Morrissey was in the city visiting friends. Mrs. Morrissey is the wife of Dr. R. A. Morrissey, who is now pasturing in Chattanooga, Tenn. She was the overnight guest in the home of Mr. & Mrs. Willie Charleston."[645]

Rev. Morrissey was a biblical scholar of the first magnitude. He authored the "Colored People and Bible History," published in 1925. The book was the first of its kind in modern scholarship to detail the genealogy of Ham in Genesis 10 and 1 Chronicles 1. This book was reviewed in *American Journal of Sociology,* Volume 32 Number 5 (March 1927), and he published the book, "What Is Man?

Henry Newby

Mr. Henry Newby was born 1833. He was one of the oldest citizens of Elizabeth City, North Carolina when he died at the home of his step-son Mr. George Reid on Friday, April 13, 1923 at age 90. Mr. Newby was one of the first members of St. Stephen Missionary Baptist Church having worshipped in a small schoolhouse and assisted in arranging for the establishment of the church. Mr. Newby served as a deacon of the church from its organization until his April 13, 1923 death. Funeral services were conducted on Sunday, April 15, 1923 at 3 O' clock. Reverend R. C. Lamb delivered the eulogy.

W. D. Newsome

W. D. Newsome of Bertie County[291] and later of Hertford County, North Carolina was free-born in 1822.[292] He married Alice A. Newson and to this union, Benjamin B., June 1, 1884-Sep. 1, 1896 and Georgia E. daughter Jan. 7, 1890-Aug. 7, 1896 were born. W. D. Newsome was a member of the Board of Managers of the 1866 Freedmen Convention. Other managers included, Caesar Johnson of "Warren, T. A. Sykes of Pasquotank, J. R. Page of Chowan, Richard Tucker of Craven, E. A. Richardson of Craven, C. D. Pierson of Craven, W. H. Anderson of Wake, J. E. Caswell of Wake, H. Unthanks of Greensboro', J. H. Harris of Wake, J. S. Leary of Fayetteville, and J. H. Williamson of Franklin County, North Carolina. [293] On Tuesday, October 3, 1866, by motion, Mr. Newsom of Hertford County was appointed to take the names and post-office addresses of the delegates attending the Freedmen's Convention. [294] During the same session, W. D. Newsome was elected as an office of the State Equal Rights League.

In 1868 new comer W. D. Newsome, won his seat only after the election in Hertford County was contested and he unseated the conservative candidate Thomas Sharpe. Other new members were John R. Page of Chowan, Richard Tucker, Edward Richard Dailey, and G. W. Willis of Craven County; Willis Bunn and R. M. Johnson of Edgecombe County; W. H. Reavis of Granville County, John R. Bryant and Charles Smith of Halifax County; George L. Mebson of New Hanover County; Robert Fletcher of Richmond County; and Willis Morgan and Steward Ellison of Wake County.[295] W. D. Newsome served in the North Carolina House of Representative as a Republican from 1870-1872.[296] During the 1871 session, Mr. Dunham, by permission, introduced a resolution in favor of "W. D. Newsom and it was adopted under the suspension of the rules.[297] Mr. Newsome was a mason. W. D. Newsome and ten other men from Hertford County, North Carolina were responsible for building a school house at Pleasant Plains, in Winton, North Carolina.[298] Some of the other men included: Maraduke Hall, William Jones, Jessie Keene, James Reynolds, Lawrence Weaver, and Willis Weaver. W. D. Newsome taught private school and Sunday school in Murfreesboro, North Carolina. The whip was often applied in Sunday school to make the pupils learn and behave according to expectations. In 1868 W. D. Newsome was teaching school in the Winton, North Carolina district. Three years later in 1871, W. D. Newsome was the vice-president of the Roanoke Missionary Baptist Sabbath School Union.

Alice predeceased W. D. Newsome on January 15, 1916, by one day. He was 94 years old, and she was 59 years old. They are buried in Union Township on Mary Saluda Road, beneath a tree and surrounded by a modern chain link fence beside a large cotton field. The epitat on their joining graves reads: "Thou God of Love beneath Thy sheltering Wing, We leave our dead to sweetly rest."

H. H. Norman

Reverend Harry Howard Norman known in North Carolina as "The Father in Israel" was born August 19, 1857 in Washington, North Carolina. His parents were Isaac Norman and the former Docus Spruill. His paternal grandmother was Rosa Norman, and his maternal grandmother was Penny Daven. Rev. Norman's ministry began in 1872. On the 3rd Sunday in July 1895 at Haven Creek Baptist Church he preached the funeral sermon of 98 year old Tony Farrow. Mr. Farrow was the oldest colored man on Roanoke Island. On Monday he preached the funeral sermon for Mrs. Rachael Etheridge, the mother of Captain Richard Etheridge, keeper of the Pea Island Life Saving Station.[303]

Rev. H. H. Norman married Mahala F. McCleese on November 15, 1878. Mrs. Mahala M. Norman quietly preceded him in death. He later married Mary F. Winslow on April 23, 1914. When the Fourteenth Census of the United States was taken on January 2, 1920 Rev. & Mrs. Molly Norman were living on South Road Street, Elizabeth City. The Norman entertained a number of young people at their home during the Memorial Day weekend. The young people highly enjoyed the excellent cream and cake. The "weesma hours" were near before the happy number dispersed."[299]

Mrs. Norman suffered a paralytic stroke on Sunday Night April 9, 1921,[300] and died the following Saturday, and was buried from Olive Branch Baptist Church on the following Monday. Rev. C. M. Cartwright officiated at the funeral that was conducted by S. P. Walston Funeral Home.[301] On the second day following Mrs. Norman's funeral, Rev. H. H. Norman left Moyock, North Carolina to hold services at Christian Home Missionary Baptist Church. From there he went to

Portsmouth, Virginia, then to Margaretville, North Carolina., to conduct revival services for Rev. J. J. Armstrong. Mr. Joseph Sawyer & Miss. Mary Sawyer were quietly married on the third Sunday in January 1922 at Rev. Norman's home on South Road Street.[302] In the early 1930's H. H. was widowed for the second time. He was now living with his widowed sister, Lucy Bryant and her children Samuel Bount 15, and Lona M. Blount on Richard Street in Elizabeth City, North Carolina.

Rev. H. H. Norman preached at Mount Olive Baptist Church, Norfolk, Virginia on November 15, 1926 for the benefit of the $1200 pew rally. On Saturday night, June 4, 1932 Mr. & Mrs. Joseph Reid gave Rev. H. H. Norman a surprise party. The next morning, Rev. H. H. Norman preached a powerful sermon to his audience at Christian Home Baptist Church. Over $50.00 was raised on the pastor's salary. Rev. Norman, pastor of Calvary Baptist Church, Elizabeth City conducted a very successful meeting during the second week of October 1932. Rev. W. H. Davis of Jamesville, North Carolina conducted the revival. [307] Rev. Norman, who had been hindered in his pastoral work because of illness, was able to be on duty again. He preached a powerful sermon at St. John's Baptist Church near Edenton, North Carolina on last Sunday.[308] Rev. H. H. Norman, D. D., closed a successful revival in September 1932 at St. John Baptist Church, Edenton. There were over 20 conversions as a result. His theme of a special sermon to candidates was "*Let Your Light Shine before Men.*" Rev. Norman pastured St. John's Baptist Church for 45 years. He was held in high esteem by the members.[309]

Reverend Norman for the next forty years went in and out before the people of God as pastor, Executive member of the Roanoke Missionary Baptist Association, Executive Member of the Roanoke Institute, and as Secretary of the same. Rev. Norman, Rev. C. M. Cartwright, Rev. Z. B. Wynn, Rev. D. J. Tate, Rev. J. A. Nimmo, Rev. W. S. Sharp, Rev. S. L. Sharp, and Mr. J. H. Perkins attended the 1926 mid-year session of the Roanoke Missionary Baptist Association which convened with Galatia Baptist Church at New Hope, North Carolina, on Wednesday, November 30, 1926.304 Reverend Norman's first pasturage of a five year term was at the Galatia Missionary Baptist Church in the New Hope section of Perquimans County, North Carolina. His second call to the pasturage First Baptist Colerain, North Carolina where he served for seven years. He was next called to the Saint John Missionary Baptist Church, Edenton, North Carolina for the next twenty five years. Mrs. Maggie Lowther, the president of the Sisters Union started preparing in November 1928 to give Rev. H. H. Norman a banquet celebrating his fortieth year pastorate. During the 1928 Advent season the elaborate reception was given in his honor. The St. John School was beautifully decorated. Fifty-two persons were present. The out of town guest were Mrs. C. M. Cartwright, Sarah Westcott, Christian Spellman, Stallis Holley of Elizabeth City, Mrs. Fannie Gilliam of Norfolk, VA.[305] While pasturing St. John's Baptist Church he concurrently preached at Haven's Creek Missionary Baptist Church, Manteo, North Carolina, Christian Home Missionary Baptist Church, and Moyock, North Carolina. Other pastoral opportunities included: Philadelphia Missionary Baptist Church, Camden, North Carolina for six years; Pleasant Branch Missionary Baptist Church, Currituck, North Carolina for six years; Chapel Hill Missionary Baptist Church, Tyrell County, North Carolina four years; Calvary Baptist Missions, Elizabeth City; Zion Hill Baptist, Plymouth, North Carolina for five years; First Baptist Belhaven, and

Snow Hill in Belhaven, North Carolina, for one year each; and Mount Carmel Missionary Baptist Church, Pasquotank County {Elizabeth City} North Carolina for 25 years. Dr. C. M. Cartwright was called to Plymouth, North Carolina to preach the funeral of Rev. Harry Howard Norman who departed this life at age 78 for the next life in the world to come on September 9, 1933.[306]

Luke Pierce

Reverend Luke Pierce was born about 1848 in Windsor, North Carolina. He is listed as a mulatto in the 1870 censes record and as a multiple race individual in the 1880 census records. He married nineteen year old Hester Williams on November 13, 1873. They were the parents of William (1875), S. D. (1876), and J. F. (1879). He listed his job in 1889 as Preacher. In 1900 his home consisted of Marcell (23), James (21), Luke (18), Daniel (15), Priscilla (13), Pearl (11), Joanna (9), Luella (5), and Lucy Pierce (3).

In 1880 Rev. Luke Pierce was an officer of the North Carolina State Convention, namely, he was one of three Vice-Presidents. Rev. Luke Pierce was a supportive member of the Roanoke Missionary Baptist Association. He was the chairman of the Sabbath Schools.[310] On the motion of Rev. Luke Pierce the forenoon proceedings of May 1878 were read and adopted.[311] On the motion of Elder Luke Pierce, the delegates from newly constituted churches were invited to come forward and present their petitions to the Association during the morning session. It was motion by Rev. Pierce at the Wednesday, May 28, 1879 Afternoon Session that the delegates from the newly constituted church be given the right hand of fellowship. By motion of Rev. Luke Pierce the May 27, 1879 Report of the Committee on Pulpit Supplies was received and adopted. It was announced that Elders Luke Pierce and Abram Mebane would fill the stand in "The Grove" at 3 P. M. The following morning Rev. Pierce motioned that no brother was allowed to speak more than 2 ½ minutes at a time on the same subject. Later in the day, Elder Luke Pierce was one of five appointed on Sabbath Schools Committee.[312] On motion of Elder Luke Pierce, a committee of five was appointed on The Memorial for the late Rev. Lemuel Washington Boon.[313]

The available minutes of the Annual Sessions of the West Roanoke Missionary Baptist Association from 1891-1894 certifies that Rev. Pierce was the pastor of three churches in the West Roanoke Missionary Baptist Association, namely: Mount Olive Missionary Baptist Church, and Saint Matthew Missionary Baptist Church both in Windsor, and Sandy Branch Missionary Baptist Church in Roboxel, North Carolina. He was called to the pastorate of the Cedar Landing Missionary Baptist Church in 1903. He remained in this pastorate until 1906. The church derived its name from the freight warehouse on the bank of the historic Roanoke River, near a grove of cedars. From the river landing and the trees the meeting place was later called "Cedar Landing Baptist Church." The boarded church was later moved to the Cedar Landing gate post.

Rev. Luke Pierce, Rev. M. W. D. Norman, T. H. Wilson, A. Robbins, Henry Houston, Samuel Hoggard, P. S. Sanderlin, Washington Allen and T. C. Bond were granted *An act to incorporate "Bertie Academy"* in the County of Bertie and state of North Carolina on the 25th day of February, A. D. 1895. Rev. Luke Pierce was called to the pastorate of Olive Branch Missionary Baptist

Church, Elizabeth City, North Carolina during the year of 1896. However, after three years of successful pastorate at Olive Branch Missionary Baptist Church, Rev. Luke Pierce of Windsor, North Carolina, tendered his resignation as pastor on August 26, 1899, effective December 31, 1899. Not one church member expected the resignation of this excellent preacher and exemplary Christian.[314] He delivered his last sermon as pastor at Olive Branch Baptist Church on the third Sunday in December 1899.[315] Reverend Pierce delivered a very forceful sermon to the Hook and Ladder Company on November 23, 1899 at Olive Branch Baptist church, the occasion being the third anniversary of the company's organization. The members were present in a body and highly appreciated the fervor and instructive remarks.[316] He was in Elizabeth City during the middle of the month, and on the third Monday of March 1900, preached at Olive Branch.[317]

Rev. Luke Pierce preceded his wife Mrs. Hester Pierce in death. She died at her home at 1438 1/2/ East Princess Ann Road, Norfolk, Virginia on Monday May 3, 1926 at 9 O' Clock A. M., following an illness of a few months. Rev. & Mrs. Pierce were active members in good standing of the Bethlehem Baptist Church, Norfolk, Virginia. They served faithfully in that church and she continued to serve faithfully until her death.[318]

E. E. Randolph

Elder Edward Eddie Randolph was born September 1849[319] in Belvedere, Upper Chowan County, North Carolina to Luke Randolph of Perquimans County, North Carolina and the former Patsie Moore also of Perquimans County. Throughout his life Elder E. E. Randolph was known as "Ned Randolph" He married Caroline Russells Barnes of Gates County, Hobbsville, North Carolina and to this union the following children were born: Exum, Mattie R., Rebecca, Lucious, Isaac, George L., Pearl, Garfield, and Webster Randolph. Ned and Caroline Randolph and family were living in Sunbury, North Caroline from the Twentieth Annual Session to 1903.[320] They lived there until Caroline's death on October 8, 1927.

In 1883 Reverend Randolph was listed as an ordained Elder in the Roanoke Missionary Baptist Association. He listed his residence in Gates County, (Sunbury), N. C. In 1885 Elder E. E. Randolph was the pastor of the Whaleyville First Baptist Church, later known as Mineral Springs Baptist Church, Whaleyville, VA. This church was a member of the Roanoke Missionary Baptist Association. Elder E. E. Randolph served as the delegate to the Roanoke Missionary Baptist Association in 1885.[321] The church reported that the pastor's salary was $64.00 for the two Sabbath preaching. The clerk was L. J. White. The membership totaled 100 members, 36 males and 64 females. The church reported the following for the year of 1884-1885: it baptized 8, received 1 by letter, dismissed 12 by letter, restored 5, excommunicated 5, and lost 3 by death.[322] In the Fourteenth Census of the Unites States: 1920, E. E. Randolph listed his job as Preaching and General Farmer. During the Wednesday Morning session of the Thirty-eighth Annual Session of the Roanoke Missionary Baptist Association held with the First Colored Hertford Baptist Church, Hertford, North Carolina Elder Randolph conducted the 9: 30 A. M. Devotional period. Elder Randolph sang hymn 344, "How Happy Every Child of Grace Who Knows His Sins Forgiven,"

He read Psalm 1.[323] Elder Randolph served as the Clerk of the Roanoke Missionary Baptist Association in 1884 under the moderatorship of Elder J. K. Lamb. Elder Edward Eddie "Ned" Randolph died May 27, 1934 at the age of 84 and was buried in the Winslow Grove Church Cemetery, Chowan County, North Carolina.[324]

Funeral services for Lucius Randolph were held at Welch's Chapel Missionary Baptist Church, Tyner, N. C., with Rev. W. H. Davis officiating. Lucius was a long time member of Welch's Chapel. He died in the Veteran's Hospital in Kecoughtan, Va. Where he had been a patient for a very long time. He was survived by his wife, Mrs. Minnie White-Randolph, two sisters, Mrs. Martha Saunders, Tyner, N. C., and Mrs. Pearl V. Blakenship of Birmingham, Alabama; one brother Garfield of Belvidere; one foster daughter, Mrs. Sheldine R. Hurdle of New York. He was a W. W. I Vet.eran.

I. B. Roach

Reverend Ivy Boone Roach was born 1847 to the marriage of Abraham and Winnie Griffin Roach of Newland, {Pasquotank County} North Carolina.[325] According to the 1850 United States Federal Census, Ivy was 3 years old and living in the home with India {17}, John {15}, Larry, {7} Charlotte, (5) Abraham, {4} and Sarah Cook {40}. In 1870 Ivy Roach's household members were listed: Anna 22, Nancy A 2, Winney 60, Juda Mitchell 40, and Emma J. 13. Ten years later, in 1880, thirty-three year old Ivy Roach was living with his wife, thirty year old Ann, and the following household members: Nancy A. C. Roach 9-daughter, Charlotte 8-daughter, Walter S. 6—Son, Francis B. 4 son, Lemuel Roach 2-son, Lovenia Roach 60, Judia Mitchell 40-sister, Lonza Barrington 12-nephew, Jordan G. Nephew.

Rev. I. B. Roach served as the Moderator of the Roanoke Missionary Baptist Association for one year 1887, and served on the Committee on Credentials.[326] Rev. I. B. Roach listed his occupation as Missionary Baptist Minister on each of the succeeding censes records. At the 1899 Session of the Roanoke Association convening at Weeping Mary Missionary Baptist Church, Jamesville,

North Carolina, Rev. I. B. Roach was elected as Moderator for his second time. He served in this position until 1909. Rev. Roach was succeeded by Rev. George D. Griffin when the association convened at Christian Home Baptist Church, Moyock, North Carolina. In 1887 I. B. Roach was called as the second pastor of the Harvey's Chapel Missionary Baptist Church, later named the Mount Carmel Missionary Baptist Church in the Newland Section of Pasquotank County, North Carolina. Due to his responsibilities as rural Negro Superintendent for several one and two room school houses in the area, and combined with his additional responsibilities as the pastor of the newly established church, Riddick's Grove Missionary Baptist Church, Belvedere, North Carolina, Rev. I. B. Roach, tenure at Mount Carmel lasted only for one year. He continued his ministry across the vast regions of Northeastern North Carolina. *The Carolinian* reported in its Wednesday, November 3, 1897 paper, that Rev. I. B. Roach left Monday to pay a brief visit to Edenton.[327] In 1903 Rev. Roach was the pastor of the Joppa Missionary Baptist Church in Hobbsville, North Carolina.

In 1910 I. B. Roach, Ann 69, Ivey H., 25, Edward L., 23, Roscoe C., 20, Franklin M. Harvey 16 Grandson, Mamie J. Harvey 14 Granddaughter, Moses S. Harvey 11 Grandson, Allen N. Harvey 9 Grandson, Lockwood C. Harvey Grandson, Chloe M. Williams 14 Adopted Daughter are members of the same household, with Ivy as the head of the household.

On her March 5, 1872 Freeman's Bank Deposit Judy Roach Mitchell, registrant #4147 asked the following questions thusly: Where born: North Carolina, Pasquotank County,: Where brought up: North Carolina, Pasquotank County; Resided: North Carolina, Pasquotank County: Age:42; Complexion, Yellow; Husband or Wife: Allen; Children: Jordan (Dead); Father: Abraham Roach (Dead); Mother: Wina (Living); Brothers & Sisters: Emma, Marrow, Ivy, and Abraham. Judy "X" Mitchell's places an X between her first and last name to verify her signature. This bank statement was signed by Harriett Halstead in the Norfolk, Virginia office of the Freedman's Bank. Ivy B and his sister Judy Roach Mitchell both list his birthplace as North Carolina.

Under his leadership, the Roanoke Collegiate Institute, located at Elizabeth City, was founded and constructed in 1896. Roanoke Hall, the largest building on the campus of the Roanoke Collegiate Institute, was named in honor of Rev. Ivy Boone Roach the foremost agitator in the early days of the school.[328] During the year of 1913 a porch was built to the Roach Hall to connect it with the porch around Roanoke Hall.[329] Rev. I. B. Roach, Steven Bowie, Mrs. Georgie Skinner, Theresa Hill attended the Inter-Collegiate and Inter-Racial Conference of the Student Volunteer Movement which convened at State College, Raleigh, North Carolina. This meeting was organized under the direction of Professor James A. Clark.[330] Rev. Ivy Roach Boone died on November 6, 1925 at 80 years old. Dr. Cartwright attended the Eulogistic Services over the late Rev. I. B. Roach, and acted as master of ceremonies. Professional Services for his funeral was entrusted to the Funeral staff of C. L. Griffin. He was buried on November 8, 1925 in the Gallop Cemetery, Newland section of Pasquotank County, North Carolina.

Tell The Angels

Tell the Angels I'll sing my soul.
Tell the Angels it won't be long;
I'll sing a new song they never heard before
How I left my troubles all below;
I'm going to sing of how he brought me through
How my head got wet with the mid-night dew;
How my soul got happy, when I came across,
How He found me, when I was lost.

C. S. Sessoms

Reverend Charles S. Sessoms was born to Edward Sessoms and the former Nannie Slaughter in the year of 1853. He married Lillie Sharp, the matron of the Albemarle Training School during March 1921. To this union two children were born: Martha, & Ada Sessoms. He was the seventh pastor of the Piney Wood Chapel Missionary Baptist Church, Bertie County, North Carolina. He was an active member of the Roanoke Missionary Baptist Association. He served as a delegate from the Bethany Missionary Baptist Church, Harrellsville, North Carolina to the 1885 Annual Session of the Roanoke Missionary Baptist Association[331] and he served as a delegate to the Twentieth Annual Session of the Roanoke Missionary Baptist Association when it convened at Providence Missionary Baptist Church, Edenton, North Carolina. He was the pastor of the Pleasant Shade Baptist Church, Franklin, Virginia. Rev. C. S. Sessom was the principal of the Albemarle Training School in Edenton.

After the Roanoke Missionary Baptist Association split in 1885 Rev. C. S. Sessoms became the Western Roanoke Association State Missionary. He reported to the Third Annual Session of the West Roanoke Association that he had visited thirty-six churches in the bounds of the Association and had endeavored to discharge his duties as a local missionary although he could not exactly ascertain from the Executive Board what the missionary duties were. Sessions continued, "I merely presumed what my duties were and went to work." He continued, "I am pleased to say our churches are making some progress. Most of them have good Sabbath schools though some fail to have books and papers which they need. Many of the pastors have organized a Foreign Mission Society in their churches. I had the pleasure to assist in organizing one at Sandy Branch. The pastor and the deacons seem alive to the cause. Many of the pastors are endeavoring to erect comfortable houses of worship. Most of the houses are very deficient. We have about only four finished churches in the bounds of the Association. I need not name them, as I am aware that the brethren know which they are. I earnestly recommend to the churches to try to secure comfortable houses of worship. I did not always find things as pleasant as I wish them in visiting the various churches. I was compelled sometimes to make more sacrifices that I desired to make. I have more than once preached in the morning and afternoon without eating anything. I have visited nearly all the pastors' churches in the Association and am sorry to say only one pastor made any preparation for me to get anything to ear or a place to lodge. I have visited 39 churches, preached 32 sermons, delivered 8 lectures, received a total of $37.00 for Foreign Missions, $1.29 for Home Missions, $26.31 in the general collection and received $29.69 for expenses.

At the funeral of Mr. William E. Burke, who died October 31, 1922, Rev. C. S. Sessoms read the resolutions on behalf of the Edenton North Carolina Businesses and Professor J. R. Flemings read the resolutions on behalf of the Building Edenton Building and Loan Association. The Gale Street Baptist Church was unable to accommodate such an aggregation of people. Rev. J. A. Lewis, pastor of Providence Baptist Church, presided.[332] Rev. & Mrs. C. S. Sessoms and daughter attended the May 1923 Annual Session of the Roanoke Missionary Baptist Association held in Weeksville, North Carolina at the Union Chapel Baptist Church.[333] Rev. C. S. Sessoms of Edenton, North Carolina, preached a sermon for No. 9 class of Cornerstone Baptist Church on the first Sunday in September 1924 at 3: P. M.[334] Rev. Sessoms left Bertie County, North Carolina and migrated to Durham, N. C., and opened his barber shop, and continued with his public and private ministry. He preached at Providence Baptist Church, Edenton, N. C., on Christmas morning, December 25, 1930. During the month of June 1933 Rev. C. S. Sessom spent two weeks visiting his mother, Mrs. N. Sessom and sister, Mrs. Ada Draper and other relatives and friends. The Moderator's Address during the May 1935 Roanoke Missionary Baptist Association Annual Session and the welcome program, which included a sermon preached by the Rev. C. S. Sessoms, constituted the work of the first day.[335] He was the guest of his sister, Mrs. Ada Draper of West Draper Street in Edenton; N. C.[336] He participated in several church services in Franklin, Virginia during the month of November 1937. On November 11, he preached at the Pleasant Shade Baptist Church, from the subject, "Such a Time as This,"[337] The collection amounted to $105. 37. At 3 O' Clock P. M., he officiated at the funeral service of Mr. Samuel Johnson. On November 14, 1937, the Historic First Baptist Church, Franklin celebrated its seventh anniversary. Among the visiting ministers who took part in the celebration were C. S. Sessoms of Durham, N. C., Rev. E. D. Harrell, pastor of the Piney Grove Baptist Church, and A. F. Bowe, pastor of the St. Luke A. M. E. Z. of Franklin. On the night of November 15, the pastor, the Rev. G. C. Lassiter was honored at banquet ceremonies. The Town Aid Club and the Hall Street Club presented the pastor with gifts of appreciation. Remarks were made by Henry Perry, president of the Town Aid Club; Mrs. Fannie Arrington, and William Duke. On the third Sunday in November, Rev. Sessoms in company with Mrs. Lula Davis, and Sam Morrow of Newport News were the guest of Mrs. Lizzie Daye on the Third Sunday in November 1937.[338] At the 1950 Annual Roanoke Missionary Baptist Association space was given to delegates and visitors for expressions. Drs. C. S. Sessoms and W. H. A. Stallings expressed themselves as being very thankful to God, for bringing they back to the spot where Dr. Sessoms was ordained to the Gospel Ministry and where Dr. Stallings pastured for many years.[339] Rev. Sessoms died on February 18, 1955. He was buried in the Vine Oak Cemetery in Edenton, North Carolina.

D. L. Simmons

Reverend D. L. Simmons was born about 1839 in Virginia. He resided in Creswell, North Carolina with his wife Julia Ann Simmons. He was a faithful member of the Roanoke Missionary Baptist Association from its inception. The Report of Committee on Permanent Organization of the Roanoke Missionary Baptist Association made the following report on Thursday Morning, May 30, 1878: that Elder D. L. Simmons was selected to preach the Introductory Sermon with his alternate, Elder Luke Pierce serving as his alternate.[340] Rev. Simmons was the delegate from the Chapel Hill Baptist Church, Columbia; Gum Neck Baptist Church, Gum Neck; St. John's, Creswell; and Zion Grove, Washington County, North Carolina to the May 1878 Roanoke Missionary Baptist Association.[341] He represented these same churches at the 1879 Annual session. He was listed on the same reports as an ordained Elder living in Creswell, North Carolina.

In the absence of Elder D. L. Simmons and Elder Luke Pierce to the Tuesday Morning, May 27, 1879, the Introductory Sermon was preached by Elder Joshua H. Flemings and his alternate Elder J. K. Lamb, from Zachariah 11: 17, followed by prayer from Elder J. K. Lamb. It was announced that Elder D. L. Simmons, and Elder E. H. Griffin his alternate, would fill the stand in "The Grove" at 11 o'clock.[342] Rev. D. L. Simmons, of Windsor, N. C., and a party consisting of Revs. W. S. Creecy, of Rich Square; W. A. Cobb of Suffolk, Virginia; G. T. Rousen, of Murfreesboro, and P. A. Bishop, of Rich Square, left Norfolk, Virginia, Monday night, August 30th 1926 for Brooklyn, New York., where the Lott Carey Foreign Mission Convention met August 31 to September 3, with Holy Trinity Baptist Church, Rev. T. S. Harden, pastor. The party reportedly remained together throughout the journey. The trip was very much enjoyed by all.[343] A committee sent by the church at which the convention met, greeted them at the church. The party was then assigned to a guest home for the convention. All members of the North Carolina party stayed in the same home. At the convention, Rev. Simmons and the North Carolina delegation met with a larger delegation from North Carolina. In Reverend Simmons estimation of things at the 1926 Lott Carey Convention, "It is an inspiration to any minister to attend the Lott Carey Convention. Everything done at the convention was done with foreign field in view." Rev. D. L. Simmons stated on his return trip home that any pastor who heard the native Russian speak, the two from Africa and the one from India speak cannot help being possessed with the true missionary spirit. Therefore, he concluded that every church should do their best for foreign missions.[344] Due to a recent illness, the third Sunday in March 1927 services at the St. Elmo Baptist Church, Windsor, North Carolina were not conducted by the pastor, Rev. D. L. Simmons. Services were conducted by Rev. T. O. Bryant.[345]

Robbin Smallwood

Reverend Robbin Smallwood was a private in the United Stated Colored Troops, Company I-14 U.S.C.H.A. He enlisted in the United States Army on February 23, 1865 and was discharged December 11, 1865. He spent a total of 9 months and 18 days. He sustained injuries during the Civil War.

He was a member of the Roanoke Missionary Baptist Association prior to the 1885 split to form the West Roanoke Missionary Baptist Association. He was listed in 1888 as a licensed minister of the West Roanoke Missionary Baptist Association. When the Association convened in September 25th-27th 1894 at the Zoar Baptist Church in Northampton County, N. C., Rev. Smallwood's name was included on the West Roanoke Missionary Baptist Association Minister's Roster. He listed his address as Quitsna, N. C.

Arajah Smith

Arajah Smith a mulatto was born December 1834 to Nancy "J" Smith of Hertford County North Carolina. He married twice, first to Ms. Emeline Smith with whom he resided in 1880. Other family members included N. J. Melteer (16) niece, M. E. Melton (7) granddaughter, J. W. Melton (5) grandson, and M. T. Combo (14) servant. His second marriage was to Ms. Elizabeth F. Combo {August 5, 1870}, the daughter of Susie Cumbo, of Ahoskie, N.C., whom he married in 1895 at the age of 25. He was 55 years old. In 1910 Arajah's house consisted of his wife and mulatto children: Solomon H., son (17), Nancy J., daughter (15), Rosa L., daughter (14, Susan A., daughter (12) Arajah D., son (11), Benjamin F., son (9) Mary D., Daughter (7), Robert J., son (5), Leonandear, son (3), and Isadore, daughter 7 months old. By 1920 Arajah Smith's oldest children are no longer in the home. The residence consisted of: Arajah, Jr., Benjamin, Mary D., Robert, Lonnie, Isa. D., and 8 year old Elizabeth.

Nineteen years after his birth Arajah Smith wrote this letter to his family friend.

Suffolk, VA May 27th 1853

David for this I wanted to write you lines to inform you that I am not well at this time. I am able to be up and that is and I hope that these few lines will find you and your family all well and so I do not think that I can come and see you until August. I will try to come then if I can come. When I come I will try to stay with you sometime and I and I wish that I could come now but I am so not well. I wish that . . . . I wish that I cannot come and I wish to hear from you so soon. As you can, please write my family as well, except myself and give my respect to all.

Arajah Smith and James M. Walden were the founders of a school located near the present site of the Phillip Missionary Baptist Church, Harrellsville, N. C. Jack Harrell gave the land and Joe Hall built the school. It was only one room. Some of the first faculty members were Tiny Nickens, Jimmie Ed. Brown, and Isaiah Boone. The principal was Fletcher Chaimons. Charles Nickens was one of the Trustees. Arajah Smith was an agent of change for the Pleasant Plains community.

In an additional to his educational interest, Arajah Smith actively represented the Church during the Roanoke Missionary Baptist Association from 1871-1885. In 1879 he reported the Statistical Table to the Association when it convened in its Fourteenth Annual Session held with the Church of Christ at New Sawyer's Creek, Camden County, N. C.; Tuesday after the 4th Lord's Day in May 1878. Rev. William Reid, Moderator & Asbury Reid, Clerk. Arajah Smith was the delegate from the Pleasant Plains Baptist church to the 1884 Roanoke Missionary Baptist Association when it convened in its Nineteenth Annual Session at the Church of Christ at Zion Hill, Bertie County, N. C. He reported to the Association that Pleasant Plaines conducted worship services twice a month. During the present 1883-1884 Associational Year 29 people were baptized and given the "Right-Hand of Fellowship" with all the rights and privileges therewith associated. In additional to his responsibilities he was also the clerk of the church. In 1885 Arajah Smith served as the clerk of Pleasant Plains. He reported to the Twentieth Annual Session of the Roanoke Missionary Baptist Association that Pleasant Plaines had a membership of 416. After 1886, Arajah Smith no longer served in the capacity of the Clerk of Pleasant Plains Missionary Baptist Church. He no longer participated in the West Roanoke Missionary Baptist Association.

Rubin Smith

Elder Rubin Smith was born July 1830 in North Carolina. The 1880 censes recorded 51 year old Rubin Smith as a white minister living in Hasletts, Gates, North Carolina. His household consisted of Reubin R. 25, Mary F., 18, Margret A., 15 and Margret Savage 75. A second censes entry included 51 year old mulatto Rubin Smith as a single day laborer. His household consisted of Reubin R. 25, Mary F., 18, Margret A., 15 and Margaret Savage 75. In 1882 Elder Rubin Smith married Sarafalia Smith of Virginia. They were the parents of Isaiah K., Leuvenia, Ella J., George M., Alma J., and Eva Smith of the Hayslett Township, Gates, North Carolina.

Elder Smith participated in many phases of the Roanoke Missionary Baptist Association. His name appeared on the 1878 list of Roanoke Missionary Baptist Association Licentiates. Rev. Smith listed a Gatesville Post Office Box as a mailing address. In 1884 Rubin Smith was listed as an ordained Elder, and has moved from Gatesville to Gates, North Carolina, and a distance of 10 miles. In 1885 Elder Smith was living on Wiggins Cross Roads in Gates. After this date his name ceased to appear in any other available records or minutes of the Roanoke Missionary Baptist Association.

Eli Thomas

Reverend Eli Thomas was born about 1843 Parksville District of Perquimans County, North Carolina. He married Kersiah Nixon on April 4, 1870. He earned his living by preaching. They were the parents of Nancy, David, Mary Thomas, and William Zachery. He was listed as an ordain Elder of the Roanoke Missionary Baptist Association.

J. J. Thompson

Reverend Jonas J. Thompson was born in Bertie County, North Carolina on Sep. 17, 1853. His preferred name was "Black Horse" Thompson. He was the third pastor called to the Indian Woods Missionary Baptist Church, Bertie County, North Carolina. He started the first building program which was a frame building with a gallery. He was called to the Woodville Plains Missionary Baptist Church which was one of the oldest African-American Churches in Bertie County although the exact date is not known. Woodville Planes was first established in Woodville and later moved to its present location in Lewiston.

In 1883 "Black Horse" Thompson was listed as a West Roanoke Missionary Baptist ordained minister. His mailing address was listed as Lewiston, North Carolina. When the West Roanoke Missionary Baptist Association convened in its seventh session in 1892 at the Philippi Baptist Church near Winton, N. C, Rev. "Black Horse" listed the following churches as pastorates: Chapel Hill, Luella, and St. Francis. The Chapel Hill Baptist Church congregation had 234 members, 97 males and 137 females. Sabbath Preaching was conducted on the 4th Sabbath. During the associational year Chapel Hill Baptist Church made the required financial reports. Luella Baptist Church had a total membership of 50. Worship Services were conducted on the 1 Sabbaths. The church neither baptized nor received any members by letter during the reporting period. The church was unable to satisfy any of the objectives of the Association. The St. Francis Congregation had a membership of 125. However, did not make the required financial reports. Rev. J. J. Thompson combined membership was 409. In 1893 Rev. "J. J. "Black Horse" Thompson was the pastor of Chapel Hill, Luella, Mill Branch, St. Francis and Weeping Mary Baptist Churches. He died on September 28, 1913.

B. Turpin

At the time of Reverend Baptist Turpin's birth Indian Woods had been a developed and thriving community of 53,000 acres given to their Indian Chief, Tom Blount by the colonial government on the north side of the Roanoke River in what is now southwestern Bertie County. The Tuscarora Indians in eastern North Carolina had previously been divided into two factions in the early eighteenth century. The Northern Tuscarora or Upper Towns were led by Chief Tom Blunt and the Southern or Lower Towns by Chief Hancock. Rev. Baptist Turpin parents were a part of the remaining Tuscarora's. In 1828, the Tuscarora still remaining in North Carolina gave up their title and rights to Indian Woods. Around 645 Tuscarora families remained; while other moved to other parts of North Carolina, Virginia, and South Carolina.

Baptist Turpin was born two years later in 1830 in Bertie County, North Carolina to a family with a strong Tuscarora heritage. He married Harriet Unknown, In 1850 his mulatto Indian household consisted of his wife and daughter; Rosetta (30),and his nieces, Harriett (7), Estelle (5), and nephew Georgia Turpin (4).

Baptist Turpin began his journey in Christendom as a deacon and trustee of the Indian Woods Missionary Baptist Church located on the Outlaw Plantation in the Indian Woods Township of Bertie County, N. C. He served under the leadership of Reverend George A. Mebane. Later in his service to the Indian Woods Missionary Baptist Church he was ordained to the full work of the Gospel Ministry. He remained an active member of the Roanoke & West Missionary Baptist Associations in the capacity of Associate minister.

Little or no academic work has been done on the Indian Woods community of which Reverend Baptist Turpin lived and died. His life and ministry displays the intersection of the histories of Native Americans, African Americans, and Europeans. As we explore and understand more about Indian Woods and the creolization that occurred in Bertie, Gates & Hertford Counties, North Carolina between African Americans, various Indian cultures, and the Anglo-Americans; we will begin to understand more about what it means to be American, Native American and African American living and preaching in the Roanoke and West Roanoke Missionary Baptist Association.

C. T. Underwood

Charles Thomas Underwood was born April 18, 1862, at Clinton, in Sampson County, North Carolina to Henry Underwood the son of Banter and Roley Crumpler Underwood, and to the former Jane Boykin daughter of George and Dinah Boykin. He attended the schools of Sampson County, North Carolina. He married the former Adeline Sellers, a daughter of Evans and Candace Sellers. They were the parents of nine children; four predeceased their parents in death. The remaining children are: Lenora, Rufus, William M., Medissa M., and Addie G. Underwood.

Reverend Underwood was licensed to preach the gospel on December 12, 1886, at the Red Hill Missionary Baptist Church, Samson County, North Carolina. He pastured Mount Pleasant Baptist Church, Harrellsville, North Carolina for three years. During the years of his pastorate he pastured no less than twenty-five churches, several of them in the Roanoke and West Roanoke Missionary Baptist Associations. While in northeastern North Carolina, Elizabeth City, Reverend C. T. Underwood was a member of the Roanoke Missionary Baptist Association and its ministerial forum.

Solomon Webb

Reverend Solomon Webb the son of Charlotte Webb was born about 1840 in Rich Square, Northampton County, North Carolina. He married Rachael Unknown. He was excommunicated from the Roanoke Missionary Baptist Association. He later joined the A. M. E. Zion Methodist denomination.

James Wilson

Reverend James Wilson, of Brooks Avenue, Elizabeth City, died December 10, 1933 after a lingering illness. Funeral services were held December 12, 1933 from the Olive Branch Missionary Baptist Church with Dr. Charles M. Cartwright officiating. Mrs. E. O. Winslow sang a solo. He was survived by his widow, two children and four grandchildren. Mrs. Sytheia Rattler of Norfolk, VA attended the funeral of her father, the Rev. James Wilson.

Thaddeus Wilson

Reverend Thaddeus Wilson born about 1831 in Merry Hill section of Bertie County, North Carolina., He married Elizabeth Unknown. His parents were natives of Virginia. His second marriage was to Alice Lynch on January 20, 1882. The committee on Pulpit Supplies gave notice that Elder Thaddeus Wilson and Charles Capps would fill he stand in "The Grove" at 11 O'clock, A. M. He was one of nine people appointed on May 29, 1879 to the Committee of Permanent Organization. Rev. Wilson was one of six people selected to investigate the case of Bethany Church against Wilson Mullen. The committee endorsed the course of action Bethany Church in turning out the brother, and recommendedS that the Association let it stand. Additionally, the committee reported that after considering the case of the ordination of Moses Wynn.

ROANOKE CENTENNIAL ANNIVERSARY

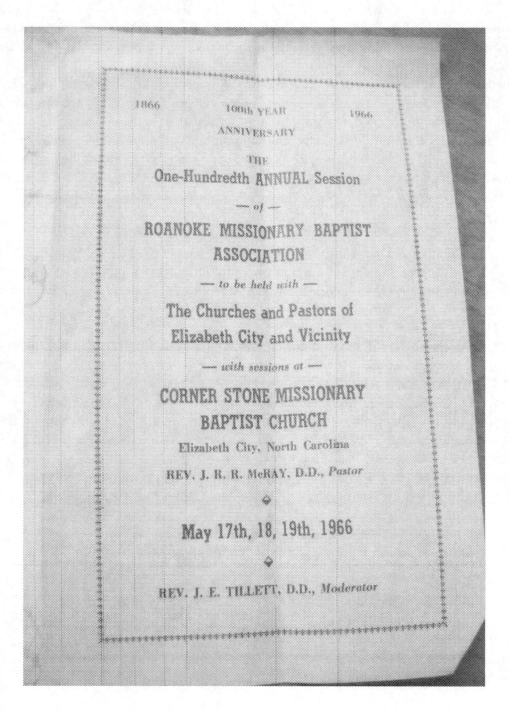

The Roanoke Missionary Baptist Association held the beginning of its centennial (100) Anniversary on May 17, 18, & 19, 1966 at the Cornerstone Missionary Baptist Church, Elizabeth City, North Carolina. Dr. J. L. S. Holloman, pastor of the Second Baptist Church, Washington, D.C., editor of the Lott Cary Herald and president of the Ministers Training Institute was the featured speaker for the launching of the centennial celebration. Dr. O. L. Sherrill, executive secretary of the General Baptist State Convention, Inc., and Dr. Joseph Edward Tillett, Moderator, delivered his annual address preceding the sermon by Dr. Holloman. Dr. James E. Cheek, president of Shaw University, Dr. J. J. Freeman and Rev. William B. Westbrook, dean of the Roanoke Institute were speakers also. Sermons were preached by the following Reverends: F. L. Andrews, W. H. Davis, C. A. Proctor, James O. Rodgers, W. J. Thompson, and R. M. Watson. Rev. M. L. Williams, promotional director of the northeastern North Carolina Baptist Fellowship led a discussion on the work included in the training programs of the Roanoke Missionary Baptist Association.

Each of the 72 member churches of the Roanoke Missionary Baptist Association held special centennial services. Many of the churches began their celebrations in 1965, and prepared church histories listing the dates the congregations were established, names of pastors and ministers sent out and the general progress of the churches since their organization. Member churches pledged a special gift of one cent per member per year, or a $1.00 as a centennial offering. This amount was pledged by the churches besides their regular contribution through the Baptist State Convention for Roanoke Institute, Shaw University, state missions, foreign missions, and central orphanage.

The One-Hundredth and One Annual Session of the Roanoke Missionary Baptist Association, convening at Saint Stephen Baptist Church, Elizabeth City, North Carolina,[346] May 23, 1967, was called to order at 10: 30 A. M. by Moderator J. R. R. McRay. The devotions were conducted by Reverends Curtis A. Proctor, and T. S. Cooper. The First Hymn was "Jesus Keep Me near the Cross". The 46th Psalm was read by Rev. Curtis A. Proctor. The Second Hymn was sung, "Pass Me Not Oh Gentle Savior." Expressions were made by Reverends J. H. Knox, Elijah Harrison Griffin, and Waitman J. Moore. Rev. S. L. Lawrence conducted the Prayer of Commitment. The theme "The Church and Social Change" of the association was announced by the moderator. The Eleven O' Clock Session was conducted by Dr. W. H. Jones, Jr. He delivered an address based on the Associational theme. The 101 Annual Key note address of the Roanoke Missionary Baptist Association was delivered by Rev. T. M. Walker. His theme was "The Three Fold Office of Christ" based on Luke 24:19 and Hebrews 8: 1-3.

Roanoke Missionary Baptist Association to Hold 101ˢᵗ Annual Session

March 23-25, 1967

At Saint Steven's Missionary Baptist Church

Reverend J. E. Tillett
Moderator

Reverend J. R. R. McRay,
Ex-moderator

9

W. M. E. U. WOMAN

The women missionaries of the Roanoke Missionary Baptist Association followed the lead of their strong missionary predecessors Elder B. J. Lenox, Elder Charles S. Sessoms, and Elder Caesar Johnson. They were strong, fierce woman who could stop you with the look at of the corners of their eyes, women who walked with majesty; who could wring a chicken's neck and scale a fish, who picked cotton, planted a garden and sew without a pattern, women who visited the elderly, made soup for the sick and shortin' bread for the babies, women like Mrs. Margaret E. Burke, of Hobbsville, North Carolina, and Hattie F. Graves, women like Nancy Rooks the great-great grandmother of the author and her daughter, Alice Rooks Butler, the maternal first cousin of Rooks Turner, the founder and the builder of the Roanoke Institute, who delivered 2000 black and white babies in Gates County, North Carolina and in Nansemond County, Virginia; woman who searched for healing roots and brewed medicines, women who darned socks and chopped wood and laid bricks, women who could swim rivers and shoot the head off a snake, women who took passionate responsibilities for their children and for their neighbors children. These women taught their daughters to take care, to take charge and to take responsibility. The women of the Roanoke Missionary Baptist Association, and in particular, the Women Missionary and Education Union taught their daughters in the Roanoke Missionary Baptist Church to learn how to get their lessons, how to survive, how to be strong. These women of the Roanoke Missionary Baptist Association were the glue that held the Roanoke Association and its Collegiate Institute together. They were the back bone of the Association and the local church.

Who were some of these women? Women like Mrs. Eldora Miller on Boston Street in Elizabeth City, North Carolina who opened her home up for the regular bi-weekly Woman's Missionary and Education Union meeting. [347] Women like Mrs. Mary Small of Elizabeth City who was appointed Field Worker for the Elizabeth City section, and whose stated aim was to give their support to Roanoke Institute and to Prof. W. M. C. Allen, president of Roanoke School. [349] There were many women like Mrs. Elnora B. Boone of Stony Branch Missionary Baptist Church, Gates, North Carolina actively and consistently held membership in the Missionary Union for more than 90 years of her 106 years of living. Many of those women were unnamed. They were women like those who attended the Woman's Educational and Missionary Union when it convened on September 2, 1932 at New Bethel Baptist church near Hertford. Rev. U. G. Privott is pastor,[350] or those unnamed women who along with Dr. & Mrs. C. M. Cartwright who attended the Woman's Missionary and Education Union at Bethel Baptist Church on the first Sunday in September 1933. [351]

They were women from each of the geographical areas of the Associations: <u>Beaufort County</u>: Mrs. Helene Freeman, & Mrs. Mabel Everett; <u>Camden County</u>: Mrs. J. E. Etheridge, Mrs. Elnora McCoy; <u>Chowan County</u>: Arizonna Flemings, Geraldine Elliott; <u>Currituck County</u>: Julia Hunt, Annie Williams, Martha Jarvis; <u>Dare County</u>: Naomi Hester; <u>Gates County</u>: Jimmy Knight, Pauline Roberts: Martin County: Marion Davis; <u>Pasquotank County</u>: Lucille Moore, Velma Sawyer, Ruth Roach, Dorothy Stallings, Willie O. Grey, Mr. George Sylvester; <u>Perquimans County</u>; Julia Winslow, Lillian Jordan, Easter Creecy; <u>Tyrell County</u>: Virginia Hill, Eva Basnight, Rasponsia Swain, Viteria Bryant; <u>Virginia Beach</u>: Hazel Bell, Ophelia Mason; <u>Washington County</u>: Katie Phelps, Mae Cola Rodgers, Nettie Norman, Pearline Rodgers, Trumilla Brickhouse.

President: Stella Bryant
Vice-President: Elessie Roach De'Boines
2nd Vice-President: Mary P. Spriell
Secretary: Carrie C. Simmoms
Assistant Secretary: Elsie H. Lassiter
Treasurer: Lenoir Spence

The Women Missionary and Education Union numerous involvements recalled a vibrate and active past. The Women Missionary and Education Union notable past activities reveal a history strewn with charitable actions towards the Free People of Color and towards the former sons and daughter of the African Diaspora. The future of the Women Missionary and Education Union is a bright one! The following entries will illuminate the way for us as we seek to understand the Past history of the Women Missionary and Education Union.

At the Tuesday Morning May 21, 1912 Session of the Roanoke Missionary Baptist Association held with the Saint John Missionary Baptist Church Moderator G. D. Griffin stated in his Moderator's Address: "that to his mind, the Woman's Education and Missionary Union is at present the most promising auxiliary within the bounds of the Association. These women did not organize for fun, they mean business." He continued, "They are demonstrating the power of the organized women. Their sessions are inspiring and helpful to the extreme. They are improving the truth of the scripture that says a woman was made for the helpmate, for indeed, they are helping us in the prosecution of our great work. They raised in their last session $120.00 and yet only a few organizations have joined them, and what is worse, not a single pastor but Rev. Bryant at whose church they met, and myself visited them to give encouragement. The President of the Institute states that but for the timely aid to this union, he would not have been able to pay the teachers their first month's salary." Rev. Griffin concluded his report by stating: "I hope that you brethren will organize local unions in your churches and have them represent in the next session which convenes at Cornerstone Church, Elizabeth City, North Carolina, and go yourself also, and help these women who labor among us." This chapter highlights some of their various activities.

The 9ᵗʰ Annual Woman's Missionary and Education Union

The 9ᵗʰ Annual Session of the Roanoke Missionary Baptist Association Woman's Missionary and Education Union convened in Moyock North Carolina on September 2, 1917. The attendance was the best in its history, spiritual enthusiasm was high and money was there too. The Roanoke Institute which is the object of the Roanoke Woman's Missionary and Education Union from an educational viewpoint of the Roanoke Missionary Baptist Association in Northeastern part of North Carolina., was freed from a debt of long standing, on September 2, 1917 when the Woman's Educational Union of the section laid more than $800 in cash on the table at their annual meeting in Moyock, North Carolina. This was the 9ᵗʰ Annual Session and it proved to be the most successful in every way. Mrs. Margaret B. Burke the President had previously asked her followers to bring up $500, and what was their glade surprise when the last figures brought up the enormous sum. There was great rejoicing among the members of Roanoke Association and the Woman's Union in particular because of the amount collected thereby freeing their beloved school of debt that had been made in 1904 when their present building was erected.[352] The ladies conducted themselves in the highest manner possible becoming Christians. The people of Moyock entertained the delegation nicely and all went well during the time the Union was in session. The only regrettable affair was the lack of railroad accommodations to bring the very large delegation home Sunday night. Extra cars were ask for in time but it seemed that Norfolk Railroad was too busy and therefore the request went by unheeded and the delegates were compelled to pack their bags into the already crowed coaches like sardines in tight boxes. [353]

The 1918 Thanksgiving Day at Roanoke Institute.

The 1918 Thanksgiving Day Celebration at the Roanoke Institute was an overwhelming success with a great concourse of people gathered and witnessed the mortgage burning scene of the old Citizens bank note against the building, which was made in 1904, by the trustees of the Association. The occasion was made possible though money raised by the Woman's Union in Moyock September 1917. Sister M. E. Burke, the very able and affable president had asked the sisters to come up to the school and they came in large numbers. Meanwhile many brethren availed themselves of the opportunity to be present too. The day came, a Thanksgiving sermon of much spiritual power and enthusiasm and very appropriate for the occasion was preached by that lofty soul and princely character young Christian minister the late Rev. Butler M. Mullen.

A wonderful dinner prepared through the kindness of the sisters of the Baptist Churches of the city and several from Camden and Currituck counties followed the sermon. A Roll of the churches was read by Rev. J. A. Mebane and contributions received, the deed of trust was read, a match was struck and applied to the "scrap of paper" by Sister Burke, as a little boy and a little girl held the tray containing the burning instrument, Rev. S. M. Price burst forth rapturously into singing "Praise God From Whom All Blessing Flow." The large audience rose to their feet, the crowd hung low, in the sky, the lights were turned on, and the strong voices of the people rent the solemn air. Men and women wept for joy: clasp their hands and threw themselves upon each other necks and there under the brilliant lights the flame of the fire licked their red tongues uncomfortably about like some red dragon, that had been going up and down the impalpable confines of this Association spreading dismay and discontent in the breast of all for fourteen years, but now writing helpless conquered, destroyed in a heap of brittle ashes by the hands of a band of loyal loving God-fearing, determined, self-sacrificing women.[354]

The 14th Woman's Union at Plymouth in 1921

Rev. C. H. D. Griffin, pastor of Central Baptist Church, Berkley, Norfolk, Va., preached for the Woman's Missionary Union at Olive Branch Church Sunday, May 29, 1921 at 8 P. M. Rev. S. L. Lawrence preached for the Woman's Missionary Union at St. Stephen's Church Sunday at 11: A. M., and 8. P. M.[355] September 1, 1921 found the woman of Roanoke Baptist Association gathered in their fourteenth annual session in New Chapel Baptist Church, Plymouth. For three days spiritual enthusiasm was at a high pitch. But this is not all about the organization; they were well dressed, orderly, deeply consecrated and intelligent. They looked happy, they were happy. It made you happy to see them happy. They were conscience of the purpose of their meeting, which was two-fold, or rather a single purpose with a most beautiful corollary. They had met to collect $2,500 to finish paying for the ten acres of land belonging to Roanoke Institute; their zeal for their goal was ably reinforced by prayers, song, testimony and spiritual fervor. What could stand in the way of these determined women of Roanoke Association? For three years they have assumed a $6,000 proposition on ten acres of land that the Roanoke Association had 30 years to pay, but the Woman's Educational and Missionary Union has almost paid this money in three years. Under the capable leadership of the president, Mrs. Margaret E. Burke, they raised this week at Plymouth $ 1,322.12. This too, it will be remembered is a period of countrywide industrial and financial depression. Bravo to them!

The sermons by Reverends R. R. Cartwright, C. M. Cartwright, J. E. Tillett, W. H. Trotman, and Henry Price were of a high and helpful order. The papers and addresses dealing with different phrases of social and missionary and education work were good. Plymouth has good entertainment. Dr. R. A. Morrissey was on hand to extend good cheer to all. In her address the President recommended that the local Union send a delegate and some money to Roanoke Institute Thanksgiving Day, to make a selection of the site for the new girl's dormitory, which they have decided to help the Roanoke Association to build when the land debt is accomplished. The next session they hope to pay the remainder. Joppa Missionary Baptist Church in Gates County near Trottsville is the next place of meeting.

The Corner Stone Baptist Church, under the leadership of Mrs. Hattie F. Graves is again accorded the honor of having represented with the largest amount which was $1, 500. Special mention is made of Mrs. Esther Holmes, of New York, who, of her own initiative, has from time to time brought money, and this time she brought $235. She is a former North Carolina woman and a member of the First Baptist church of Hertford. Great is her zeal for Roanoke Institute. There was no change in officers, Mrs. M. E. Burke, president; Mrs. Hattie Graves, secretary; and Mrs. Virginia Bowe, treasurer; each county being represented by a vice-president. They are looking towards Elizabeth City Thanksgiving Day. [356]

WOMAN'S UNION AT PLYMOUTH

According to the September 10, 1921 edition of the Plymouth Journal and Guide, September 1, 1921 found the women of Roanoke Missionary Baptist Association gathered in their fourteenth annual session in New Chapel Baptist Church, Plymouth, North Carolina. For three days spiritual enthusiasm was at a high pitch. But this is not all about this organization; they were well dressed; orderly deeply consecrated and intelligent. They looked happy, they were happy. They were conscious of the purpose of their meeting, which was two-fold, or rather a single purpose with a most beautiful corollary. They had met to collect $2,500 to finish paying for the ten acres of land belonging to Roanoke Institute; their zeal for the goal was ably reinforced by prayers, song, testimony and spiritual fervor. What could stand in the way of these determined women in the Roanoke Association. For three years they have assumed a $6,000 proposition on ten acres of land that the Roanoke Association had 30 years to pay, but the Woman's Educational and Missionary Union has almost paid this money in three years. Under the able leadership of the president, Mrs. Margaret E. Burke, they raised this week at Plymouth $1,322.12. This too it will be remembered is a period of countrywide industrial and financial depression. Brave For Them! The sermons were excellent.

18th Annual Woman's Missionary & Education Union

The 18th Annual Woman's Missionary and Educational Union Auxiliary to the Roanoke Missionary Baptist Association of North Carolina convened at the Shiloh Missionary Baptist Church in Camden County, N. C. during September 1925. The able Dr. R. R. Cartwright, pastor, had provided that hospitality for the delegation for which he is noted. His members and the surrounding people vied with each other in their efforts to entertain the large audiences and visiting host. It will be recalled that this auxiliary paid for eight acres plot of land and present it to Roanoke Institute in May at the Association in Columbia, North Carolina. This cost $6, 280.00 which they paid in 7 years. Their aim now is to assist in paying for the erection of a building on Roanoke Institute campus. In the meeting at Camden $969.00 was raised.[357] Sermons were preached by Reverends Z. B. Wynn, C. L. Griffin, and Dr. R. R. Cartwright. Enthusiasm was at a high mark all the time. The people were orderly and showed signs of prosperity and intelligence. The work is divided into primary, junior and senior divisions. Mrs. E.B. Burke is president; Mrs. Hattie T. Graves, secretary; Mrs. Virginia Bowe, treasurer. Each county of the six affiliating has its own president or vice, who cooperates closely with the Unions. Mrs. Ester Holmes, New York, New York and Mrs. Mattie Chavis, Philadelphia, PA brought money. The next session goes to Mount Carmel Baptist Church, (Newland) near Elizabeth City.[358]

Woman Missionary & Education Union Annual Session

The Woman's Missionary and Education Union held its 26 annual session at Corinth Baptist Church, Jarvisburg, September 1-3, 1933. It was a success from both a financial, spiritual and attendance standpoint. The W. E. M. U. had a baby contest on September 28, 1934 for the benefit of the annual union. A brief program was given before awarding of the prizes. The first prize went to Frederick White, son of Mr. & Mrs. Edward White. Elbert A. Covington was winner of the second prize. He was the son of Mr. & Mrs. Murry Covington. Little Arthur Britton, son of Shock Britton, won the third prize. Mrs. B. E. McRay, president was the mistress of ceremonies. The 1934 session was conducted at Union Chapel Baptist Church Friday before the first Sunday in October, 1934. Mrs. B. L. Hinton returned from Jarvisburg where she attended the session of the Woman's Missionary Union, and she returned to her work as a member of the Roanoke school faculty. Mrs. M. E. Burke of the Union and Mrs. Sarah Reid, vice-president and the Rev. S. R. Hill all of Gates County passed thru Elizabeth City on Monday enroute from the recent session of the Woman's Missionary and Educational Unions. Fourteen ushers from Shiloh Chapel Baptist Church rendered service during the session.

37th W. M. E. U. Anniversary

The Woman's Missionary and Educational Union celebrated its 37th anniversary at the Cornerstone Missionary Baptist Church. Rev. J. R. R. McRay was the host pastor. A Roanoke Missionary Baptist Association Memorial Service was held in honor of the first president, Mrs. Hattie Graves, and other deceased members. Among those participating on the program were Patti Barcliff, Mrs. Pattie Blanchard and Mrs. Katie Bryant. Mrs. Willie Spellman and Prof. C. F. Graves, founder of the union gave an address. Music was furnished by the missionary choir with James E. Norman and Miss Vivian White, his assistant, at the organ.[359]

1941

Those Fist Baptist Hertford Missionary Baptist Church members attending the 1941 Annual Session of the Roanoke Missionary Baptist Association at Zion Tabernacle Missionary Baptist Church in Corapeake, North Carolina were: Isaac Barnes, Mrs. Miles Bembry, Ollie Bembury, Jennie Bonner, Johnnie Collins, Jerry Creecy, Katie Creecy, Lue Creecy, Aletha Dail, Irene Dail, Mr. & Mrs. W. N. Douglas, Alberta Eason, C. L. Eason, Mannie Everette, Fannie Hall, Rev. J. A. Harrell, Anna Holley, Minnie P. James, Della Jordan, Laura Lowder, Laura Lowe, Sarah Moore, Sylvadore Overton, Mr. & Mrs. Ike Riddick, Jane Simpson, Bertha Smith, Hazel Smith, Mrs. Essie Stewart, Fred Stewart, Amy Thompson, C. B. Thomas, Alice Weaver, Dan Weaver, Emma White, Hattie Williams, Alphonso Winslow, John Winslow, Mss Mary Winslow.

Since I Met Jesus

Since I met Jesus there's a burning, O such a burning within.
It holds me with an unseen power,
And turns me away from all sin.
It changes me from day to day
As I trod along this narrow way.

Since I met Jesus I keep toiling, yes, in the sunshine and rain.
But the service that I am giving
Will not be given in vain.
He fixed it so a long time ago
That to heaven I will surely go.

Since I met Jesus
Since He blest this old soul of mine
Makes me want to run on-Hallelujah to the end.

His yoke is easy,
His burdens are light.
If I walk where He leads me
I'll always be right.
So I'll cherish the race that I'm running with haste
And by His grace, I'll make it home someday.

10

PRESIDENTS OF THE W. M. E. U.

Mrs. S. H. Bryant

Mrs. Stella Lee Halsey Bryant was born on January 16, 1925 to Lincoln Lieutenant Halsey and the former Bertha Alena Lewis of Columbia, (the section known as Travis) North Carolina. Her paternal grandparents were Professor James Lawrence & Caledonia Lewis. Her maternal grandparents were Robin and Virginia Halsey. Both sets of grandparents were from the Columbia area. The Halsey and Bryant families were members of Chapel Hill Missionary Baptist Church. Mrs. Stella Bryant married Melton Wesley Bryant and to this union one daughter Bertha Delores was born.

Stella received her early education from the Travis Elementary School. She was honored as the first black and the youngest student to have graduated from the seventh grade at Travis School. She was an honor graduate with a B. S. degree from the Elizabeth City Teachers College; Elizabeth City, North Carolina; further studies were completed at the Temple University, Philadelphia, Pennsylvania. Mrs. Bryant's teaching career extended from the one and two rooms Negro school houses of Tyrell, & Hyde Counties. She taught 6 years in Creswell, 36 years in Columbia, and 6 years in Hyde County. Later, Mrs. Bryant became the principal of the Swam Quarter Elementary School.

Mrs. Bryant was active in the religious, civic and social activities including throughout North Carolina. Mrs. Bryant served as president of the Woman's Missionary and Education Union of the Roanoke Missionary Baptist Association for twenty-one years. She actively participated in the District 9 of the North Carolina Woman's Convention; Deaconess Department of the Lott

Carey Home and Foreign Missions; Board of Education, Executive and Finance Boards of the Roanoke Missionary Baptist Association, and the Spruill Singers. The other members of the Spruill Singers were: D. T. Spruill, manager and pianist; Madams Geneva Melton, Amphia Spruill, Clara Bowser, and Avilla Griswell.

Margaret E. Burke

Mrs. Margaret Ellen B. Burke was a native of Hobbsville, North Carolina and the president of the Woman's Missionary and Education Union. During the 9th annual session Mrs. Margaret B. Burke the President asked her followers to bring up $500, to free the beloved Roanoke Institute School of debt that had been made in 1904 when their present building was erected.[360] At the 1918 Thanksgiving Day Celebration at the Roanoke Institute there was an overwhelming success of people gathered and witnessed the mortgage burning scene of the old Citizens bank note against the building. The occasion was made possible though money received by the Woman's Union at Moyock September 1917. Sister M. E. Burke, the very able and affable president had asked the sisters to come up to the school and they came in large numbers. In 1921 there was no change in officers, Mrs. M. E. Burke, president; Mrs. Hattie Graves, secretary; and Mrs. Virginia Bowe, treasurer. [361]

Mrs. E. Cartwright

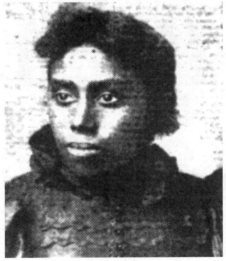

Mrs. Elizabeth Cartwright was a native of Merry Hill, North Carolina. She was born to Mr. & Mrs. Lawrence Bembry. She joined the Providence Missionary Baptist Church in Edenton, North Carolina and was a charter member of the Gale Street Missionary Baptist Church, Edenton. Mrs. Cartwright attended the Edenton North Carolina Public Schools, and the State Normal School, Plymouth, North Carolina. She married Reverend Charles M. Cartwright, pastor of the Olive Branch Missionary Baptist Church, Elizabeth City, North Carolina. To this union two daughters, Addie and Fannie L. Cartwright were born. She served as the pro-tempt president of the Roanoke Women Education and Missionary Union during 1903-1907. In 1921, she was elected Queen of the East, Grand United Order of Queen of the Orient. Mrs. Cartwright died June 7, 1951. Funeral services were held June 11, 1951 with the Rev. J. R. R. McCray delivering the eulogy. Others taking part in the service were the Rev. J. E. Trotman, Invocation; the Rev. A. W. Lamb, Prayer; Dr. M. S. Rudd, Scripture; Rev. T. S. Cooper, Mrs. Alive Vaughan, soloist; C. F. Graves, Mrs. Ida Bouge, and Rev. G. Z. Mizell, Benediction.[362]

Mrs. J. A. Walson-Ferebee

Mrs. Jean Althea Roach Walston Ferebee was born May 31, 1937. She is the daughter of the late Benjamin Roach, the granddaughter of Walter S. Roach and the great granddaughter of Rev. I. B. Roach all of Pasquotank County. She is a product of the Pasquotank County North Carolina Public Education System, and the mother of seven, one daughter and six sons. Presently, Mrs. Ferebee is a member of the Mount Carmel Missionary Baptist Church, Newland, North Carolina; vice-president of the Sunshine and Junior Missionary Board; the President of the Women Missionary and Education Union of the Roanoke Missionary Baptist Association; Executive Board member of the Roanoke Institute; member of the Lott Carey Convention, Inc., member of the Woman Baptist State Convention of North Carolina; and member of the Eastern Star Prince Hall Affiliated. Other church involvements include membership in the following church activities; missionary; senior choir and senior usher board member. Additionally, Mrs. Ferebee formerly served on the Publicity Department for the Baptist Informer News Paper and the served under the leadership of Dr. Julian McDonald. Mrs. Ferebee retired in 1999 from the Elizabeth City School System as a Teacher's Assistant.

Somebody Bigger Than You and I

Who made the mountains, who made the tree, who made the river flow to the sea, And who hung the moon in the starry sky? Somebody bigger than you and I. Who made the flowers bloom in the spring, Who writes the song for the robin to sing, And who sends the rain when the earth is dry? Somebody bigger than you and I.

Mamie R. Griffin

Mrs. Mamie Roach Griffin was born in Pasquotank County, North Carolina about 1899. She was a member of the Mount Carmel Missionary Baptist Church in the Newland District of Pasquotank County. She married Marvin W. Griffin, son of Reverend Elijah Harrison Griffin and the former Emily Whitehurst of Pasquotank County. To this union a son, Joseph D., and three daughters were born: Wendell G., Marie G. and Avis Griffin.[363] Mrs. Griffin graduated from the Roanoke Institute and the State Normal School, in Elizabeth City, North Carolina.[364]

The Woman's Missionary and Educational Union met at St. Paul's Baptist Church, Sunbury, North Carolina, Rev. E. H. Griffin, pastor, elected Mrs. Alice Trotman of Elizabeth City, President. Other officers elected were: Mrs. Mamie Griffin vice president; Mrs. Mary Griffin, Secretary Mrs. Katie Bryant assistant secretary, and Mrs. Caroline Boone, treasurer. The retiring officers were: Mrs. Sarah Reid, president, Mrs. K. P. Roberts, vice president, and Mrs. Blanch Hinton, secretary.[365] During the 44th (1952) session of the Women's Educational and Missionary Union at Union Chapel Baptist Church, Weeksville, N. C., Mrs. Mamie Griffin was serving under Mrs. Alice V. Trotman as the vice-president of the Women Education and Missionary Union.[366] In 1954 the Annual Session of the Woman's Educational and Missionary Union was held from October 2-3, at the New Sawyer's Creek Baptist Church, Belcross, N. C., Mrs. Mamie Griffin was the newly elected president who succeeded the late Mrs. Alice Trotman. Mrs. B. E. McRay served as her vice-president.[367] Mrs. Griffin delivered her annual address entitled, *"Living Victorious Through Christ."* In 1960 Mrs. Griffin's Missionary cabinet consisted of Mrs. B. E. McRay, vice-president; Mrs. Mary Christian, secretary; Mrs. Nellie Clarke, secretary; Mrs. Nezzie Clarke, assistant secretary, and Mrs. Eleanor Taylor, treasurer.[368] The officers of her cabinet remained the same during the 53rd (1961) annual session held at the Philadelphia Baptist Church, Camden County, North Carolina.[369] The theme of discussion at the 95th Annual Session of the Roanoke Missionary Baptist Association when it convened in Gates County at the New Middle Swamp Missionary Baptist Church on Wednesday morning the 23 day of May 1961 was the "New Frontiers in Social Justice." The theme discussion was led by the Rev. Asa Bell. This was followed by the Woman's Educational and Missionary Union Hour with Mrs. Mamie J. Griffin, president.[370] Shortly before the convening of the 96th Annual Session of the Women Missionary and Education Union of the Roanoke Missionary Baptist Association at the Roanoke Institute, Elizabeth City, North Carolina, Mrs. Mamie Roach Griffin was widowed. In May 1962 her husband, Marvin W. Griffin became the victim of an automobile accident.

During the week of June 20th 1954 Mrs. Mamie Griffin was visiting her children in Philadelphia and Brooklyn, N. Y.[371] Mrs. Mamie Griffin's influence on education can be seen in the lives of her daughter's Marie's children, Eddie Moore, Jr., and Rita Moore Jordan, who excelled in their professional lives. Eddie Moore, Jr., served as the president of one of the oldest Historical Black Colleges or Universities in Virginia, the Virginia State University in Petersburg, Virginia, and Rita, retired as an educator from the Philadelphia School System. Rita returned back to Pasquotank County, and back to worshipping with her parents at the family's home church, the Mount Carmel Missionary Baptist Church, Pasquotank County, North Carolina.

Blanche L. Hinton

Mrs. Blanche L. Armstrong Hinton was born on June 1, 1871 to Tony & Eliza Armstrong of Gates County, North Carolina. On May 8, 1897 she married Mr. Alfred Hinton (1876) son of Jack & Agnes Smith Hinton of Gates County. The Hinton family resided at Roanoke Avenue, Elizabeth City, North Carolina with their only daughter Blanche Hinton (Blanche's daughter, Blanche Hinton married Avon Howard, son of Grant Howard and Lula Howard of Hobbsville in 1907. They resided in Elizabeth City, North Carolina). Alfred was a common labor, but they lived well and prospered. Mrs. B. L. Hinton was the mother of John Darden, Suffolk, Virginia; grandmother of Ernell & Willard Howard & Mrs. Earl Spence of Elizabeth City, North Carolina; Alphonos & Ersell Howard of the East Coast.[372]

Mrs. Hinton was an active member of two churches within the Roanoke Missionary Baptist Association: the Lebanon Grove Baptist Church, Gatesville, and the Olive Branch Baptist Church, Elizabeth City, North Carolina. She was elected assistant secretary of the organization and at the time of the death of Mrs. Hattie F. Graves filled the position of secretary. Mrs. B. L. Hinton was a member of the Roanoke Institute Faculty and an active president and supporter of the Women's Missionary & Education Union of the Roanoke Missionary Baptist Association. She was one of the first 20 members in the organization of the Woman's Missionary and Educational Union. Mrs. B. L. Hinton was affiliated with the Middle Ground Union, the Church School Union. She was the second woman elected to the Trustee Board of Roanoke Institute, where she served until hindered by severe poor heath which compelled her to resign.

Mrs. Blanche Hinton and husband Alfred Hinton motored to Gates County on the First Sunday in November 1927 to attend the closing joint session of the Roanoke Missionary Baptist Union Meeting held over the Gatesville Creek at Lebanon Grove Baptist Church. They were accompanied by Mr. Mankey Lassiter and Mr. James Eggleston. Mrs. Blanche Hinton left Monday to resume her teaching at the Wickam School, near Shiloh, Camden County, N. C.[373] Mrs. Blanche L. Hinton and Mr. Alfred Hinton and Miss Minnie Hinton, motored to Hill Point, Suffolk, Virginia on August 1, 1931 to see Mr. Alfred's father, Mr. Jack Hinton and family. Mrs. Hinton motored to Gates County, North Carolina during the week of August 7, 1931 to visit her brother and other relatives.[374] She was accompanied by her daughter, Mrs. Blanchard Hinton Howard, and children, and Miss. Nellie Clarke.[375]

Alfred Hinton, the spouse of Mrs. Blanch Hinton died at his home, 696 Euclid Street, on May 21, 1932, after a brief illness.[376] Mrs. B. L. Hinton placed the following *In Memoriam* in the Negro News paper. It was picked up by the local *Norfolk Journal and Guide;* In memory of my dear husband, Alfred Hinton who died two years ago May 21. *"I miss you every moment, you have left me here alone, but someday I hope to meet you, There no more to mourn."* Blanche L. Hinton, Wife. Elizabeth City, N. C.[377] Mrs. Hinton motored to Gates County during August 1932 to visit her brother and other relatives. She returned the following week from Gates County where she went to attend the funeral of her brother, Joseph Hoskins. Mrs. Hinton returned to Elizabeth City from a visit to her brother at 1180 County Street, Portsmouth, Virginia. According to Mrs. B. L. Hinton Roanoke Institute is doing fine with its night and day sessions of school.

During her November 1933 visit to the Progressive Baptist Convention in Tarboro, North Carolina Mrs. B. L. Hinton required immediate attention from the emergency room. Among those attending that session from Elizabeth City were: Dr. C. M. Cartwright, Professor M. L. Collins, Ella Corbritt, Rev. C. L. Griffin, Robert Hadley, Rev. G. W. Lamb, Sirena Mackney, Rev. J. R. R. McRay, Rev. W. J. Moore, J. L. Perkins, and Mary Small.

Mrs. B. L. Hinton had as her guest on June 18, 1934 Mr. & Mrs. Elton Hall, little John Elton, and Mrs. Luray Sharp. Mrs. Hall was formerly Miss Johnetta Moore and was a close friend of Mrs. Hinton. Mrs. Patience Hall and daughter, Addie were callers at the home of Mrs. B. L. Hinton on Roanoke campus on Thursday, May 10, 1934. Mrs. Hinton was all smiles over the little token presented by Mrs. Hall.[378] Mrs. Hinton motored to Pleasant Branch on the Third Sunday in November 1934 to witness the closing of the Union Meeting. She spoke in the interest of the Woman's Educational and Missionary Union. She was accompanied home by the Rev. S. H. Jenkins and S. H. Perkins.[379] Mrs. Hinton was active in The Community Needle and Thimble Club; she rose to prominence in this club from the position of Advisory Committee member in 1942[380] to the position of president in 1948.[381] During February 1950 Mrs. Blanche Hinton spent a few days in Elizabeth City with Rev. & Mrs. B. C. Ellis.[382] During July 1950 Mrs. Blanch Hinton who spent some time out of the city, returned to her daughter's on South Martin Street. She attended the 1950 Baptist Training Unit and Sunday School Convention which convened at South Mills, N. C. during the week of July 23, 1950.[383]

Blanche L. Hinton survived her husband by twenty-two years and six months. She died October 2, 1954. She was survived by her adoptive son, Marshall; five grandsons, there granddaughters and other relatives.

I'm Willing To Run

Use Me Lord in Thy service,
Draw me nearer, draw me near, everyday, Lord-
Lord you know that I'm willing to run all the way.
If I falter while I'm trying,
Don't be angry Jesus, I truly believe, you'll let me stay, Lord:
And I'll be willing just to run all the way.

Mrs. E. H. Lassiter

Mrs. Elsie Horton Lassiter is a native and resident of Sunbury, North Carolina, and the wife of Reverend Algernon Lassiter. Rev. & Mrs. Lassiter and their only child Dorothy are lifetime members of the Saint Paul Missionary Baptist Church, Sunbury. Mrs. Lassiter is a venerable missionary with a proved record of service. She received her education from the Gates County, North Carolina Educational System. She attended and participated in numerous Continuing Educational Units through the North Carolina State General Baptist Convention; the National Baptist Convention, U. S. A. Inc; the Roanoke Missionary Baptist Association and the Lott Cary Foreign Missionary Convention.

Mrs. Lassiter's life demonstrates a special call of our Lord and Savior Jesus Christ to the work in Christendom through her community, her local church and the Roanoke Missionary Baptist Association. Her tenderhearted work within Christendom is immortalized in the hymn *Count on Me*.

> The Lord has need of workers, to till His field today,
> so kindly He has led me to walk in Wisdom's way;
> I pray for grace to help me with all my heart to say,
> O blessed Savior, count on me.
> Count on me, Count on me,
> for loving-hearted service glad and free;
> Yes, Count on me, Count on me,
> O Blessed Savior, Count on me.

Mrs. Lassiter's response to the Master's Call "for workers to till his field" has been answered in many spheres of the Baptist State Convention of North Carolina and its local affiliations, namely: Youth Church Mother in 1964 under the pastorate of Rev. Elijah Griffin; Missionary President and President of the Pastor's Aid; member of the S. B. Lewis Church Beautification club; and a member of the Saint Paul Senior Choir. Mrs. Lassiter was installed as president of the Roanoke

Missionary Baptist Woman's Missionary and Educational Auxiliary in 1989 under Moderator Rev. William T. Davis. She served in that position for three years. In this position Mrs. Lassiter initiated the Roanoke Missionary Baptist Fellowship Banquet for the Woman's Missionary and Education Auxiliary Baptist Association and friends. The T. S. Cooper Elementary School, Sunbury, hosted these fellowship banquets. The Late Mrs. Dorothy Stallings, City Council of Elizabeth City, North Carolina was the guest speaker for the second fellowship. Additional opportunities of service included her untiring service with Dr. Shirley Bullock on the Publicity Committee for the Baptist Informer Newspaper form 1993-1997, and service on the Executive Board during Dr. Maggie White, State President 1991-2001 and service with Dr. Julius McDonald from 2001-2005. Presently, Mrs. Lassiter is a member on the Roanoke Institute Trustee Board, Executive Board Member of the Roanoke Missionary Baptist Association; Historian and member of the Board of Christian Education Committee of Roanoke Missionary Baptist Association; Executive Board member of the Woman's Baptist Home and Foreign Missionary Convention of North Carolina.

Mrs. Mary Sharpe presented Mrs. Lassiter as the guest speaker for "*A Voice From The Women*" the at the One Hundred Thirty-Second Annual Session {1998} of the Roanoke Missionary Baptist Association held with the Saint Stephen's Missionary Baptist Church, Elizabeth City, North Carolina. Mrs. Lassiter stated that there is a constant war of misunderstanding going on, especially in African American families because families are failing to follow God's Blueprint.[384] Mrs. Lassiter, continued, "Every Christian has a responsibility to be committed to God's Work. Some people rather hold on to this sin sick world than to grasp on to Jesus Christ and Eternity." Mrs. Lassiter concluded her message by simply stating," Acknowledge God and he will direct your path."

Thomas A. Dorsey's song, "*I'll Tell It Where Ever I Go*", is a very befitting summary of Mrs. Elsie H. Lassiter's life's motto. *If I was dying with just one word to say, I'd speak it for Jesus and then breathe my life away.*

Mrs. B. McRay

Mrs. Beatrice Bright McRay was a native of South Mills, North Carolina, and the wife of Reverend J. R. R. McRay, pastor of the Cornerstone Missionary Baptist Church, Elizabeth City, North Carolina. Mrs. McRay was the President of the Roanoke Association Women's Educational Missionary Union from 1963 to 1966 and for more than 25 years the president of the Cornerstone unit of the Women Educational and Missionary Union. She was an organizer and officer of the Alliance of Ministers Wives and an active participator of the Cornerstone Missionary Baptist Church where she was a Sunday school teacher over 45 years. Mrs. McRay died January 20, 1966 and was eulogized by Reverend George L. Brown at the Cornerstone Missionary Baptist Church, Elizabeth City, North Carolina.

Cora A. P. Thomas

Missionary Cora A. Pair-Thomas was born in Knightdale, Wake County, North Carolina on September 8, 1875 to Rev. Harmon & Ailee Pair. The Pair family resided at Marks Creek. By 1900 Cora and three of her siblings: James D., Lula N., Mary V. Pair were teaching school in Raleigh, N, C, while William D., John H., Lee R., Harman J., Martha, Blondie S., Lillie U., and Bingerman Pair were working on the farm. Cora graduated from Shaw University (Raleigh, N. C.) in 1895 with a higher Education Diploma. Between 1904-1906, she took post-graduate courses in missionary training at the Theological School of Fisk University (Nashville, TN). Ms. Pair acted as the principal of the Oxford North Carolina Orphanage for Negro Children.[385] In November 1908 she married a Jamaican named William Thomas.[386]

Cora Pair was the first missionary sent to Brewerville, Liberia, Africa by the Foreign Mission Convention to establish the Lott Carey Baptist Mission. She selected for the theme of her missionary ministry the following poem: *Be strong, we are not here to play, to dream to drift; We have hard work to do and loads to lift Shun not the struggle, face it; Tis God's gift, be strong, be strong. Be strong, it matters not how deep entrenched the wrong, How hard the battle goes the day how long Comes the song, be strong, be strong.*

With the assistance of Rev. J. Oliver Hayes, Sr., a native of North Carolina and pastor of Zion Grove Baptist Church, Brewerville, Lott Carey Mission started as a day school for boys in the Zion Grove Baptist Church. Classes were held from the First through Eighth grades. Zion Grove and Salem Baptist Churches in Brewerville purchased the present site that Lott Carey Baptist Mission occupies. The first building erected on Campus was "The Chapel" in 1914. The upstairs area was used as the girls' dormitory while the downstairs area was used for classes and vesper services.

The Woman's Convention of North Carolina, in its annual session at Reidsville, 1907, voted the entire support to Miss Cora A. Pair, one of the young women of North Carolina who made known her call to the mission field of Africa. In 1908 she set sail for the Liberia to spend herself in the work of saving the lost Africans at any cost. In her absence; at the meeting of the Lott-Carey Convention which met in Washington City September 2, 1908, the first quarter's salary of Miss Pair, $267, was paid in by the Women's Convention. No object appealed more readily to the generosity of the North Carolina women than Foreign Missions.

The Fifty-first (1935) Session of the Women's Baptist Home and Foreign Missionary Convention of North Carolina was held at the First Baptist Church, High Point, N. C. It was one of the most successful in its history. The attendance was unusually large and every section of North Carolina was represented by the delegates and visitors. The president stated that the senior department of the convention has for a number of years wholly supported Mrs. Cora P. Thomas.[387] The Thursday evening session of the 1966th Annual Session of the North Carolina Baptist State Convention held in Wilson, North Carolina at the First Baptist Church, the Rev. B. F. Jordan, pastor, on November 1-3, 1933, was a great occasion. It was foreign missions night. The foreign mission sermon was preached by the Rev. J. A. Harrell, D. D., of Hertford, N. C. It was a masterly effort, and had a telling effect. Dr. J. H. Randolph, corresponding secretary, followed the sermon with a strong address on foreign missions. He, on concluding, presented Mrs. Cora Pair Thomas, of Brewersville, Liberia, who was preparing to return to Africa. She made a very interesting talk on the needs of her missionary station.[388]

In a letter to the *Norfolk Journal and Guide* Rev. C. C. Somerville set forth the views of a committee appointed by the general board of the Baptist state convention. In addition to Rev. Somerville other members of the committee included: Revs. A. C. Croom and L. W. Wertz, Miss Mary A. Burwell, and Dean J. L. Tilley of the Shaw University department of Theology. Rev. Somerville views, and that of the committee were in answer to a statement published in a August 7, 1937 issue of the Journal and Guide by the Rev. G. W. Watson, D. D., pastor of the Bank Street Church, and president of the Baptist Ministers Conference of Norfolk, Portsmouth and Vicinity, in which he gave his views on the type of man who should succeed the late Dr. C. S. Brown.

COMPLETE TEXT OF LETTER "North Carolina has been loyal to the Lott Carey Foreign Missionary Convention ever since its organization; much of this spirit of loyalty was due to the influence of our fallen chieftain, the late venerable Dr. C. S. Brown; and today North Carolina pays the salaries of four of the full time missionaries; Mrs. Cora Pair Thomas, Miss Minnie C. Lyons, Mrs. M. L. Walker, and Mr. Joseph Parker. From this fact it would appear that North Carolina is just about furnishing everything for the ongoing of the Lott Carey Convention, especially since there are only a small number of full time missionaries under the auspices of the convention. Let it be known to the whole world that North Carolina is determined to come to Norfolk in September with the idea of saving if possible the organization of the great Lott Carey. However, North Carolina is not especially interested in blindly following the program of gynocracy which has dominated the Lott Carey Convention in recent years. Neither is it satisfied with the policy of nepotism as now practiced.

SYSTEM OF MATRIARCHY The Lott Carey convention too long has been controlled by the system of matriarch. We are cognizant of the splendid work done by our "sisters" but what we want is a "he-man" to lead, and not a group of "henpeck" men awaiting the bidding of the matriarchs. After careful study North Carolina has unanimously gone on record as endorsing the candidacy of Dr. G. O. Bullock of Washington, D. C., for the presidency on one condition-that is, that other members of the Bullock family will retire from all executive positions in the Lott Carey Convention and Women's Auxiliary, in case he is elected. We believe that our candidate and his church have contributed a larger amount of finance to the Lott Carey throughout the years than any other individual church in this convention; his loyalty and zeal for foreign missions have been unexcelled; and his Christian character as a gentleman is unimpeachable; his vision of leadership is clear.[389]

William and Cora Thomas worked together at the Lott Carey Mission for thirty-three years with a few furloughs to the United States. During that time William Thomas served as superintendent of the mission and principal of the Baptist boarding high school as well as preacher and teacher at the Lott Carey Mission School in Brewerville. He died in Liberia on September 4, 1942 and was buried on the mission station. The couple had four sons, all born in Brewerville. After her husband's 1942 death she was designated the superintendent of the mission, a position she filled until 1946 when poor health forced her to leave. [390] Mrs. Cora Pair Thomas returned from Africa to represent African Missions during the 1949 annual session of the Roanoke Missionary Baptist Association.[391]

David Meserve Thomas, son of Mrs. Cora Pair Thomas of Raleigh, North Carolina and the late Dr. William Henry Thomas was appointed principal of a mission school in Liberia, operated by the National Baptist Foreign Mission Convention. He was ordained to the ministry at services held Sunday night, October 5, 1937 at First Baptist Church, Raleigh, N. C. Dr. O. S. Bullock, pastor, delivered the ordination sermon. The charge was made by the Rev. J. H. Jackson, and theprayer was offered by the Rev. S. F. Daly, both of the Shaw University School of Religion.[392]

Mrs. Thomas was in Elizabeth City spending time with Mrs. Florence B. Rayner, They were students in Missionary Training School, Nashville, Tennessee over 40 years ago.[393] Mrs. Cora Pair Thomas was visiting her sister, Mrs. Bonnie Slade of Wake County during October and November 1951. She left by air on Wednesday November 3, 1951 for Liberia, Africa where she lived for 37 years and to visit her two sons Harmon Cary and David who were born there.[394] She died of malaria while on a pilgrim back to Liberia in 1952.[395] She was buried on the Lott Carey Mission School campus next to her husband.

Sarah A. Reid

Sarah A. Eure Reid was a mulatto born in Gates County, North Carolina about 1871 to Jethro Eure and Victoria Eure. Her siblings were Margaret S., Francis L., Martha C., Emma V., Ella S., Roxanna Eure, and Lucious Banks. They were the maternal grandchildren of Martha Burke, of Gates County. On June 1, 1904 Sarah A. Eure married William M. Reid, a mulatto, born about 1877 to William E Reid and Odelia A. Reid of the Reynoldson District of Gates County. William's siblings were: Olive B., Octavia D., Earl C. F., Alonza L., Ulyses E., Robert A., Julia E., and Oscar Reid. Sarah & William Reid and their family resided in Gates County with their children: Alvah Reid, Sarah V., William E., Evelyn O., and Olive B. Reid. During 1910 the family resided in the Hunter's Mill section of Gates County.

Sarah A Reid was a member of the Roanoke Missionary Baptist Association and the president of the Women Missionary and Education Union of the same. She made a presentation of the Women Missionary & Education Union during the Auxiliary Hour at the Seventy-fourth (1940) Annual Session of the Roanoke Missionary Baptist Association held with Pool's Grove Missionary Baptist Church, Woodville, (Perquimans County) North Carolina during the week of May 21-23, 1940. Her presidency spanned twenty years. She was succeeded by Mrs. Mamie Roach Griffin. Her August 7, 1958 funeral was attended by Mrs. Rosa B. Gibbs, Hertford, North Carolina; Mrs. Ellen Manley, Mrs. Adeline Clark, and Alvah Reid of Winfall, North Carolina. Mrs. Reid funeral and burial were conducted at the Mount Sinai Missionary Baptist Church, Holland, Virginia.

He's My Light

He's my light, the man of Calvary
And He's got His arms around me.
I am glade to know that He love's ever true.
Power and might are His possessions.
He'll forgive, all my transgressions,
He died for me, that no other could do.

He's my sight, He's my light.
I do not worry If its day or night.
By His guiding light,
He makes my pathway bright, every step of the way.
He paid the price that I might have a right to the tree of life.
And dwell with him forever.
For He's my light.
He's my sight, He's my light.
I do not worry If its day or night.
By His guiding light.

C. C. Somerville

Reverend Clanton Clay Somerville was born March 16, 1859 in Warren County, North Carolina to Richard Somerville and the former Mary Trapp. His paternal grandfather was Fred Somerville. He attended the State Normal School at Salisbury, North Carolina. In 1886 he graduated from the Shaw University, Raleigh, North Carolina with a Bachelor of Arts degree. He earned the Doctor of Divinity degree from the Livingstone College, and the McKinley University conferred the L. L. B. degree on him in 1892. He and his wife, the former Addie Louise Brown, daughter of Henry and Flora Brown of Salisbury, North Carolina, and their children: Galileo L., Mary L., Julia B., Lillian B, Wendell C., Olympia and Annetta F., accompanied him in the fulfillment of those responsibilities. After the death of Addie, Dr. Somerville married the former Mary Howell also of Salisbury, North Carolina.

He was converted to Christianity in 1875 and joined the Warrenton First Baptist Church. At the 1887 Annual Session of the Rowan Missionary Baptist Association, Somerville was ordained to the full work of ministry. Eleven years later, in 1887, at the same session, he preached from the subject Impartiality of God's judgment. His first pastorate was the Emmaus Missionary Baptist Church, Statesville, North Carolina. After a four year ministry with this congregation, Rev. Somerville went to the Reedsville First Baptist, Reidsville, North Carolina. Dr. Somerville was the Moderator of the Rowan Missionary Baptist Association. He was chosen as the District Missionary of the North Carolina Baptist State Convention and assigned to the work in the northeastern part of the state which included the Roanoke Missionary Baptist Association.

On January 20, 1897, Dr. Somerville and Rev. J. A. Whitehead of Raleigh, North Carolina conducted the second session of the New Era Training Institute at the Cornerstone Missionary Baptist Church.[397] On Tuesday, July 22, 1899, Dr. Somerville and Rev. J. A. Whitted conducted another New Era Institute for ministers of the Roanoke Missionary Baptist Association at the Roanoke Institute; He was accomplished by Professor A.W. Pegues, Ph. D. *The Carolinian News Paper* reported that a number of ministers from out of town were in attendance and all felt that they had benefited by the very excellent instruction given them.[398] In 1899, he was called to the First Baptist Church Charlotte, North Carolina where he remained until 1905 when he accepted the pastorate of the Ebenezer Baptist Church, Portsmouth, Virginia. He preached a special sermon on the subject of *Law and Order*, in the preservation of which, he declared, rest the Negro's best hope. Somerville declared that every good citizen must observe the law, and the colored man must respect those charged with the execution of the law. He remained at Ebenezer for 17 years, resigning the charge in 1922. Following his resignation, he founded the Mount Olivet Baptist Church. During November 1923, after an unanimously vote he accepted a call to the pastorate of Union Baptist Church, Main Street, Cambridge, Massachusetts.[396] In November 1923 Rev. Somerville attended the North Carolina Baptist State Convention and the Shaw Day Campaign Meeting where he was a featured speaker. He remained with Union Baptist Church three years. Returning to Portsmouth, he was re-elected to the pastorate of Mount Olivet and served as its pastor until June 1944, when ill health and the infirmities of old age forced his retirement from active pastorate. While at Cambridge, the scholarly minister studied at Harvard University.

Dr. Somerville was an active member of the Roanoke Missionary Baptist Association and his name regularly appeared within its minutes. He was very frequently appointed to various organizations and committees. He was appointed to the Committee on the Moderators Address in 1906. He was present at the Tuesday, Afternoon May 19, 1914 Annual Session and presented his paper *the Vigil* to the assembly. He was present during the Tuesday Morning May 19, 1915 annual session and recognized. On Thursday May 20, 1915 Professor C. F. Graves thanked the association that they had taken note of and it is that North Carolina the inimitable Virgil or more correctly speaking C. C. Somerville, who has told the world with his paper of the work of Roanoke Missionary Baptist Association and the Roanoke Institute. Dr. Somerville was thanked for his kind words of sympathy and good will about the Roanoke Institute, *the Search Light*, the Baptist Union-Review, and many other items of interest expressed in *the Journal and Guide* for the notice taken of the work in this particular section of North Carolina.[399] During the Fifty-Fourth Annual Session (1920) Dr. Somerville, editor of *the Vigil*, was present and very pleasantly entertained the body while he talked of his paper.[400] Two years later, in 1922 Dr. Somerville was among the visiting brethren attending the Fifty Sixth Annual Session with Corinth Baptist Church, Jarvisburg, North Carolina; he was invited to the front and seated.[401] During the Wednesday Evening Session the devotions were conducted by Revs. C. C. Somerville, D. D., C. M. Cartwright, D. D., and H. H. Norman, D. D. Prayer was offered by Dr. Somerville.

For 38 years, Dr. Somerville opened a printing business which provided employment for most of his eight children. His daughter, Mrs. Lillian S. Jones managed and operated the day to day business affairs. For several years, Dr. Somerville published a four page weekly news paper, the "*Virgil*", which was circulated through a number of states. Dr. Somerville won fame as a pulpiteer and lecturer, having traveled extensively in both capacities. He was a familiar figure in the General Baptist Convention of North Carolina and the Baptist General Convention of Virginia and their associations, having been connected with them for more than a half century. It was at these conventions and associations that he distributed various booklets of his own compositions. Many of these were based on his experiences while traveling over the country. He is well remembered by his illustrated lecture, "A Rooster and Two Dead Heads."[402]

Dr. Somerville departed this life Thursday morning, March 2, 1944 at his residence, 812 Columbia Avenue, Portsmouth, Virginia. Five days later, on Tuesday afternoon, March 7 1944, an impressive funeral was conducted at Zion Baptist Church, Portsmouth, Virginia for Dr. Clanton Clay Somerville Virginia by the Baptist Minister's Conference of Norfolk, Portsmouth and Vicinity of which Revered Somerville was a veteran member. Interment was at Lincoln Memorial Cemetery. Scores and scores of telegrams and messages of sympathy attested to his esteem in which the aged and highly respected manner was held.[403]

Alice Trotman

Mrs. Alice Trotman was born February 10, 1907 in Plymouth, North Carolina to Ernest & Melizza Johnson. She and her siblings: Alfred, Theodore, Samuel, Leemon, and Rebecca Johnson joined Zion Hill Baptist Church during her youth, and on moving to Elizabeth City, united with Olive Branch Baptist Church. She married Reverend W. H. Trotman in 1924. They were the proud parents of four children, John Erwin and Mable Trotman, Hurbert Randolph and Hoover Trotman preceded her in death. She was the step mother of Elmer Trotman, Stephen Trotman, William, George Trotman and Mrs. Josephine Trotman West. She was called to Plymouth, N. C. during the week of April 10, 1938 because of the death of her mother.404 On March 14, 1939 Mrs. Alice Trotman was a banquet hostess to the Missionary Society of Olive Branch Baptist Church. Mrs. Mary J. Small, president presided. Dr. C. M. Cartwright, pastor, made impressive remarks. Mrs. Trotman presided at the piano.

Mrs. Alice Trotman was an outstanding church worker at Olive Branch. She was the vice-president of the Missionary Institute of the Roanoke Missionary Baptist Association; president of the local Alumni Association of the Roanoke Institute; president of the Community Missionary Club; member of the Ministerial Alliance of Elizabeth City; a worker of five districts of the State Baptist Convention of North Carolina. She was a member of the Home and Foreign Executive Committee of the State Women's Missionary and Educational Convention of the State of North Carolina. Additionally, she was an instructor in the Missions and Educational Department of the Sunday school and the B. T. U. Convention of the Roanoke Missionary Baptist Association. Additionally, she was an instructor of the Missions and Education Department of the Sunday School and the B. T. U. Convention of the Roanoke Missionary Baptist Association.

Mrs. Alice Trotman, Misses Mable Trotman, and Majorie Bryant spent the 2nd weekend of April 1939 visiting Ernest Johnson and Miss Rebecca Johnson, father and sister of Mrs. Trotman. Rev. & Mrs. W. H. Trotman motored to Tarboro, N. C during October 25-30th 1940 to attend the District Convention of Eastern North Carolina which convened at St. Stephen Baptist Church. They were accompanied by Miss Mildred Carter. Two of the high lights of the 44th session of the Woman's Educational and Missionary Union held at Union Chapel Baptist Church, Weeksville, N. C., on Oct. 4 and 5, 1952 were: First, the annual address given by President Mrs. Alice V. Trotman. Her theme was "Christian Called to be Missionaries." THE MAIN POINTS she stressed were: "We must be filled with the Holy Ghost. We must pray for guidance. We must have the spirit of self-giving. We must have a desire to sacrifice. Second, Mrs. Trotman's son, Rev. John Ervin Trotman preached the Memorial Sermon. He was accompanied by his junior choir, junior ushers and junior trustees. A total of $ 1,225.53 was raised, including $27 for the sick.[405] At the 46 Annual Session of the Women's Education and Missionary Union held from New Sawyer's Creek Baptist Church, Belcross, N. C., October 2, and 3, 1954. Mrs. Mamie Griffin succeeded the late Mrs. Alice Trotman.

Mrs. Alice Trotman died March 8, 1954 in Elizabeth City, North Carolina after having been stricken on March 5 with a cerebral hemorrhage. A full page of the Elizabeth City edition of the Journal and Guide printed her funeral service on Sunday afternoon, March 14, 1954 over three thousand persons overflowed the auditorium annex and lawn of the Olive Branch Missionary Baptist Association to witness her final rites. There were more than 350 cars in the funeral procession. It was the largest ever held in Elizabeth City. Numerous floral arrangements expressed the high esteem in which she was held. The eulogy was delivered by Rev. Joseph Edward Tillett, Moderator of the Roanoke Missionary Baptist Association, based upon Acts 13:36. The senior choir sang, with Mrs. Ella Bryant, organist, and sols were rendered by Mrs. Hattie Mill and Mrs. Pauline Wynn. Rev. S. W. Hill gave the invocation, and the Scripture Lesson was read by Rev. J. A. Barrington-Jackson. The tributes on behalf of the Roanke Missionary Baptist Association was paid by Rev. J. R. R. McRay. Mrs. Mary Griffin represented the Woman's Missionary Education Union: the Rev. M. L. Williams paid tributes on behalf of Olive Branch Baptist Church; the Rev. J. F. Banks offered prayer, and Mrs. Laura McMurren read the obituary and acknowledged condolences.

Hattie N. Ward

Mrs. Hattie Nixon Ward was a native of Washington County, North Carolina as were her parents, Granville and Mary Nixon. She was a member of the Mount Lane Baptist Church, Washington County during her youth. On moving to Elizabeth City, North Carolina she joined the St. Stephen Missionary Baptist Church in 1910 under the leadership of Rev. Mr. Johnsons, and became the bride of Mr. Weldon W. Ward. Mrs. Ward's religious interest and involvements include the following: Member of the Roanoke Missionary Baptist Association; treasurer of the Woman's

Missionary Education Union; member of the Helping Hand Club; and other organizations far too numerous to list. Mrs. Ward left Elizabeth City on Saturday, December 2, 1922 for her Christmas vacation which included visiting relatives in Roper, Plymouth and Washington, and New Burn, North Carolina.[406]

Mrs. Pattie Wynn

Mrs. Pattie Hargett Wynn, wife of Reverend Z. B. Wynn and daughter of Mr. Morgan Hargett of Bertie County, North Carolina was one of the best known laundry ladies in Elizabeth City, North Carolina. Mrs. Wynn was a member of Saint Steven's Missionary Baptist Church, and the President of the Woman Missionary Education Union. Mrs. P. Wynn quietly predeceased her husband in death on Tuesday, September 12, 1922 at their Parsonage home.[407] Funeral services were held at Saint Stephen's Church on Friday, September 15, 1922 at 3 o' clock. Rev. R. C. Lamb pastor of the church officiated and was aided by Rev. C. M. Cartwright of Olive Branch Missionary Baptist Church and Rev. H. H. Norman of Saint John Missionary Baptist Church, Edenton, North Carolina. Resolutions were read by the secretary of the Court of Calanthe of which she was a member and the several auxiliaries of the church.[408]

What Is Life

Life Is A Challenge	Meet It
Life Is A Gift	Accept It
Life is an Adventure	Date It
Life is Sorrow	Overcome It
Life is a Duty	Perform It
Life is a Game	Play It
Life is a Mystery	Unfold It
Life is a Song	Sing It
Life is an Opportunity	Take It
Life is a Journey	Complete It
Life is a Struggle	Fight It.
Life is a Goal	Achieve It

"Life Is A Story In Volume Three,

The Past

The Preset and

The To-Be"

11

Deacon Alexander & Mrs. Deborah Ellis Founders
of the Ellis Temple Missionary Baptist Church Winfall, North Carolina

Deacon Ellis was born May 1844 to Nancy Ellis in Gates County, North Carolina. He married Cinthy M. Hobbs on March 26, 1861. The marriage was performed by John C. Trotman, witnessed by Henry L. Eure, with Bondsman Fletcher H. Russ. He next married the former Deborah Reddick the daughter of John & Deborah Riddick of Powellsville, Hertford County, N. C. Both sets of parents were North Carolinians. In 1870 the Alexander & Deborah Ellis were living in Gatesville, N. C., and earning their living as a farmer. Their house hold consisted of Briant (6), Median (3) and John (1). Their 1880 house hold consisted of Bryant (15), Mediann (13), John A. (11) Renia Ann (9), Emily (7), Margaret A. (5) James (3) Issac G. (2) Ludia (1) Their 1900 household consisted of Isaac T.(1877), Lydia (1880), Indiana (1882), Benjamin C. (1885) Harriett (1893), Meda Rumba (Sept 1870) and Alexander Rumba-grandson (1897). There were 10 children born to this union. Mr. Ellis enlisted on June 22, 1861 in Company C., North Carolina 2nd Calvary Regiment.

When Alexander Ellis moved from Gates County, North Carolina to Winfall, North Carolina in 1895 there was no Missionary Baptist Church in the local area. So he built Ellis Temple Missionary Baptist Church. Deborah Ellis was living with her daughter, Hattie Lightfoot and son-in-law, Henry Lightfoot, in 1920. Reverend W. H. Ruffin of Harney Street, Elizabeth City, North Carolina was called to the pastorate of the Ellis Temple Missionary Baptist Church during August 1925. Rev. Ruffin was married to the former Ida Lamb, daughter of Henry Lamb of Philadelphia, Pennsylvania.

Benjamin C. Ellis, a former resident of Winfall, and of New York City, and Greensboro, N. C., preached his first sermon at the Ellis Temple Baptist Church on September 6. 1936. J. Martin offered prayer. His sermon was on, *The Coming of the Holy Spirit in Power.* Mr. Ellis's father Alexander Ellis founded the church and Mr. Ellis himself was a deacon of the church. Rev. B. C. Ellis and family left for New York City where they planned to live indefinitely. Rev. Berk R. Newby and family occupied their home until their return.

12

CHURCH HISTORIES

Mineral Springs Baptist Church

The Mineral Springs Baptist Church is located in Nansemond County, Virginia in the very picturesque town of Whaleyville was organized in 1869 with Mrs. Mary E. White of Whaleyville as one of the founders.[409] This church was a member of the Roanoke Missionary Baptist Association in 1885 with the pastor Reverend E. E. Randolph serving as the delegate to the Roanoke Missionary Baptist Association.[410] The church reported that the pastor's salary was $64.00 for the two Sabbath preaching. The clerk was L. J. White. The membership totaled 100 members, 36 male and 64 female. The church reported the following for the year of 1884-1885: it baptized 8, received 1 by letter, dismissed 12 by letter, restored 5, excommunicated 5, and lost 3 by death.[411]

The Reverend E. E. Randolph of Gates County, North Carolina; Reverend A. A. Graham, Reverend J. Raymond Henderson, Reverend W. Preston Jones, and Reverend George Speight pastured this church. The names of many of the early pastors and founders were unattainable. Deacon James H. Langston served as head deacon from 1869 to 1923. A biographical sketch of him follows. In 1925, Mr. James Edward Sweat was ordained as deacon and served in that capacity for 19 years of which 17 of those years he also served as the Sunday school superintendent.[412] Consequently, only a glimmer of the early history of this church could be reconstructed.

On Sunday morning, January 8, 1922 the following Sunday school officers were elected: Mr. Junius Langston, Superintendent; (Mr. Langston served in this capacity several years and gave his best service and much time to the work.); Miss Annie Wiggins, secretary; Miss. Linnie Lee, organist. The teachers for the year: Mr. Johnnie Haywood, Mr. Jessie Wiggins, Mrs. Alma Drake, Miss Elsie Brown, Mrs. L. A. Watson, Mrs. Smith and Mrs. Haywood.[413]

The Mineral Springs Church was taxed to its seating capacity on Friday evening, May 4, 1922 with patrons and friends of the Whaleyville Graded school, of which Mrs. Helen B. Hunter was principal, to witness its closing exercise. The evening program consisted of a cantata, "The Greenwood Fairies," by primary grades of which Miss. Nannie Harrison is teacher. "Drills" and "Pantomime" by the intermediate grades, Misses Pearl Cooper and Flossie Walden teachers. Short plays, "The Stolen Commencement Dress," by the seventh B. Grade," The Troubles of a Bachelor," by the fourth grade; "The Trials of an Editor," by members of the fifth grade, "A Cure for Neuralgia" by the sixth grade B. grade, Choruses by the school.[414] The program was well chosen and rendered to the credit of the pupils and teachers of the school. There were people in attendance from the North Carolina towns of Winton, Ahoskie, Drumhill, Harrellsville, and from the Virginia areas of Holland, Suffolk and Portsmouth. Mrs. Mary E. White, (one of the founders of the Mineral Springs Baptist Church) died at her Whaleyville home on May 19, 1926. The funeral Services were held the following Thursday afternoon at 2:00 P. M. at Mineral Springs Baptist Church of which she had been a member since its organization. The services were conducted by the Reverend T. J. Johnson, of Suffolk. His sermon was a touching tribute of the life and character of the deceased. After the sermon a solo was sung. "Christ Is All." Left to mourn her calling to that great beyond were eight children: Mrs. J. R. Allen, Whaleyville: Mrs. Ida Rainey, Norfolk; Mrs. Ambrose White, Richmond; Mrs. Virginia Rodgers, Portsmouth; Mr. Bartimons White, Nurney; Mr. Norman White, Mrs. J. C. Crocker, Suffolk; and Mrs. J. B. Simmons, Ivor. Other family members included 36 grandchildren and eight great grandchildren. The floral tributes were beautiful and numerous. Interment at the family cemetery.

The Mineral Springs Baptist church celebrated its Sixty-first Anniversary and the eight of its pastor, Reverend W. Preston Jones beginning on Sunday Night, November 2, 1933. At 8:00 P.M. on November 13, 1933, a Pageant. "Taking Pictures from Our Church Album was presented. The Reverend Platt and his congregation from Suffolk, Virginia provided music.[415] Reverend W. P. Jones and the Mineral Springs Church family observed its 71st church anniversary on November 11-13, 1942. On Wednesday night the Missionary Circle and Pastor's Aid had charge. The T. A. Club and Sunday school conducted Thursday's program, and the usher board and choir Friday night's. Regular services were held November 15, and at 3:15 p.m. the Union Baptist Church and choir rendered services.[416]

Reverend W. P. Jones began his twenty-second pastoral year at the Mineral Springs Church on April 1943. During the Eleven O' Clock Worship Service, he was surprised when the Reverend J. H. Smith, his senior choir, deacon board, and the members of Mount Olive Baptist Church of Virginia Beach, marched down the aisles. Reverend J. H. Smith, pastor of First Baptist Church, Lynnhaven, Willow Grove, Norfolk, Lebanon Grove, Gatesville, N. C., delivered the message. He was accompanied by Mrs. S. E. Smith and Mrs. R. W. Forbes of Piney Grove Baptist Church of Creeds, VA. Others on the program were Miss C. L. Pratt, Mrs. White of Elizabeth City, N.C., and J. E. Sweatt and James Faulks. This occasion was made even more special with the purchase of a Hammond organ. Reverend Jones also currently pastured the Mount Olive Baptist Church, Virginia beach, and Little Piney Grove Baptist Church, Creeds; VA This special program was organized by his wife, Mrs. Jessie Welch Jones.[417]

James H. Langston

Deacon James H. Langston was born in Whaleyville, Nansemond County, Virginia about the year of 1835. He married the former Ms. Primmie Faulk and to this union was born nine children: Maggie, Arena, Alma, George T., Alexander, Charles A., Primmie, Pearlie C., and James C. Langston. He became a deacon at the Mineral Springs Baptist Church in 1869.

The Langston family held a lavished party at their beautifully country home in Somerton, Virginia, on August 16, 1921 that included a reunion of old friends and their friends from North Carolina, Virginia, and Alabama. The ages of the families united ranged from three to eighty-eight. In additional to the Langston Children the following were present: Dr. & Mrs. W. E. Reid, their children, Cornelia, Beulah. And Edna: Mrs. Lottie Reid, her daughter Mrs. T. H. Reid and her two grandchildren Thomas Jr., and Alice Reid, all of Portsmouth: Mr. Warren Green, Mrs. Omedia Knight, Mr. & Mrs. Walter Green and children, Florence, Leon, Edna and Hunter, Mrs. Lula Copeland all from Gates, N. C.: Mrs. Mary Reid Smith of Winton, N. C., Mrs. Nora Reid and daughter Alice and son, Howard, from Holland,: Mss. Hortense Burke and Mrs. Faustine of Portsmouth; Mr. Larry Langston and Mrs. B. H. Howell, Somerton: Mrs. Charles W. Green, son Charles, niece, Lottie Young, Mrs. E. C. Cooper and Mr. J. W. Barrington, of Tuskegee, Alabama; Mr. James Green of Norfolk: Mrs. T. Langston and daughter, Thelma of Whaleyville:

Mrs. Frank Minter, formerly Texie Greene, of Cleveland, Ohio: Miss Euna Copeland, and Master Doyle Skeeter and Joanna Denton of New York City. Other guests were Mrs. John Corprew, Mr. Edinburgh Corprew and Miss Virginia Spivey of Portsmouth, Virginia. Deacon Langston remained in this position until he was called from labor to reward on September 21, 1921.

Mount Carmel Missionary Baptist Church

The Mount Carmel Missionary Baptist Church is shrouded in the pre-history of the Harvey Chapel Missionary Baptist Church. This church came into existence in the year of our Lord 1863, as a direct result of Reverend Miles Harvey and Reverend Charles Capps. These men decided to construct a house of worship for the residents of the Newland section of Pasquotank County, North Carolina. Reverend Miles Harvey and Reverend Charles Capps provided religious instruction to this band of people until September 30, 1864. On the first Sunday in October 1864, the members of Harvey's Chapel Missionary Baptist Church elected the former abolitionist Elder Charles Hodges as their first pastor. Immediately after Elder Hodges acceptance of the pastorate of the Harvey's Chapel, he announced the "plans to build God a House of Worship." He exclaimed, "The Bush Shelter has served its purpose and now is the time to focus our attention on Self-Help and Independence as we look into the face of God and erect Him a House of His own."

In 1867 the decision of the Founding Fathers of the Roanoke Missionary Baptist Association was that the Harvey Chapel Baptist Church should host the 2nd Annual Roanoke Missionary Baptist Association. The Elder Lemuel Washington Boon was the moderator, John T. Reynolds, Clerk and Elder Joshua A. Fleming, the Assistant Clerk for that setting. The available records do not indicate who preached the annual sermon.[418] The next year, in 1868, The Roanoke Missionary Baptist Church was compelled to revolt the preaching license of Miles Harvey, who was suspended "until he has retrieved his former character and reputation in the church."[419] After the expulsion of Rev. Miles Harvey from the Roanoke Missionary Baptist Association, the Harvey Chapel Church changed its name to the Mount Carmel Missionary Baptist Church.

Mount Carmel's service to the Roanoke Missionary Baptist Association has not waned since 1867. During the Forty-Ninth Annual Session of the Roanoke Missionary Baptist Association held with St. Stephen's Baptist Church in 1914, Mount Carmel reported with $10.01.[420] Rev. A. D. Moore financial report to the Forty-Ninth Annual Session held with the First Baptist Church, Hertford, N. C., May 18-20, 1925 included $11.55 towards Roanoke Institute, and a prior report of $27.55 they had sent in to the association before May 1915.[421] The clerk of Mount Carmel for this annual session was W. W. Archie, and the delegate was T. W. Stewart.[422] At the Fiftieth Annual Session held with Providence Baptist Church, Edenton, May 23-25, 1916 Mount Carmel reported to the Association that that they had a membership of 500, 236 males, and 265 females. They had baptized 49 members, returned 9 former members, excommunicated 3, and lost 5 by death. The value of the building was $4500. They had raised $527 from 1915-1916. Rev. Moore's salary was $2. 50 per Sunday.[423] Mount Carmel sent in $18.00 to the Association in 1918. They brought in $8.70 to the session and made another apportion of $40.00 to be used at the discretion of the Roanoke Missionary Baptist Association. In 1919 Mount Carmel reported to the Association that they had gained 14 by baptism; restored 3 to membership; gained 1 by letter; lost 5 by death; total membership was 451, 137 members attended Sunday School.[424] In 1923 Mount Carmel met its financial responsibility obligation to the Roanoke Missionary Baptist Association. They mailed the Association $37.00 prior to the setting and brought in $18. 20. At that session Mount Carmel reported having baptized 36 members, restored 4, lost 3 by death, and maintained a membership of 366. The property was valued at $10,000.[425] In 1924 John W. Wood of Hertford, North Carolina was the clerk of Mount Carmel and L. H. Hall and W. N. Douglas was the delegates to the Fifty-Eight Annual Session held with the New Bethel Baptist Church Perquimans County, North Carolina, Rev. W. F. Brinkley, pastor May 20-22, 1924. Three years later, Mrs. P. E. Williams of Elizabeth City was the clerk of Mount Carmel, and C. L. J. Griffin was the delegate the Roanoke Missionary Baptist Association.

Mrs. Della Reid and Misses Hattie Reid and Nellie Bass attended revival services at Mount Carmel during September 1921. Messrs. Isaiah Reid, George Reid, Henry Hines, W. F. Riddick, Charlie Mouring, James Simpson, Isaac Brickhouse, Rev. W. H. Freeman, and D. W. White motored to Mount Carmel to attend the closing of the revival. The revival was one of the best in the history of the church. Forty-one were baptized. Miss Essie Mackey attended the Annual Session of the Woman's Educational Union which met at Mt. Carmel during September 1926. The weekend of May 27, 1927 brought many pleasant memories to the Mount Carmel Church family and community. The Golden Crown Quartet consisting of Mr. L. James, M. Reid, and C. Cross of New York and the Jubilee Singers also of New York rendered an enjoyable program at Mount Carmel on May 27, 1934. Mr. & Mrs. J. W. Boone of Rich Square were in attendance for this service. They were the Sunday dinner guest of Mrs. Boone's parents, Mr. & Mrs. W. R. Griffin. Dr. G. D. Griffin and family of Camden, N. J., were visiting the home of Mr. & Mrs. Miles W. D. Griffin. The Rev. W. D. Griffin and the Rev. J. R. R. McRay were highly entertained in the home of Mr. & Mrs. J. J. Griffin. Mr. Melton Williams and Mr. Charlie Brite motored to Norfolk, Virginia on Monday, May 28 on business. Professor & Mrs. W. S. Creecy of Rich Square was also the guest of Mr. & Mrs. J. J. Griffin while attending the Roanoke Missionary Baptist Association.

Dedicational services were well attended at Mount Carmel on the first Sunday afternoon in April 1963 with Rev. E. H. Griffin, choir and congregation of the Saint Paul Missionary Baptist Church, Sunbury, North Carolina. Welcome was extended by Mrs. Rosetta Williams, response by Deacon Jones of St. Paul. Mrs. Ruth Roach read a paper and Miss. Vendetta Owens sang a solo, accompanied by her brother, Franck Roach Jr. Mr. Joseph R. Williams, deacon was the worship leader. Rev. E. H. Griffin's subject was "Giving unto the Lord." Dinner was later served in the dining hall. [426]

Several of the former presidents of the Women's Educational and Missionary Unions were members of the Mount Carmel Church Family. Thus, Mount Carmel hosted several special functions on behalf of the presidents and that auxiliary. Thanksgiving 1921 was memorialized at Mt. Carmel Baptist church in a very commendable way. The Woman's Missionary Union of the church under the leadership of Mrs. C. J. Woodhouse made a special effort to raise and provide a special charity fund for the needy and distressed, and all the unfortunate ones in the Newland community were provided with a Thanksgiving dinner and such other gifts as their fund would allow. Many of the Newland and South Mills residents were delighted that they had something to rejoice about.[427] An extra Session of the Women's Educational and Missionary Union was held at Mount Carmel Baptist Church on April 3, 1951. Rev. J. E. Tillett delivered the sermon. A special collection was made for the rebuilding of the Roanoke Institute of Elizabeth City, a unit of Shaw University.[428] Mrs. Hattie Armstrong represented Mt. Carmel at the Annual Women's Educational Missionary Union held at Corinth Baptist Church in Jarvisburg. Mrs. Mamie J. Griffin a member of Mount Carmel was the president. Mrs. Edna Moore, who supervised the usher boards, represented the ushers, and Mrs. Rosa L. Roach was the mother of the Sunshine Band. Just prior to attending the session Mrs. Moore had returned from visiting her daughter, Mrs. Floretta Sutton in Atlantic City, N. J. She was accompanied by her granddaughter, Gwendolyn, Eddie Griffin, Walter Griffin, and Bruce Williams of Norfolk.[429] The Woman's Education and Missionary Union held its annual meeting at Mount Carmel Baptist Church during the week of October 3-6 1955.[430] The One-Day Session of the Woman's Educational and Missionary Union to the Roanoke Missionary Baptist Association was held on April 5, 1966 at Mount Carmel. The session opened at 10 a. m. with a Welcome Address by Mrs. Mary Williams. The sermon was preached by Rev. T. M. Walker, pastor of Olive Branch, Elizabeth City. The Junior Unions and the Sunshine Bands participated in the session. The officers of the Union are: Mrs. E. B. McRay, president, Mrs. Stella Bryant Vice-President, Elnora Taylor treasurer, Mrs. Mary L. Christian secretary, and Mrs. Nezzie Clark, assistant secretary.[431] The Sixtieth Annual Session of the Woman's Educational and Missionary Union was held with the Mount Carmel Baptist Church on October 5-6 1968. Reverend W. A. Davis was the pastor.[432] The members of St. John Baptist Church attended the Union. Mrs. Angela Rodgers marched as Queen during the session representing St. John Baptist Church.[433]

Funeral services for Mr. Oscar Temple were held from the Mount Carmel Church on March 5, 1936. He had been a member of the church since 1915. Mr. Temple was born about 1868 and raised in Newland where he lived until 1935. He was about 70 years old at the time of his March 1, 1936 death. He married seventeen year old Fannie Ellen "Jennie" Hinton on November 29, 1889. Seventeen children were born to this union. Mr. Temple was noted for his activities in educational work. He was particularly interested in farm demonstrations. He served as president and vice-president of the State Farmers' Conference. Mr. Temple was survived by seven of his 17 children, two sons, and five daughters. Reverend W. H. Trotman officiated. Short talks were given by some of the most distinguished leaders of the Roanoke Missionary Baptist Association, namely: Joseph Brothers, Melvin Griffin, Mrs. B. L. Hinton, J. T. Raynor, Mrs. Rosa Roach, and J. H. Skyes.

Funeral services for Mrs. Nancy Harvey were held at Mt. Carmel Missionary Baptist Church, December 23, 1941 with Rev. W. P. Jones of Fentress, VA, officiating. Mrs. Harvey died December 20 in Brooklyn, N. Y., where she had made her home since 1922. She was the daughter of the late Rev. Ivy Boone Roach. Funeral services for William Arthur Stallings, who was instantly killed when a truck in which he was riding enroute to Baltimore, Maryland, overturned, were held at Mount Carmel on June 19, 1943. The Reverend J. C. Davis officiated. He was assisted by the Reverends C. L. Griffin and Eddie Spence. The obituary was read by Mrs. Rosa L. Roach. Mrs. Mary Sharp sang a solo. Mrs. Mary Griffin conducted the funeral program. Mr. Stallings was a member of Ramón Gilead Baptist Church. He was survived by his parents, Rev. Willie & Vera Stallings; two sisters, one brother of Newland, N. C., four aunts, grandparents, and a host of other relatives. Mrs. Nettie Banks Thornton of Baltimore, Maryland, formerly of Newland was killed in an automobile wreck in Little Rock, Arkansas while traveling with her son to Texas for a visit. Her son Otis escaped uninjured. Prior to the southwestern trip, Mrs. Banks visited her father and Mrs. Sarah Carver in Newland. Funeral services were held October 10, 1954 at Mount Carmel with the Rev. Curtis A. Proctor officiating. He was assisted by the Revs W. J. Moore, pastor and M. H. Hinton. Others participating in the service were Charlie Moore, Ms Ina M. Moore, and Mesdames Rosa L. Roach, and Mary G. Williams. Mrs. Thornton was survived by her husband, Judge Thornton; two sons, James and Otis Thornton of Baltimore, Maryland, and one daughter, Alma of Massachusetts. Mrs. Thornton was also survived by her father, Preston Banks, of New Land; two brothers, Haywood, of Baltimore, Md., and Mayo of New Land N. C.; and an uncle Joe Banks, of New Land, N. C. Interment was in the family plot in New Land.[434]

Rev. Dr. Linwood Morings Boone, D. MIN., was installed as the 17th Pastor of the Mount Carmel Missionary Baptist Church on November 6, 1994 at 6: 00 P. M. The Reverend John Henry London, Jr., pastor of the First Baptist Church, Hertford, N. C., presided, and conducted the Call To Worship; Invocation by Rev. Timothy Hicks, pastor of Stony Branch Baptist Church, Gates,; Hymn; "Lift Every Voice and Sing," Scripture Readings:, The First Lesson *Joshua 1:1-8* Rev. Jerry Boone, associate of Stony Branch Baptist Church, Gates; The Second Lesson *Jeremiah 1:4-10*, Rev. William Wiggins Pastor of Ballard's Grove Baptist Church, Eure, N. C., The Third Lesson, 1 Peter 5 1:3, Rev. George Smith, Pastor of Pleasant Grove Baptist Church, Suffolk, Virginia; Prayer: Rev. George Munden pastor of Galatia Baptist Church, Weeksville, N. C., The Words of Welcome by Deacon J. C. Williams, chairman of the Board of Deacon's at Mount Carmel Missionary Baptist Church; The Welcome Response by Elder Raynor B. Wilson, St. Timothy Church of Christ Holiness, U. S. A., Newport News, Va.; Greetings by Elder Melvin Austin, New Bethel Cathedral Church of God In Christ, Hampton, Virginia,; The Recognition of Clergy, Rev. Leon Credle pastor of New Sawyers Creek Baptist Church, Camden, N. C., Solo Mrs. Viola Parker, New Mount Joy Church of God In Christ, Suffolk, Virginia., Offertory Appeal by Rev. John Felton, pastor of First Baptist Church, Gates, N. C., Offertory Music Mount Carmel Choir, Offertory Prayer, Rev. Ralph Martino, Shiloh Baptist Church, Alexander, Virginia.; Doxology, "All Things Come of Thee O Lord.", Introduction of Clergy, Rev.William Sawyer pastor of New Bethel Baptist Church, Hertford, N. C., The Installation Message, Rev. William T. Sawyer,

Text: Matthew 14: 22-33 *"Six Things To Remember When The Storm Comes"* Pastor of Shiloh Baptist Church, Shawboro, N. C., The Invitational to Discipleship, Rev. Ronald Goodwyn, Balm of Gilead Baptist Church, Suffolk, Virginia., The Installation Service The Consecration Prayer by Rev. Jasper Horn, pastor of Providence Baptist Church, Edenton, N. C., The Pastoral Litany, Rev. Robert Eaton, Pastor, Union Baptist Church, Newport News, Virginia,; The Charge to the Church, Rev. Joseph E. Griffin, Portsmouth, Virginia,; The Charge to the Pastor, Rev. David S. Whitehurst, Pastor of Bagley Chapel Baptist Church, Winfall. N C., The Presentation of the Bible, pastor, Rev. Bruce Childs, pastor, Popular Lawn Baptist Church, Surry, Virginia., The Presentation of the Bible by Rev. Bernard Lloyd, First Baptist Church, Hampton, Virginian., The Presentation of the Keys, Trustee Linwood "Lee Bell" Williams, The Remarks by the Moderators, Rev. Rick Banks pastor of St. Steven Baptist Church & Rev. Charles Turner, pastor of Samuel Chapel Baptist Church, Elizabeth City, N. C., Presentations, Pastoral Remarks, Rev. Linwood Boone, Benediction by Rev. Horace McPherson pastor of Whitesville Grove A.M.E. Z., Elizabeth City, N. C. Music provided by Mr. Winford Simpson, and Mr. Vincent Beamon. Rev. Boone's pastoral remarks were preceded by his singing, "I Am on the Battlefield for My Lord." He was accompanied by the Gates County Caravans consisting of Bertha Ryans, Vivian Howell and Willie Mae Gatling.

The following men have serve as Pastor of the Mount Carmel Missionary Baptist Church. Reverends Miles Harvey; Rev. Charles Hodges 1 year; Rev. Ivy Boone Roach-1 year; Rev. Elijah Harrison Griffin-15 years; Rev. Harry Henry Norman-13 years; Rev. George D. Griffin 2-years; Rev. A. D. Moore-15 years; Rev. William A. Cobb 15-years; Rev. Sampson Lane 7-years; Rev. W. Preston Jones 4 years; Rev. Ulysses G. Moye—4 years; Rev. Waitman J. Moore 17 years; Rev. Joseph E. Griffin 4-years; Rev. W. A. Davis-17 Years; Rev. David L. White 4 years; Rev. E. J. Lillard 2 years; Rev. Linwood Morings Boone, D. MIN. 7 ½ years; Rev. William J. Smith 3 years; Rev. Michael Barcliff.

The North Carolina General Warranty Deed made on the 29 day of April, 1988, by and between the grantors, Harold Vann Boothe, and wife Adele Forbes Boothe and the grantee Mount Carmel Missionary Baptist Church conveying to Mount Carmel Baptist Church the land on which the church was situated.[435] Fire destroyed the Mount Carmel Missionary Baptist Church on the third Sunday morning, April 2010. According to the pastor, Michael Barcliff, "The church was almost 148 years old, and we lost a lot of rich traditional history." Firefighters labeled the cause of the blaze as 'undetermined,' but officials say they were able to eliminate any suspicion that the fire was intentionally set. "We are satisfied based on the fire scene examination as well as interviews of witnesses and other parties that the fire was not arson," said Elizabeth City Fire Marshall Barry A. Overman in a released statement April 30. According to that statement, officials were able to narrow the "origin" of the fire to an area within the church where several factors lead to the determination to support an accidental type cause.

Stony Branch Missionary Baptist Church

The arrival of the mulatto free born Boon families and their descendants in Gates County are scantly recorded in the local and State Archives. The first Boon on record in Gates County was James Boon born about 1745, in Hertford County, N. C., and the head of a Gates County household of 1 "other free" in 1790. At the time of his 1790 death, he had a, twelve-year-old "orphan" son Thomas Boon. The Boon households listed below were residents of the Reynoldson District of Gates County from 1793-1830. The difference between a Free Born, and a Free Negro are telling. A Free Born person had no slave ancestry, whereas, a Free Negro person derived his freedom from purchase, or manumission. The Reynoldson Boon's were Free Born.

Name	Birth Year
Boon, Abram	1793
Boon, Cherry	1800
Boon, Wilkerson	1800
Boon, Dempsey	1809
Boon, Kizar	1810
Boon, Anzilla	1814
Boon, Betsy	1818
Boon, John	1818
Boon, Polly	1820
Boon, Sophia	1820
Boon, Elimine	1825
Boon, John	1825
Boon, Sally	1830

The Gates County, North Carolina Court stated that no free Negro could reside in Gates County without first having obtained a permit from the Board of Commissioners, which was only granted after the Board had been satisfied "that the applicant supports honest, industrious and peaceful character." The permit was to be forfeited upon misbehavior, and the offender was to pay a fine of $4. In 1844 fourteen free Negroes were indicted by the grand jury for coming into Gates County, from Virginia without Gates County's permission. What the court did with these Negroes cannot be ascertained but what is reasonably certain is that they did not leave the county. The names of those indicted were, Boon, Brown, Collins, and Copeland. John C. Boon and wife, Martha "Patsy" Reid Boon, the parents of William Aldred Boon for whom this book is dedicated, were among the Boon's who entered North Carolina from Virginia prior to 1845. Twelve years later, 1857, the Boon's, were prominent founders of the New Hope Missionary Baptist Church, Gatesville, N. C. It is more than conjecture to state that the Boon names listed above; the founding Boon's of the New Hope Church, and the Boon's in the Reynoldson District of the Stony Branch Missionary Baptist Church were one big happy family. A brief genealogical research will reveal their close affinities. The attitudes of the Reynoldson District Boon's were very similar to those attitudes found in Hertford County. This is not surprising since the Reynoldson District was carved out of Hertford County in order to form Gates County. Boon's in the Reynoldson District of Gates County, North Carolina often lived in closed and isolated communities, as did their relatives in Hertford County. They shared a common ancestry whether through blood or marriage. Family lines of descendants were often blurred by the repetitions of the same names, and often by having one or more paternal and maternal grandparents in common. The Boon's and their descendants were free born, and had lived in the Reynoldson District a minimum of one-hundred fifteen years before the outbreak of the war of the Rebellion in 1861. The 1850 census records verified the fact that many of the Boon's were literate, home and property owners.

The Reynoldson free mulatto Boon families had a history different from the mass of other Negroes in the area, they gradually became identified more or less with the Negro group and provided many of the leaders for the church, school board and ministry. In this respect the Reynoldson Boon's may be distinguished from those families of Negro, Indian white ancestry, living in isolation. The Boon's and their descendents generally formed the upper class in the Negro group, the families of mixed bloods often regarded themselves as an altogether different race. In some instances their consciousness of being a different race from the Negro expressed itself in the naïve reference to themselves as "a different kind of folks," The Boon's formed their own enclaves and named them Boon Town, and Blind Neck. In all probably, the Boon's were the founders of the Stony Branch Missionary Baptist Church. They were free born; lived in close proximity with the dominate culture; had little or no restrictions of movement; and they had both the means and the resources to perform such a feat. Furthermore, traveling the ten miles to worship with their free born relatives at New Hope Baptist Church was not always practical or safe. Nor was crossing the Chowan River by ferry and then traveling the 10 miles to attend worship with their free born relatives at the Pleasant Plains Baptist Church in Hertford County practical.

The first House of Worship for the Free born Boon family in the Reynoldson Township of Gates County, North Carolina was probably crudely constructed out of bull-rush reeds, bushes, limbs and boards on the property of Betty Eure. This House of Worship was located in the Betty Eure curve which is within one mile north of its present location on Gatlington Road. The name Stony Branch was selected because of the stones that plentifully rolled along the creek side of the House of Worship. Adjacent to the first Stony Branch Church was the old Serum Church. The second house of worship and perhaps the first building of its kind for this beloved community was constructed prior to May 1866. The third house of worship as shown above and as it is inscribed on the cornerstone was dedicated on October 12, 1895, presumably by the Odd Fellows as its lodge was at the opposite side of the campus complex. The oral history states that David Rooks built this church. He was assisted by his wife's cousin, Wilson Boone.

Some of the slave residents of the Reynoldson Township worshipped at the white Piney Grove Church, located in the Reynoldson section of Gates County. The slave members of the Gatlington Community also in the Reynoldson Township were allowed to conduct their religious services and their communion services at the white Piney Grove Church, Reynoldson, North Carolina. However, on June 22, 1866, after the war of the rebellion ended in a defeat for the south, returning ex-confederate soldier Julius Howell, objected to this longstanding practice.[436] Accordingly, these former slaves made arrangements for their own church building between John Gatling's home and the river. It is uncertain how these former slaves were integrated into the worship experience of the Free-Born Boon family at Stony Branch. We know that they were integrated into this existing church because the 1869 minutes of the Roanoke Missionary Baptist Church reported that on Friday June 2, 1869, Elder Lemuel Washington Boone, Rev. William Reid, and Elder Henry Hays were selected as the Presbytery of the Roanoke Missionary Baptist Association for the purpose of constituting Stony Branch Church, Gatlington, North Carolina as a Missionary Baptist Church,[437] duly organized according to the rules of the said association. Please note that the 1869 minutes reported the proceedings of the previous year, 1868, and beyond. At lease two years later on November 26, 1870, Piney Grove Church granted letters of dismissal to the following former slave members in order that they could join a church whom they referred to as Stony Branch Chapel.

Mary Benton	Anna Eliza Eure	Hasty Gatling	Jane Lawrence
Celcia Cross	Caroline Eure	Jack Gatling	Sarah Parker
Henrietta Cross	Easter Eure	Nancy Gatling	Anthony Riddick
Mary Cross	Harry Eure	Julia Ann Howell	Priscilla Sears
Julia Cross	Jiles Eure	Tiggy Howell	Lucy Williams
Lucy Cross	Sarah Eure		

It is evident from the 1869 report of the Roanoke Missionary Baptist Association that the members of the white Piney Grove Baptist Church either did not know about the presbyter visit to the already established Stony Branch Baptist Church or did not care enough to address the presbyter visit to the Stony Branch Baptist Church. It is not factual that the Stony Branch Baptist Church was birth out of the white Reynoldson Church as is commonly reported and believed.

The Stony Branch history as given by the innocent church historian of the Pinry Grove Baptist Church really victimized Stony Branch's prehistory. An innocent historian is one who regarded the text as a complete presentation of the truth on the subjects he treats. He neither thought of his own prejudices, nor of the prejudices of others and the ignorance of authors. Many of these repeaters of history will not relate a fact that is favorable to Negro. For instance, the historian of the Piney Grove Baptist Church readily stated that the Negro belonged to their church as a slave, but will omitted the fact that the Reynoldson Negro could have very well participated in the Nat Turner's rebellion, or that the Negro repeadly rebelled against slavery. This writer will ignore Gabriel Prosser's plot of 1800, and Vesey's planned revolt of 1822. He will omit Nat Turner's rebellion of 1892, so significant that it caused the formulation of black codes in all of the slave states, some of which prohibited Negroes to preach, as was the case and cause of the Piney Grove Negroes being expelled from their lily white church. This same repeaters of history said nothing of L'Amised Insurrection of 1839 or the Creole Affair of 1841. These incidents tend to prove that the Negro did not readily submit to slavery, that he fought for free himself; that he was not only a slave, but a hero. These facts historical facts are often omitted just as the presbyteia visit to the already Stony Branch Church in 1867 was omitted from their history, either because of ignorance or prejudice or both. Text with such omissions cease to be histories, but become propaganda. The innocent histroain in not making a critical analysis of these books teachers them as history. In so doing, the church historian teaches that throughout American history, the Negro was a slave and never a master, that he was always driven and he never led. That he was a coward and not a fighter. Such as this the innocent teacher imparts without question.

It is not factual that the Stony Branch Church owes its founding to the New Middle Swamp Baptist Church, Corapeake, N. C. However, it is accurate to state that those ex-slaves attending the Piney Grove Baptist Church were dismissed on November 26, 1870. The records do not suggest how nor where the Gatlington & Reynoldson Negroes worship between the exodus and prior to the 1868 certification of the establishing of the Stony Branch Church.

On May 18, 1877 Mills H. Eure entered into a contract with the members of Stony Branch to lend to the said members one acre square of land on which the church was presently located. The contact contained the following stipulations: the property could be used as long as it remained a place of worship; when the land was dispensed with as a place of worship, said land shall return to Mills H. Eure his heirs assigns.[438] Mills H. Eure personally appeared before R. B. G. Cowper, Clerk of Superior Court of Gates County on September 4, 1880 and acknowledged the execution of the foregoing deed.[439] The original of the foregoing Deed was delivered to L. P. Hayes, the Register of Deeds and registered by him on the 10th day of September, 1880.[440] A third church building was erected on the fore-mentioned grounds of the Stony Branch Baptist Church on the property of Mills H. Eure on October 12, 1895.

On September 20, 1882 John J. Gatling described the Gatlington area where Stony Branch Baptist Church was located as a forest that contained three types of pine trees: long-straw, medium-straw or ordinary, and the short-straw or rosemary; several varieties of oak trees named in order of the prevailing varieties—red, white, post, black jack, water, Spanish, turkey, chinquapin, and the over-cup. According to Gatling's descriptions, Gatlington also had a large supply of ash; gum, sweet, black, and papaw; poplar, persimmon, juniper, cypress, cedar, a sprinkling of mulberry, holly, maple, dogwood, sour-wood, elm, beech, and birch trees. He concluded this interview by stating that fully three fourths of the area of this county is covered by forest, including old fields. There is a large quantity of pine timber and a good deal of oak. The pine, oak, and cypress are being rapidly cut and in a few years will all be gone.

R. Cross

Reverend Robert C. Cross who was born about 1850 in the Gatlington section of the Reynoldson's District of Gates County, North Carolina. He married a mulatto woman, the former Sarah A. Ryan about 1870. During September 1870, Reverend Cross is employed as a Turpentine Hand in Beaver dam Township of Rockingham Township in the County of Richmond, North Carolina. Ten years later on July 10, 1880 Robert and his mulatto wife Sarah Ryan Cross were living in Gates County; and he was earning his living by working on the farm. The Crosses employed their daughter Irma Cross as a servant. (Irma married Wille Leroy Boon, the son of William A. Boon and Caroline Parker Boon, of the Reynoldson District of Gates County, North Carolina.)

Reverend Cross is the first known minister associated with the Stony Branch Missionary Baptist Church. He was paid $60.00 for his once a month preaching. He served as the delegate from the Stony Branch Church to the Thirteenth Annual Session of the Roanoke Missionary Baptist Association with it convened with at New Bethany, Hertford County, N. C. on the Tuesday after the 4th Lord's Day in May 1878. His report included the fact that Stony Branch's worship services were held on the 3rd Sunday of each month. The church had a total membership of 83 people; of which 2 members had been gained in 1877 through baptism, and 2 members had excommunicate in 1877 for unspecified infractions. The Sunday school had 27 members. There were not any members received or dismissed by letter. More importantly there were no deaths reported during the preceding year.

The Minutes of the Nineteenth (1884) Annual Session of the Roanoke Missionary Baptist Association held with the Church of Christ at Zion Hill, Bertie County, N. C., on the Tuesday after the third Lord's Day in May, 1884 records the fact that the Stony Branch membership had grown to 156 active members. Isaac Eure and Jiles Eure were the delegates to the Association [441] The next year, (1885) Rev. Cross's congregation had gained 26 new members, and had lost 3 by death. Thirty-nine of them had been baptized into the faith,[442] and had been given the Right-Hand of Fellowship. Frank R. Smith and Henderson Eure were the delegates. By 1886 Rev. Cross reported to the Twenty-First Annual Session of the Roanoke Missionary Baptist Association convening at the Church of Christ at Antioch, Camden, N. C., which the congregation had grown to 166 active members.[443] Rev. Richard Cross's pastorate ended in 1896.

In 1920 Reverend Cross was gainfully employed as a wagon loader for a logging firm. In 1930 Reverend Cross is widowed and living with his 74 year old brother Frank Cross and his wife, the former Henrietta Small daughter of Nancy Small of Gates County, in the Reynoldson District of Gates County, North Carolina. He remained a faithful and supportive member of Stony Branch and the Roanoke Missionary Baptist Association. He died in the Gatesville Township on July 22,1931. He was 84 years old.

The Stony Branch Baptist Church maintained a positive and supportive role of the Roanoke Missionary Baptist Church from its inceptions. Its Missionary objectives of Baptism and Lord's Supper (Communion) were clearly adhered to and practiced. The Annual Second Sunday in September Homecoming Service was antecedent to Baptisms. Dressed in their calico frocks and straw bonnets women from across Reynoldson area would bring their best culinary delights to the annual home coming. Baptisms occurred on the third Saturday in September following the Annual Tract to The Meeting, (referred to the Annual Revival) in which repentant sinners were converted after hearing strong and powerful sermons by the various revivalist, and by the promptings of Brother Joseph "Bread" Goodman and William "Bill" Scott as they canvassed the Mourner's Bench during the week of morning and nightly preaching. Baptisms were officiated by the pastor and the deacons at the Max Wharf in the Chowan River, the Creek, or the Gatlington Wharf. Newly baptized members received the sacraments of the Lord's Supper on the Third Sunday of the month. Thereafter, they were full pledged members with all the rights and privileges of membership.

Rev. J. C. Saunders

Reverend Joseph Cephesus Saunders was born on March 12, 1861 in Gates County, North Carolina to Reverend Abram Saunders. Rev. Saunders began his ministry at Stony Branch in 1896. He remained with this church until 1932. Revered Saunders's pastorate at Stony Branch was a fruitful one. The membership increased to 299 during the 1903 fiscal year. The following people were listed as members of Stony Branch: Ross B. Boone, Wilson M. Boone, Annie L. Daughtery, Charles Daughtery, David Eure, Jet Eure, Martha Eure, Sarah Eure, John Johnson, Mary Johnson, Alice Parker, Jerry Parker, Lazarus J. Parker, Martha A. Parker, Mary A. Reed, Asbury Reid, Gracie A. Scott, ___ M. Scott, Henry Smith, Victoria M. Smith, Ida C Wilson,

Risup Wilson, and Maria Wilson. (Many of these member names were the former ex-slaves and former members of the white Piney Grove Baptist Church in Reynoldson.) This increase was due to 28 people being baptized into the faith and 6 former members being restored to their Christian Commitment, and 1 person gained by letter from another church of like faith. The Sunday school class had 90 pupils and the Rev. J. C. Saunders received $80.00 for the Third Sunday Preaching.[444] Rev. L. J. Parker of Dort, (Parker town in the Reynoldson section of Gates County) North Carolina was the delegate to the 1906 Association meeting convening at Providence Baptist Church, Edenton, N. C., on May 22-24, 1906. Per the Statistical Report of the Forty-First Annual Session (1906) Stony Branch increased her pastor's monthly salary to $100.00 for the 3rd Sunday Preaching. Rev. Saunders leadership and preaching abilities resulted in an increase of 28 new members this year; 19 by baptism and 9 by letter. The membership was composed of 143 males, and 130 females, making a total membership of 273 members.[445] When the Association convened at in its Forty-Second (1907) Annual Session at Corner Stone Missionary Baptist Church, Elizabeth City, North Carolina Stony Branch did not report any attritions or gains in membership. However, she did report that 11 members had been excommunicated, and a total of 74 males and 98 females' names were still on the membership roll. The pastor's Third Sunday Preaching salary had increased to $180.00.[446] The 1907 Financial Report indicates that Stony Branch met its financial Obligations towards the Objects of the Association by paying $3.00 towards the Associational Expenses, $6.00 on the new building; $50.00 on the Orphan/Asylum and $50.00 on State Conventions.[447] Stony Branch met its obligations to the Objects of the Roanoke Missionary Baptist Association in 1909 when she contributed $50.00 for the Association Expense, $50.00 for the Building expense; $50.00 for the Roanoke Institute; $100.00 Home & Foreign Missions $50.00 Orphan/Asylum.[448] Rev. L. J. Parker of Gates was the delegate to the Roanoke Missionary Baptist Association, and the clerk of the church. Stony Branch changed its Sunday worship service from 3rd Sunday to the First Sunday during 1915 and reduced the pastor's monthly income to $150.00. The 1919 Roanoke Missionary Baptist Association Annual Church Assessment reports that Stony Branch exceeded her assessment again this year.[449] All day services at the Popular Lawn Baptist Church, Surry County, Virginia were good. Rev. J. C. Saunders and administered the Lord's Supper at 12:30 P. M.[450] Mr. W. M. Gatling served as the delegate to the Fifty-Second Annual Session when it convened at Philadelphia Baptist Church, Shiloh, N. C., on May 20, and 22nd, A. D. 1919. He reported that Stony Branch had excommunicated 19 members and had raised $550.00 since January 1, 1919. The Minutes of the Fifty-Fourth Annual Session of the Roanoke Missionary Baptist Association held with New Hope Baptist Church, Gatesville, North Carolina on May 18 to 20, A. D. 1920 reflect in the Finance Report that Stony Branch sent in $8.80, and brought in $47.20 which totaled $56.00. The church had been assessed at $52.50; however, the church exceeded the Assessment amount by paying $3.75 above the assessed amount.[451] On the 3rd Sunday in October 1920 the church observed the annual *Roanoke Institute Day* and paid the assessment amount of $52.50 in addition to contributing $35.00 to the Board and $17.50 to the Association.

The Statistics of the Roanoke Missionary Baptist Association for 1920 reveal that Stony Branch Missionary Baptist Church held worship service on the Third Sunday of each month with Rev. J. C. Saunders doing the preaching. The membership grew by 17, baptized 16 members, and restored 1 to its membership. The total church membership was 300, which was composed of 125 males and 175 females. Of that amount 49 people attended Sunday school. The total value of the debt free church property was $1200.00. The church collected $801.00.[452] Rev. Lazarus

Junious Parker was the delegate to the Association and W. M. Gatling of Gates, N. C., was the church clerk. The Corresponding Secretary, Foreign Mission Board received from Stony Branch Missionary Baptist Church at the May 23-25, 1922 Annual Session of the Roanoke Missionary Baptist Association held with the Corinth Missionary Baptist Church, Jarvis burg, North Carolina the sum of $ 3.00.[453] They had previously sent in an additional $38.00. Rev. J. C. Saunders, the pastor, brought in another $14.50 during the reporting period of the association.[454] This made the total amount of $ 55.50 for this Association. The delegate to the Association was Luke Gatling and the church clerk of Stony Branch was Wilson Boone of Gates, N.C.[455] Rev. Saunders was known in Virginia as Dr. J. C. Saunders. His contemporary in Virginia was Rev. Israel Cross the founder of eight Baptist churches. Rev. Saunders of Corapeake, N. C. stopped in Elizabeth City, N. C. on first Sunday in November 1922 enroute from the Union Meeting at Belcross, N. C. He was the guest of Mr. & Mrs. Robert Riddick.

Rev. Joseph Cephesus Saunders was the 7th pastor of the Middle Swamp Missionary Baptist Church, Corapeake, North Carolina. His tenure was from 1891-1929. He concurrently pastured the Popular Run Baptist Church, Sleepy Hole, Virginia, from 1907-1932, the New Middle Swamp Missionary Baptist Church, Corapeake, North Carolina for thirty-two years, and Joppa Baptist Church, Hobbsville, North Carolina. Rev. Saunders had a ministry that totaled 96 years. Rev. Saunders died July 6, 1932 and is buried in the New Middle Swamp Memorial Park.

The Stony Branch Chapter 3032 of the United Order of True Reformers Unity-Temperance Charity was founded December 1902 under the pastorate of Rev. J. C. Saunders with the following twenty six members: Ross B. Boone, Wilson M. Boone, Annie L. Daughtery, Charles Daughtery, David Eure, Jet Eure, Martha Eure, Sarah Eure, John Johnson, Mary Johnson, Alice Parker, Jerry Parker, Lazarus J. Parker, Martha A. Parker, Mary A. Reed, Asbury Reid, Gracie A. Scott, William Scott, Henry Smith, Victoria M. Smith, Ida C Wilson, Risup Wilson, and Maria Wilson. The original founding document is in the personal collection of Donald C. Cross, the maternal grandson of Wilson Boone and the paternal great grand nephew of Jerry Parker. Jerry Parker's wife Caroline Eure becomes the great grandmother of Donald Cross. Wilson Boone served as a deacon and trustee of Stony Branch Baptist Church.

He's Able To Carry You Through

He's able to carry you through. No matter what the world may do.
Try Jesus for He satisfies;
He's waiting to hear your cry,
Trust Him in everything you do, For He'll bear the load for you.
He's able to carry you through.

Rev. H. A. Smith

Reverend Henry Augustus Smith was born August 13, 1875 in Mintonville Township of Gates County, North Carolina to Fletcher Smith and the former Mary Jane Robbins. The Smiths were married by the Gates County Justice of Peace, James Walton. Rev. H. A. Smith married the former Dinah Burke, the daughter of Louisa Burke of Gates County, on April 24, 1903 in Gates County. Rev. & Mrs. Smith were the proud parents of Mary L., Edna M., and Nellie Smith. Rev. Smith had one sibling, Francis Smith born about 1869 in Gates County.

The Revival Services at Harrellsville Chapel closed on Friday night, September 7, 1925 with eighteen candidates for baptism. Rev. G. C. Lassiter, the acting pastor, was there throughout the week. The services were conducted by Rev. H. A. Smith, of Hobbsville, N. C. Rev. & Mrs. Lassiter and children spent the week with relatives. They left on Tuesday for Windsor, N. C. On the first Sunday in October 1925 services were excellent and spirit filled. Rev. Smith, who had recently accepted the pastorate of the Harrellsville Chapel Baptist Church delivered an inspiring sermon. Rev. Bembry Archer filled the pulpit at night and delivered a wonderful message. Reverend Smith preached at Harrellsville Chapel on the first Sunday in November 1925. At the close of the service dinner was served to the visiting friend's which included Dr. & Mrs. W. B. Sharp of Little Hertford. At 3: 00 P. M. Rev. Smith's the Installation Service were held. The Installation Sermon was preached by Rev. Grover C. Lassiter, of Hertford, N. C. Music was by the choir of the First Colored Baptist Church, Hertford, N. C. There were many out of town. Rev. Smith conducted the October 15, 1939 funeral of Robert Sharp, the son of Rev. & Mrs. C. B. Sharp. Funeral services were conducted at the Harrellsville Chapel Missionary Baptist Church. Mr. Sharp was survived by his father, one sister and two brothers. On the second Sunday in July 1923 Reverend Smith pastor of the Roduco First Baptist Church preached a very inspiring sermon. He later attended the Woman's Missionary and Educational Union at Lebanon Grove Missionary Baptist Church. The following month, August 1927, Rev. Smith secured the services of Rev. J. H. Skinner, Hertford, N. C., to carry on the Revival Services. He preached forceful and stirring sermons. The collections were good during the day and during each night.

Rev. Smith was called to the pastorate of Stony Branch prior to 1933. It was reported in the July 1, 1933 edition of the *New Journal and Guide* that "The Rev. Henry Smith was at Stony Branch on the 3rd Sunday in June of which he is pastor." On October 2, 1937 Mr. Luke Gatling reported to the *Norfolk Journal and Guide* that the Reverend A. B. Askew of Norfolk, Virginia conducted the Revival under the pastorate of Rev. H. A. Smith. Revival Services were conducted at 11: 00 A. M., and at 7: 00 P. M. The following reverends attended those services: Joseph Melton of Goldsboro, N. C., G. C. Lassiter of Franklin, Virginia., J. D. Farrar of Newport News, Virginia., Joseph Goodman of Suffolk, Va., John Applewhite of Gates, N. C., and H. L. Mitchell of Gatesville, North Carolina. The revival was interesting and very inspiring. Seventy-eight dollars was received in the offering and 30 souls were saved from sin.

Reverend Smith preached the annual sermon of the Roanoke Missionary Baptist Association when it convened at Galatia Missionary Baptist Church, Elizabeth City, North Carolina. Rev. Smith concurrently pastor Roduco First Baptist, Roduco, North Carolina; Harrellsville Chapel Missionary Baptist Church, Harrellsville, North Carolina and Stony Branch Baptist Church, Zion Grove, Bertie County, North Carolina.

Rev. Smith's wife, Dinah Burke Smith was a maternal relative of Alice Butler Parker, Asbury Reid, William Reid, Rooks Turner, and of many of the founding families of New Hope Missionary Baptist Church, and of the founding families of the Pleasant Plains Missionary Baptist Church. David Rooks, the one armed builder of Stony Branch Missionary Baptist Church was Dinah's maternal relative and members of the blue blood members. The Blue Veins were a little society of colored persons organized in Northern and Southern cities shortly after the Civil War. Its purpose was to establish and maintain social standards among a people whose social condition presented almost unlimited room for improvement. By accident, combined perhaps with some natural affinity, the society consisted of individuals who were, generally speaking, more white than black. Some envious outsiders made the suggestion that no one was eligible for membership who was not white enough to show blue veins. A second unspoken required of membership was the distinction made between those born free before the Civil War, and those who were shot free by the Civil War. Therefore, no slaves were ever admitted for membership.

Rev. Skinner was a friend from Rev. Henry Augustus Smith's youth. Rev. Smith preceded his friend, Rev. John H. Skinner in death by four years. Rev. Skinner's funeral was conducted at New Bethel Missionary Baptist Church, Bethel, N. C. where he was a member. Reverend Skinner pastured the following churches: First Baptist Colerain, Wynn's Grove Missionary Baptist, Bertie County, Pilgrim's Chapel, New-Burn, N. C., Cedar Landing, Windsor, and Spring Hill, all in North Carolina. Remarks were by the Rev. A. J. Cherry and the eulogy was delivered by the pastor, Rev. S. L. Lawrence. Thomas Downing sang a solo. Survivors included two sons, John H. Skinner Jr., of Virginia Beach, Virginia; Clarence B. Skinner of New York City; two sisters-in law; four grandchildren; one sister, Mrs. Clara V. Holly of Hertford, N. C. Rev. Henry Augustus Smith died May 24, 1962. He was buried in the family plot in Hobbsville, North Carolina.

Rev. F. L. Lee

Reverend Frank L. Lee, Sr., was born March 31, 1920 to the late Jonah and Lena Sharrock Lee in Bertie County, North Carolina. Rev. Frank Lee, Sr. was a graduate of Scotland Neck High School. He later attended Elizabeth City State University and Shaw University, Raleigh, North Carolina. Rev. Frank Lee, Sr. was the former pastor of Beacon Light Missionary Baptist Church, St. Matthews, Stony Branch Missionary Baptist Church, Gates, North Carolina, Beautiful Zion, Lewiston, North Carolina, Mill Branch, and St. John 2ⁿᵈ Baptist Churches, Hertford County, North Carolina. At the time of his demise, he was the pastor of Mount Sinai Baptist Church in Como, North Carolina and Creeksville Baptist Church in Conway, North Carolina.

He served 15 years as Town Councilman for the town of Aulander and Mayor pro-tern of Aulander. He was the Moderator for four years for the Northampton County Missionary Baptist Association, Northampton County Council for Ministerial Education for 30 years, member of Northampton County Union for 40 years, Moderator of West Roanoke Union from 1986-1998 and numerous other affiliations. He sang base in the Bertie County Male Chorus. His favorite Song was" I'm Gonna Sit down by the Banks of the River." Rev. Lee preached the closing sermon at the 1965 Annual Session of the Roanoke Association when it convened at the First Baptist Church Hertford. He selected for a topic "Keep Your Promise with God" He highlighted the following points: 1.) Keep the lines of communication open between the soul and God. 2.) The joy of Christian Alertness. 3.) Confidence in the protection of God.[456]

Rev. Lee began his pastorate at the Stony Branch Missionary Baptist Church in 1960 largely through his singing in the Bertie County Male Chorus. He was introduced to Stony Branch by his long time friend Genie Lazarus Parker, and sisters Alice, Lucille, and Pearla Parker. Genie's parents, Rev. Lazarus J. & Mrs. Alice Butler Parker had previously befriended Rev. Lee's parents Jonah and Lena Sharrock Lee in Bertie County, North Carolina.

On Sunday evening October 20, 1968 Rev. Frank L. Lee was the guest preacher for a service honoring Mrs. Lorene M. Gatling, the worthy matron of the Nansemond Chapter 31 Order of the Eastern Star of Virginia, Prince Hall Affiliated. The service was held in the basement of the Tabernacle United Church of Christ, Sixth Street & Norfolk Road, Suffolk, Virginia.

Reverend Frank L. Lee departed this life for heaven on Sunday, June 1, 2003. Left to cherish his life are: his wife, Marie Marsh Lee of the home; one son, William Lee (Rosa) of Aulander, N. C.; three daughters, Irene Foster of Aulander, N. C.; Lena Askew (Cleveland) of Simpsonville, KY; and Ada Brown (David) of Roosevelt, N. Y. (he was preceded in death by son, Frank Lee, Jr. and daughter, Mazie Mattie); ten grandchildren; nine great grandchildren; and one great-great-grandchild; daughter-in-law, Gloria Lee of Windsor, NC; one sister-in-law, Claudia Marsh of Portsmouth, VA and a host of nieces, nephews, cousins, and many friends.

Rev. Elbert Lee presided at the funeral of Rev. Frank Lee. Other participants included: the Old & New Testament readings by Rev. Cornell A. Watson, Sr., solo's by Curtis Chapman and Tracy Watson, Acknowledgements by Rena Tann & Deacon Paul Cooper of Mount Sinai Baptist Church, Sandra Williams & Deacon Robert Reese, First Baptist Creeksville, Linwood Melton First Baptist Aulander. Music was provided by the SBC Inspirational Choir. The newly elected pastor of Aulander First Baptist, Rev. Dr. Stevie Lawrence delivered the Eulogy to an overflowing grieving congregation of 200 or more. Rev. Frank Lee was interred at the Aulander First Baptist Church Cemetery located on the property of First Baptist Aulander. Professional Funeral Services were entrusted to the staff of Wilder's Funeral Home located at 816 Commerce Street, Aulander North Carolina.

Rev. W. A. Cotton

Reverend Willie Allen Cotton was born April 29, 1924 in Halifax County, North Carolina to Walter and the former Lillie Norfleet. He was the paternal grandson of George & Annie "Anna" Edmonds Cotton of Halifax County, North Carolina, and the maternal grandson of Madison Norfleet and the former Rebecca Caldwell Norfleet. He and his siblings Rebecca, Hebert, Elvie Cotton attended school from their Conocanary, Halifax County home. Rev. Cotton married the former Dorothy V. Smith on September 19, 1945 and to this union six children were born: Willie Jr., Dorothy M., Mamie L., Shirley A., Isaac L., Walter A. Cotton, and Reginald Newsome.

Rev. Cotton was a W. W. II Veteran. After his honorable discharge from the Armed Forces, he began an employment journey with the Mutts-Willoughby Funeral home. This relationship lasted until his death. Additionally, Rev. Cotton was a notary; and a well known public servant; a substitute school teacher; Forest Ranger; a life-long member of the National Association for the Advancement of Colored People; a member of Ancient Free and Accepted Masons, and the Order of the Eastern Star. His lodge members served as Honorary Pall Bears for his Tuesday, November 23, 1999 funeral conducted by Reverend Robert L. Knight at the Scotland Neck Municipal Auditorium, Scotland Neck, North Carolina.

Among Rev. Cotton's many pastorates are Bethlehem Baptist Church, Jarrat, Virginia; Calvary Baptist Church, Yale, Virginia. In 1972 he succeeded the Reverend Frank L. Lee of Aulander, North Carolina as pastor of the Stony Branch Missionary Baptist Church, Gates, North Carolina. During his pastorate Rev. Cotton's favorite "Yule-tide" sermon was *"No Room at the Inn"*. His favorite song was *"You Can't Hurry God."* Rev. Cotton ordained the Dr. Linwood Morings Boone, D. MIN., and Rev. Jerry Boone, Jr. He remained with the Stony Branch congregation until September 1986. In adulthood, two of Reverend Willie Allan Cotton's son Willie & Walter followed him into the gospel ministry. The Willie Allan Cotton family consists of twenty grandchildren, three step-grandchildren; twelve great-grand children.

The Stony Branch School

On October 13, 1919 Hallard A. Boone and Wilson M. Boone-Reynoldson Township appeared before the Gates County Board of Education and asked for better school facilities for their children. These men reported that there were about thirty children in this vicinity within school age. They came before the Board requesting better public schools for their race. However, there is no record of the request being honored. Consequently the Stony Branch members were undaunted in their efforts for better education for their children. Therefore, on October 1, 1928, Nine years, 11 months and twenty days later, The Board was compelled to hold an emergency consultation meeting over the conditions prevailing at the STONY BRANCH HALL SCHOOL. The superintendent reported in that meeting that "the negroes of this district had no house in which to hold school for the present year." The board ordered "that ½ acre of the land be brought from Mr. Carlton Savage for the schoolhouse to be placed on for these Negroes." The Stony Branch Negro families had petitioned the School Board for permission to either move the WIGGINGS HALL SCHOOLHOUSE or the SANDHILL SHOOLHOUSE located on the property of Bonnie and Helen C. Eure Boone's property formerly owned by Mr. Savage, and they would do the work. Permission was granted for them to do the work and move the building at their own expense.

Wilson Boone and Abram Lassiter, the Stony Branch Negro committee members were not happy that they were required to move their school and then rebuild it on its present site without any money from the County to assist with its construction. They were aware that the white County schools did not have to labor under such educational inequities and duress. On February 4, 1929, the Board approved the $500.00 loan application for the Stony Branch Negro School and reported the same to the Board in its April 1, 1929 meeting. On September 2, 1929, the board passed a resolution to the effect that the old Stony Branch Negro schoolhouse be exchanged for ½ acre of land provided no cost for surveying, deed, and etc. It was motioned that $50.00 be considered an acceptable sale price for the building if it was not exchanged for the land. On November 7, 1929 the Board ordered that a carpenter be employed to help Stony Branch Negroes erect their schoolhouse. Due to the building not being completed on time, and resignation of many of the Negro teachers in the county, the September 1933 school year at Stony Branch did not start on time.

The 1935-1938 School Committee consisted of Abram Lassiter, Rev. L. J. Parker and James Saunders. Their first July 6, 1936 responsibility was to make and accept local bids for furnishing wood delivered in right lengths to Stony Branch for the cost of $10.00 per year. The committee approved the employment of Emma Jenkins at its June 6, 1938 meeting. Mrs. Jenkins immediately began to deal with the attrition rate of the Stony Branch children by communicating with the Board of Education. On November 4, 1940, the Superintendent read a letter from the teacher at Stony Branch School stating that children from seven families who lived in the Stony Branch District are going to Rooks School. No action was taken on this matter. On December 2, 1940, The Superintendent read a letter from Emma R. Jenkins, teacher at Stony Branch Negro School, stating the children of six families, living in the Stony Branch School District and much nearer to Stony Branch School than any other, were going to Rooks School and Ariel School. By motion made by Mrs. Marian Nixon and seconded by R. E. Williams, the Superintendent was ordered to write each family and require them to send their children to Stony Branch School. This action is to become effective after January 1, 1941. Apparently the Stony Branch members did not agree with the written communications of the school board. On January 6, 1941, The Superintendent reported that the parents who had requested to transfer their children from Rooks School to Stony Branch School had asked to continue to send their children to Rooks School because they were living in a section which had been considered a part of the Rooks School District since the consolidation of the Sand Hill School; they had contributed their means for the improvement of Rooks School; they wanted their children to get the advantage of the contributions they had made, and by traveling wood paths, their children had no farther to walk to Rooks School than they would to Stony Branch. In view of these facts, the Board rescinded its action taken on December 2, 1940, which required these children to transfer to Stony Branch School.

On May 5, 1941, the Superintendent reported that there were only 14 pupils enrolled at Stony Branch School and the teacher had stated that there were not any other pupils to enroll. The attendance record for the first month showed an average daily attendance of 11 pupils. Upon visits of the superintendent on two successive days, he found no pupils present the first day and 8 pupils present on the second day. The Superintendent was authorized to order the Committee of the Stony Branch school and other interested patrons to appear before the Board of Education in a special meeting to held at 7:30 P. M. on Wednesday, October 15, at which time it would be decided whether a school could be continued at Stony Branch. October 15, 1941, the Stony Branch Committee, which had been requested to appear before the board, and explain why only one family with 4 children had recently moved back to the Stony Branch District, two families with six children now attending Aerial School lived in the Stony Branch School District and should attend Stony Branch; and two families with 4 children living in Stony Branch District in the direction of Rooks School had not started their children to any school, and there was one other family with 3 children which should attend Stony Branch, these additional children would bring the total enrollment to 31. They asked that the school be allowed to continue to operate. Motioned made by R. E. Williams and seconded by Mrs. Marian Nixon was passed to allow the Stony Branch School to continue to operate, provided the enrollment could be brought up to the number stated by the Committee as belonging to Stony Branch School; and ordering the Superintendent to write Jerry Parker, John Tom Johnson, Pricilla Johnson, Len Saunders, Zomack Boone, and James Saunders requesting them to send their children to Stony Branch School in an attempt to bring the enrollment to a number which would justify the continuance of the operation of the school. The Superintendent was ordered to write to each parent in the district and urge them to send their children to school regularly.

There are two similar instances of students from one district attending schools in another district without the knowledge or support of County School Officials. One such case happened to Gates County's neighbor, Pasquotank {the Newland School District and the Camden County Schools}. The Newland School District and the Camden County School District are within five miles of each other. The particulars of the case are as follows: The Camden County Superintendent of Schools E. P. Leary received a letter from the State Board of Education directing the Board of Education of Camden County "to take appropriate action at once to stop the unauthorized attendance of pupils by means of private transpiration from the Newland School District of Pasquotank County to South Mills in Camden County." Superintendent Leary refused to comment on the letter other than to say that he has turned it over to the Board of Education for action. When contacted, Board Chairman W. I. Sawyer of South Mills refused to make any comment. However, it was learned that a meeting of the School Board was scheduled for Saturday afternoon September 14, 1946 to discuss the situation. The residents of South Mills stated that they understood that between 25 and 30 pupils living in Newland were being carried to South Mills by means of bus which was obtained by the residents and parents of Newland for that purpose. The letter which was dated September 7, 1946 and signed by Controller Paul A. Reid reads: "The State Board of Education at a meeting September 5, 1946, adopted a resolution relating to the attendance of certain Pasquotank County children at South Mills Schools, as follows: "That the Board of Education at Camden County be notified that appropriate action be taken at once to stop the unauthorized attendance of pupils by means of private transportation from Newland School District of Pasquotank County to South Mills School in Camden County." Signed Paul A. Reid. [457]

A recent opinion by Attorney General Harry McMullan was to the effort that the state board of education has the authority to pass a rule or regulation requiring the attendance of children of school age to schools of the district in which they live. The South Mills residents were not sure whether the students attending South Mills School from Newland were of high school age or grammar school age, but some expressed the opinion that they were of both ages. A similar instance was reported in Kinston, North Carolina, in which the State Board of Education took more drastic action and virtually ordered the Grifton School authorities to stop taking students from Lenoir County to the Pitt County School. The Pasquotank County School enrollment figures released on Thursday, September 12, 1946 showed a total of 48 pupils enrolled in the Newland School and Superintendent M.P. Jennings estimated that between 20 and 30 Newland school children were going to the South Mills School. On November 8, 1941, the Superintendent stated that the two families who had been requested to send their children to the Stony Branch School had asked that they be allowed to continue to send their children to other schools-one family to Rooks and one to Arial; because his children had to cared for by his sister and his sister lived on the way to Rooks School, Lin Saunders was allowed to send them to Rooks. John Thomas Johnson was ordered to send his children to Stony Branch. The February 3, 1947 minutes reveal that the Superintendent called attention to the low membership at the Stony Branch Colored School. He stated that there had been 24 pupils enrolled in this school, but losses around January 1 caused the membership to fall to 16 pupils. Only 13 pupils were in average daily attendance during the fifth month of school.

The Gates County Board of Education unanimously decided on July 19, 1948 to consolidate the one and two room school houses located at Stony Branch Missionary Baptist Church and at Aerial, Rooks, Buckland, Newberry, and Roduco into one school. The abandoned white Gates School building would accommodate the Negro elementary children. It was unanimously decided to carry the Ballard's school children to Reid's Grove; and the Hudgin's Branch children to Corapeake. On July 26, 1948, the Stony Branch School and the physical equipment were closely inspected. The Superintendent was instructed how to dispose of the equipment in the abandoned buildings. August 2, 1948 several people voiced their opinion, some pro some con, on the matter of consolidation and the use of the abandon buildings by the Negro race. Attorney Kenyon Wilson from Elizabeth City spoke for those opposing consolidation and the use of abandon buildings by the Negro race. On December 30, 1948 the Stony Branch Church School was sold at a public auction to C. C. Savage for $410.00. On January 3, 1949 the Superintendent was instructed to request insurance agencies to cancel insurance on Stony Branch.

D. T. Spruill

Reverend Dallas Thomas Spruill was born on September 12, 1900 to Walter Spruill and the former Ellen Owens of Columbia, North Carolina. On July 4, 1929, he married the former Amphila Baker daughter of the late Samuel Augustus Baker & Katie Baker of Tyrrell, North Carolina.

The ladies of the Plymouth Parent-Teacher League gave a surprise banquet in honor of Professor and Mrs. Dean on June 8, 1929. Tables were spread to serve sixty. Just as Professor & Mrs. Dean entered the school building the lights were turned off and as they were being ushered in by Mr. Dallas Spruill, the lights were again turned on and everyone stood while the boys and girls gave the college yell in honor of Prof. Dean. A joint reception culminating the anniversary services of

Rev. George T. Rouson, pastor of Mount Sinai Baptist Church; Nebo Baptist Church, and First Baptist Church, all of Murfreesboro, North Carolina. Following the services at First Baptist, the members and friends of the three churches marched to the school auditorium for the joint reception. After a short march played by Mrs. Virginia Williams of Conway, Rev. Dallas Spruill and others spoke on his behalf.

Rev. Mr. Dallas Spruill taught school for several terms at the Stony Branch School in the Reynoldson District of Gates County. Mr. Spruill was a principal at the Travis Elementary school, Travis, North Carolina. In 1937 Mr. D. T. Spruill, the principal of the Mount Sinai School made remarks on behalf of the faculty for the funeral of Deacon I. J. Cooper. Five hours before his death, Deacon Cooper gave a warranty deed to the Mount Sinai Church. In additional to the ground for the church, he donated the property and gave the county the parcel of land on which the school was built.

Rev. Dallas Spruill accepted the pastorate of the Pleasant Grove Baptist Church, Belhaven, North Carolina during June 1968. He conducted the funeral of Mrs. Annie Sykes Eichelberrey on July 14, 1968 He preached at Mount Sinai Church, Como, N. C. for his brother-in-law, Rev. George Rowusen. During the week of October 30 through November 3, 1968, Rev. Dallas T. Spruill conducted services at the Salem Missionary Baptist Church for its 102nd church Anniversary. He was accompanied by his choir, usher and congregation. He was a president of the United Citizens of Tyrell County, North Carolina. He was a member and the president of the Plymouth Economic Improvement Association. He died June 1976.

The Deacon's Board

A. T. Ash

Deacon A. T. Ash was born on December 10, 1910 to Alberta Ash (the son of Robert & Sally Boone Ash) and Elnora Peele Ash, daughter of Thomas N., and Dolly Peele of Nansemond County, Virginia. He married Laura Eley (daughter of Peter Eley and Elizabeth "Lizzie B. G. Eure, daughter of Daniel & Mary Eley)" of Reynoldson Township of Gates, North Carolina. There were three children born to this union, namely: Vivian, Jacobi and Garland Ash. He married Marie Chalk (April-30, 1922-March-16-1983) of Nansemond County, Virginia. No children were born to this union. Deacon Ash served as a deacon of the church for many years.

William "Bill" Parker Boon

Deacon William "Bill" Parker Boone was born about 1890 in Gates County, North Carolina. He was the son of Joseph Boone (and the paternal grandson of Washington and Jerusha Boone) and Mary Howell Boone of Nansemond County, Virginia. He was the husband of Geneva Boon, daughter of John Jackson Boone, II, and Garfenia Boone of the Reynoldson Township. There were two sons born to this union: Anthony and Nathan Boone. Deacon Boon was an active deacon of the Stony Branch Missionary Baptist Church. He fully exercised the office of the deacon.

Wilson C. Boon

Deacon Wilson Columbus Boon was the son of John Jackson Boon (grandson of Abram Boon and Cherry Boyette), and Caroline Eure Boon, daughter of Jack Eure & Chloe Jenkins) residents of the Reynoldson Township of Gates County, North Carolina. He was born March 4, 1875. He married Ludie Armstrong (John Richard Armstrong) daughter of Jimmie Jernigan and Mary

Howell of Hertford County, North Carolina. Deacon Wilson & Ludie Virginia Boon were the progenitors of the following children: nine children: Dorothy M., Wilson W., Mollie, Clyde, Hillie, Mattie L., Cecil C., and Effie G. Boon. Deacon Boon remained faithful to the office of the deacon, although he was visually impaired. Deacon Wilson Columbus Boon died on October 16, 1933 at age 58 years, 7 months and 12 days.

Jiles Eure

Deacon Jiles Eure was the son of Cloe Matilda Eure, and the spouse of Lena Boone, daughter of John Jackson & Caroline Eure Boone of Gates, North Carolina.

Titus Eure

Deacon Titus Eure the son of Henderson & Lillie Channie Eure of Gates, North Carolina. He married the former Edith Bagley, the daughter of Robert Bagley and the former Essie Boone Bagley of Gates, North Carolina. Deacon Eure was appointed to the Deacon's Board under the leadership of Rev. Frank L. Lee.

John Amos Farrow

Deacon John Amos Farrow was the oldest child of Sam Farrow and Joanna Gatling. He was born June 1887 in Roduco, North Carolina. He and his siblings: Benjamin J., Fibbie, Carry, Lucy and Sam M. Farrow attended the one room house in Roduco, North Carolina. They were members of the Shepherd Grove Missionary Baptist Church, later known as First Baptist Roduco. John A. Farrow married Neice Charlotte Davis (born October 1890), on March 19, 1911. She was the daughter of Thomas "Tom" Davis (1865) and the former Anna Harriett Daughtery (1868), daughter of Anna Liza Parker in Gates, North Carolina. In 1900 Thomas and Chaney were living in the Reynoldson District of Gates County, North Carolina. Niece Davis's siblings were Mattie, Larcie and James Davis. Deacon John A. and Niece Davis Farrow were dutiful members of Stony Branch Baptist Church. Deacon Farrow was appointed to the Deacon's Board under the ministry of Rev. Henry A. Smith. Deacon John A. & Niece G. Farrow were the parents of thirteen children: John Edward, Nellie, Rosa, Bertel, Louise, Willie Esque (Tes), Thomas Earl, Willmetter, Ethel, Betty Jean and Ervin Gray and Walter Ray (Twins) Farrow.

Albert Lee Hinton

Deacon Albert Lee Hinton was born May 2, 1888 to son of Tobe Hinton of Gates County, North Carolina. He second marriage was to the former Mary Holland of Nansemond County, VA. There were no children born to this union. He received his heavenly crown for faithful service on February 27, 1981.

Linwood "Lin" Saunders

Deacon Linwood "Lin" Saunders was born October 1902 to David Saunders and Alice "Allie" Eure of the Reynoldson district of Gates County, North Carolina. He married Willye Parker, daughter of Jerry Parker and Martha Ann Boone of Gates, North Carolina. They were the parents of Cleddie May, Joseph DeBrough, McTroy, and Willie Edward Saunders. His second marriage on January 3, 1945 was to Lillar Vaughan, daughter of Robert Major Vaughan and Queen Eley of Gates, North Carolina. They were the parents of Charlie Linwood, Jr., Wendell, Melinda Jane, Queen, Jessie Frankie, Leslie Laverne, and Timothy Vann Saunders. He died on October 9, 1969.

James "Jim" Saunders

Deacon James "Jim" Saunders was born to David Saunders and Alice "Allie" Eure of the Reynoldson district of Gates County, North Carolina. He married Susie Sears and to this union five children were born, namely: James, Larry P., Carrie, Martha and Vanzola Saunders. Deacon Jim Saunders is remembered as a very devoted Christian. According to the oral history of Stony Branch, Jim Saunders was a "Praying Man." If the heavens were brass, and you could not get a prayer through, Jim Saunders was the man to call. The God of the Heaven's would respond to his call.

Harvey Gilbert Smith

Deacon Harvey Gilbert was the son of Gilbert Smith and Lizzette Wilson of Nansemond County, Virginia. He graduated from the Gates County North Carolina Education System. He married the former Lucy Lassiter, daughter of Abram Lassiter and Nettie Sears of Gates County. Deacon Smith & Mrs. Smith were the parents of Gerald and Darious Smith, and the spiritual adoptive parents of Linwood Boone. Deacon Smith was a lifelong member of the Stony Branch Missionary Baptist Church. He was added to the Board of deacon's during the pastorate of Rev. Frank L. Lee. Deacon Harvey Smith was the president of the Non-Denominational Sunday School Union of Nansemond County, Virginia and Gates County, North Carolina, and he served his God and His County by joining the Armed Forces. Deacon Smith was a dutiful member of the Deacon's and Laymen Union of the Roanoke Missionary Baptist Association. He was gainfully employed by the City of Suffolk Virginia Department of Highways. Deacon Harvey Gilbert Smith's sudden death was a surprise to all.

Robert Major Vaughan

Deacon Robert Major Vaughan was the son of Taylor Vaughan and Elmira Jenkins of Hertford County, N. C. He married Queen Eley, (daughter of Peter Eley and Elizabeth "Lizzie B. G. Eure, daughter of Daniel & Mary Eley)" of Ronaldson's Township of Gates, North Carolina on January 24, 1915. The Vaughan's were the parents of Lizzie Mae, Lilliar Maria, Rose Eley, Della, Mattie Gay, Ineva, and Ora Vaughan. Deacon Vaughan or "Papa" as he was called by his family faithfully served the parishioners of the Stony Branch Baptist Church for more than forty-years.

William "Henderson" Eure

Mr. William Henderson Eure was born 1862 to Mills Eure and Isabel Eure of the Reynoldson District of Gates County, North Carolina. He was the maternal grandson of Hasty Gatling of the Gatlington District of Gates County. In 1870 thirty-two year old Isabel Gatling is living in her home with her eight year old son Cader Gatling and her 80 year old mother. She is earning her living as a domestic servant. Ten years later, Henderson Eure has joined the family. Mr. Henderson Eure often represented the Stony Branch Church at official functions; conventions and during the Roanoke Missionary Baptist Associations. His name was closely associated with the early success of the church.

The Stony Branch Odd Fellows-1940's taken in front of the Odd Fellow Hall on the campus of Stony Branch (Thanks to James Ronell Gatling son of Luke Gatling) Left to right standing: Unknown, Jim Saunders, Charlie Linwood Saunders, Luke Gatling, Willie Samuel Morings, Unknown, Second row seated, Unknown, Risup Wilson, Unknown, Larry Saunders.

The Stony Branch Odd Fellow Hall as depicted in this 1940 era picture was one of three buildings that composed the Stony Branch Camp. The date that the Odd Fellow Hall was constructed on the site remains unattainable, as are the names of most of its members. The Stony Branch Grand United Order of the Odd Fellows was the only hall located in Gates County. The Grand United & Independent Order of Odd Fellows was the largest black fraternal organization in antebellum America. In its complex initiation rituals, initiates were told that 'Adam was the first member, and that the order was coevolved with the advent of man." The rituals effectively declared that all human descended from Adam and were "of one blood," which counteracted racist beliefs in polygenism.[458] Members were encouraged to develop business contract and leadership skills, and were involved in a variety of reforms. Wives and widows were honorary members and participated in celebrations. Many of these wives, widows and women were also members of the Independent Order of True Reformers[459] chapter 77 at Stony Branch.[460] However, the most important function of the Stony Branch Missionary Baptist Church Grand United Order of the Odd Fellows was to generate a feeling of black pride and comradeship.

The Stony Branch Odd Fellows did not attend the August 1921 Grand Lodge Meeting in Rock Mount, North Carolina. The attendance was smaller than it had been for the previous 3-4 years. Many other subordinate lodges were not represented. Communications from these lodges reveal that depleted treasuries, due to the low price of farm products and lack of employment for wage earners, were responsible to a large extent for their failure to send delegation. [461] The Stony Branch Odd Fellows were on the campus of the Waters Institute, Winton, North Carolina for the November 25, 1925 annual Thanksgiving service held in the school auditorium. They were also invited to participate in the 12: O' Clock Cornerstone lying. The ceremony was observed by the Grand United Order of Odd Fellows, directed by the Winton Lodge No. 2907. The lodges at Bertie, Hertford and Northampton Counties were also invited to take part in the ceremonies. The exercise was followed by a Thanksgiving dinner.[462]

Mrs. E. B. Boon

Mrs. Elnora Boon was born April 24, 1900 to the Mr. William A. Boon and the former Mrs. Edith Victoria Caroline Parker Boon of Gates, North Carolina. She was the maternal granddaughter of Mills Parker and Mary Ann Boone Parker and the maternal great granddaughter of Dempsey and Anzilla Boon of Gates, North Carolina. Mrs. Boon married Patrick Boon of Virginia. They were the parents of four children: James Obie, Lydia Marie, Clarine and Canzata Boone. She attended a one room school house located adjacent to her homestead. Mrs. Boon joined the Stony Branch Missionary Baptist Church in the Boon-town section of Gates County at an early age, and remained an active member of the Missionary Department for more than 90 years. She was frequently chosen to give recitations for woman's day, missionary day, church anniversary and pastoral anniversaries. Her recitation committed to memory from her childhood seldom had less than ten stanzas.

Until the 1940's the name Boone was typically spelled without the "e" "Boon. Mrs. Boon was very conscientious about the education of her children. Lydia Marie died at an early age. Her other children are all college graduates: James Obie Boone graduated from the historic Hampton Institute, Hampton, Virginia; Clarine Boone graduated from the Elizabeth City Teacher's College at Elizabeth City, North Carolina and Canzata Boone graduated from the historic Virginia State University, Petersburg, Virginia. These children also earned graduate degrees from historic black colleges and universities.

Mrs. Boon was a very active democratic all of her life. On voting days, Mrs. Boone and son James Obie would work the voting pools, and or serve as transportation for those who would not otherwise have a means of getting to the polls to cast their vote. Regrettably, Mrs. Boon did not live to see the historic election of the first black USA president, Barack Hussein Obama; she died at age 106 in 2006.

Rev. L. J. Parker

Reverend Lazarus "Lad" Junius Parker was born to the union of Jerry Parker, Sr., and the former Harriett Carolina Eure the Reynoldson District of Gates County, North Carolina. Harriett Caroline was the supposed white daughter of Dr. Green, of the Reynoldson District. Jerry's siblings were Clara Matilda Eure known by some as Clarrisy Myrtle and known to others as "Puss" Eure. Clara Matilda Eure was the sister of Caroline Eure, wife of John Jackson Boon, all of the Reynoldson, North Carolina. Jerry's other sibling Jiles Eure was a resident of the Reynoldson. Other siblings are still being identified.

It is evident by the religious involvement of Rev. Lad Parkers siblings, the Parker family were trained in Christian service by their parents. His siblings were meaningfully involved in Christian service. His oldest brother, Wiley W., was the head deacon at Saint Mark Missionary Baptist Church, Portsmouth, Virginia until his January 12, 1942 with more than 50 years of service in that position. His sister Ann Liza Parker Daughtery was one of the founding members of the Sheppherd Grove "Roduco First Baptist" Missionary Baptist Church, Roduco, North Carolina. Her name appears with much frequency as a supporter.

"Lad Parker's" paternal grandparents were Jack Eure and Chloe Jenkins Eure of Gates, North Carolina. Lad married the former Nancy Alice Butler, daughter of David Butler and Nancy Alice Rooks of Gates County. Lad Parker was the Assistant Pastor of the Shepherd Grove (First Baptist Roduco) Missionary Baptist Church, Roduco, North Carolina under the pastorate of Rev. Henry Augustus Smith, the husband of his wife's cousin. Lad and Alice Butler were the parents of Nancy Pearla Victoria Eugene, Lucille, Alice Bertha, Constancevilla, and Genie Lazarus Parker. Rev. Parker served the Stony Branch Baptist Church in the capacity of Sunday School Superintendent, Church clerk, and delegate to the Roanoke Missionary Baptist Association.

Lad and his daughters formed the Parker Singers to accompany his during his preaching opportunities. The Parker Singers were one of the earliest quartets in Gates County or in any of the surrounding counties. A few of their favorite selects were; *Beautiful Isle of Somewhere, Fade, Fade Each Earthly Joy, Tell The Angels, When They Ring Those Golden Bells,* and *Life Is Like A Mountain Railroad,* sang by Alice Bertha.[472] Rev. L. J. Parker of Gates was the delegate to the Roanoke Missionary Baptist Association, and the clerk of the church. Rev. Lazarus Junious Parker was the delegate to the Association and W. M. Gatling of Gates, was the church clerk.[473]

Union Chapel Missionary Baptist Church

The Afro American Missionary Baptist Church of the Weeksville District of Pasquotank County, North Carolina was started in 1848,[474] although the land remained in the hands of Matthew J. Reid and wife Minnie A. Reid, and G. G. Markham and wife, Bessie L. Narkham until 1919, at which time the parties of the second part: A. W. Sharp, James E. Boon, Tim Bowe as Trustees of Union Chapel Baptist Church colored, paid the sum of Seventy-five dollars to the first part for the tract of land.[475] Worship Services were held on the 3rd Sunday of each month from 1848-1950's. The original wooden structure was located on the old highway Number 34.

The parents of John Shannon (1840-1933) and the parents of Margie Boone Shannon (1843-1933) were members of the first founding families of the first church. It is recorded in the *Union Chapel's History Book, Our People: Yesterday, Today & Tomorrow,* Union Chapel Baptist Church that John and Margie Boone Shannon were founders. They were perhaps founders of the second church. This is based upon the fact that the Union Chapel was founded when John was eight years old, and Margie was five years old. *The Norfolk Journal and Guide* reported in its January 4, 1947 Elizabeth City Edition that Mrs. Susie Overton (94), (daughter of Alfred & Edith Morris) funeral was held at Union Chapel Baptist Church with Rev. W. J. Moore, pastor, and the Rev. C. L. Griffin officiating. As a pioneer member of Union Chapel Mrs. Overton was active until the infirmities of old age slowed her up.[476] Mrs. Susie Overton was born about 1852. In 1864 when John was eight years old, and Margie was five years old and Susie was nine years old the church moved to its second home at 111 Union Chapel Road, and changed its name to Union Chapel Missionary Baptist Church. In 1905 this structure was torn down; and unnamed members of the church and community donated the land behind the old church to be used as a church cemetery. It was replaced and dedicated on the 3rd Sunday in March 1906,[477] and wired for electricity during October 1928.[478]

The Union Chapel Missionary Baptist Church is the oldest existing church within the Roanoke Missionary Baptist Association. The Mother Church, Haven Creek Missionary Baptist Church, Manteo, North Carolina is the second oldest existing church within the boundaries of the Association. The now abandoned church of Harriett Jacob's in Edenton, North Carolina, known as the Providence Baptist Church, Edenton, North Carolina built in 1820.

In 1884 Mr. J. J. Johnson was the delegate from the Union Chapel Church to the Nineteenth Annual Session of the Roanoke Missionary Baptist Association. He reported that Union Chapel had a sustained membership of 206 members, 76 males and 130 females. During this reporting period the church received 11 members by baptism; lost 2 by death; restored 13 members back into membership; and dismissed 2 letters.[479] Union Chapel hosted the 1902 Annual Session of the Roanoke Missionary Baptist Association with Rev. B. W. Dance preaching the Introductory the sermon.[480] P. C. Nixon was the delegate to the 1903 Annual session. Martin Lamb of Weeksville, N. C. was the clerk of the church, and Reverend Andrew Moore was the pastor.[481] The Union Chapel Choir sang at the Antioch Missionary Baptist Church, Jarvisburg, North Carolina on the 4th Sunday in February 1917 for the Installation Service of Reverend Butler M. Mullen.[482] Rev. R. C. Lamb was called to the pastorate of the Union Chapel Church in June 1921. He began to hold services immediately.[483, 484]He was installed as pastor of Union Chapel Baptist Church on Sunday, October 15, 1921. The Installation Sermon was preached by Rev. P. P. Eaton, pastor of Cornerstone Missionary Baptist Church, Elizabeth City, North Carolina. Music was the Saint Stephen church choir.[485] Rev. A. G. Tillery conducted a revival meeting at Union Chapel during the last week of August 1927. There were sixteen baptized Sunday at Greenleaf Landing, after which the pastor Rev. U. G. Privott preached on the subject *Follow Jesus.*[486] Rev. T. A. White and the New Sawyer's Creek Missionary Baptist Church congregation motored to Weeksville on the third Sunday in June 1933 and worshipped with the Union Chapel Church of which Rev. W. J. Moore was the pastor.[487] Immediately following the morning worship service, the Reverend Waitman Moore was installed as pastor of Union Chapel on the Third Sunday in June 1933. The Installation Sermon was preached by Rev. T. A. White, pastor of New Sawyers Creek Baptist Church, Bellcross, N. C. He was accompanied by his choir which rendered music for the service. Collects during the three nights of service was over seventy dollars.[488]

The Woman's Missionary Union sponsored a program at Union Chapel on the first Sunday in September 1933.[489] Rev. A. W. Lamb and congregation worshipped with the Union Chapel on October 14, 1933 at 3: 00 P. M.[490] The Sisters Union of Union Chapel rendered a program at Union Chapel for the benefit of the Union on the third Sunday in September 1934.[491] The Woman Educational Mission Union had a baby contest September 28, 1934 for the benefit of the annual union which met October 5th at Union Chapel. A brief program was given before the awarding of the prizes. The first prize went to Frederick White, son of Mr. and Mrs. Edward White. E. A. Covington was winner of the second prize. He was the son of Mr. and Mrs. Murry Covington. Little Arthur Britton, son of Mr. and Mrs. Shock Britton won third prize. Mrs. Beatrice Brite McRay, president, was the mistress of ceremonies.[492] The Sunday school at Union Chapel completed the interior painting during October 1934.[493] The following day, the Reverend D. W. Lamb, pastor of St. John Baptist Church, and 150 members including his choir worshipped at Union Branch on October 14, 1934. An offering of $62.00 was lifted.[494] Rev. B. C. Ellis preached for the Juniors of Union Chapel on the 4th Sunday in June 1939. He used for his subject, *The Marriage of Tomorrow.*" He was accompanied by the choir from Ellis Temple Missionary Baptist Church.[495] On the first Sunday in July 1939 Rev. E. R. Cooper and his choir, deacons, ushers and members of the Union Chapel Church rendered service to a packed house at the Galatia Missionary Baptist Church at Durant's Neck, North Carolina for the benefit of the Usher Board. There were about 13 car loads from Union Branch. At 7:30 P. M., Rev. Cooper with his choir and congregation were back at Union Branch for the evening service. The collection was a good one.[496] Rev. Moore preached at Union Chapel on the second Sunday in June 1945 from the subject: {*The Necessity of Light,*: based on the text: "He was a burning and shinning light," Later in the afternoon, Rev. Moore preached the Installation Sermon and performed the ceremony installing the Rev. J. T. Johnson as pastor of Palmyra and Ramoth Gilead churches, two separate churches, and on different Sundays. Union Chapel choir, under the direction of Mss. Edith Mackey furnished music for the occasion. Deacon J. T. White gave the welcome address at Ramoth Gilead. At this church, Rev. Johnson has made extensive additions to the church. Rev. Johnson was also a business-man, having connections in Elizabeth City where he had an excellent reputation.[497] The youth choir of Olive Branch Church and the junior choir of Union Chapel Baptist Church gave a concert March 6, 1949 at Union Chapel Baptist Church, The youth choir made the trip in buses and was accompanied by a group of members of Olive Branch Church, Miss S. E. Mackey was the organist and director of both chairs.[498] A successful revival was conducted by the Rev. D. W. Lamb, pastor of Tyne Street Baptist Church, Suffolk, Va. During the revival, the Rev. Lamb preached from the following subjects: *"The Value in Going to the Prayer Ground:" "Women at the well," What Will Happen When the Revival Comes," The People Ate Too Many:" The Value and The Power of God:" "When Was Jesus at His Best,"* and: *How Death Drops Out of the Sight."* The pastor, Rev. W. J. Moore, baptized and also preached.[499] Rev. Raymond Griffin and congregation of Oak Grove Baptist Church at Backwater, Va., was the guest of Rev. W. J. Moore and the Pastor's Aid of Union Chapel during the week of December 11-16, 1950.[500] The August 1952 revival meeting at the Union Chapel ended on a successful note, and the Rev. D. W. Lamb, the young pastor of the historic Tyne Street Baptist Church of Suffolk, Virginia filled the Union Chapel pulpit the next Sunday. Rev. W. A. Moore was unable to be present.[501]

On the 3rd Sunday in October 1932 The Sister's Union of Union Chapel rendered a musical at the Whiteville A. M. E. Church. The play was titled, "The Holy City." The Sister's were well received by the large and appreciative audience.[502] The Silver Crest Singers sang at Union Branch on the 4th Sunday in October 1932 at 3:00 P. M. Mrs. M. V. Overton, president, and James Norman, president. The following Friday and Saturday, October 28-29, 1932, Union Chapel hosted the Union Meeting.[503] The Royal Light Quartet of Norfolk, Virginia presented a special service for the benefit of Union Chapel. The program was held on the first Sunday in July 1933. The service was sponsored by I. L. Shannon, secretary and T. R. Lamb.[504] Rev. Moore preached from the subject, *"A Man's Place"* at 11 A. M. Sunday. At 3 P. M., the ushers from Union Chapel, Mount Zion, A. M. E. Z. and Pitts Chapel Churches were present. Rev. Moore sang an impressive solo, "Time." The revival services began on the second Sunday in August 1933.[505] The Annual Protracted Revival Services began at Union Chapel this Sunday. Services were held in the afternoon and evenings. The pastor Rev. Waitman Moore was assisted by Rev. W. H. Smith of Norfolk, Va. Mr. John Hyter, his brother Roosevelt, and wife of New York, were spending a few days with their father, Rev. Matthew Hyter of Weeksville, and attending the revival at Union Chapel.[506] The Volunteer Singers of Christ of St. Galilee Disciple Church rendered a musical program at Union Chapel Baptist Church to a capacity house on August 13, 1939.[507] The Galilee Gospel Singers rendered a program at Union Chapel Baptist Church. Annie Freshwater, a member of Union Chapel Choir, was sick during January 1941.[508] The Choir Union held its regular meeting at Union Chapel. A brief program was conducted with the following choirs taking part: Miss Marjorie Bryant, Mrs. Ruth Leggings, Mrs. Shirley Hardy, president was mistress of ceremonies. The participating choirs were: Union Chapel and the Missionary Choir of Cornerstone Baptist Church; Choir No.2, of Mount Lebanon A. M. E. Zion Church, Holy Trinity Methodist Church Choir, and the Treble Clef Choral Club participated.[509] The Pasquotank

County Choir Union celebrated its second anniversary on February 29, 1944 at Cornerstone Baptist Church. The Union Chapel Choir participated. A reception was held in the church dining room after the program. Mrs. S. S. Hardy, President.[510] Rev. S. L. Britton preached for the Men's Union at Union Chapel.[511] The Peerless Four sang at Union Chapel on Sunday evening, August 4, 1946 for the benefit of the Pastor's Aid Club. Mrs. Mattie Taylor was president of the club.[512]

Deacon Henry Shield a well known citizen and church member died at his home Saturday, December 1, 1928, after being sick for seven years. He was eighty one years old and had been a member of Union Chapel for 55 years, serving on the Deacon's Board since 1912. At his funeral Mr. Delay White spoke on his life as a deacon while Mr. W. M. Britton spoke of him as a lodge member. Rev. Joseph Godfrey spoke of him as a church member. The funeral was conducted by Rev. J. H. Johnson who chose for a text: Job 14:4; subject: *"A Great Change."* A solo was sung by Mrs. Mary F Mullen Boon and another by S. S. Price.[513] Rev. Moore conducted the funeral of Mrs. Maggie Boone Shannon one of the founders of the Union Chapel Missionary Baptist Church died on June 23, 1933. She was 76 years, and three months. Mrs. Shannon died at the home of her daughter, Mrs. Addie Lamb of 13 Dawson Street, where she had lived almost two years and seven months of her illness. Mrs. Shannon was survived by five sons, two daughters, three brothers, 18 grandchildren, and six great-grand children. Mrs. Shannon's was preceded in death five weeks ago by her husband John Shannon.[514] [515] Her siblings Luke Boone, & Laura B. Wilson, of Norfolk, Virginia; Margie B. Jones of Gregory, N. C., and Mary B. Jones, New York City.[516] Deacon S. S. Price died February 28, 1935 at Weeksville. He was a chorister of Union Chapel. His remains were interred in the Union Chapel Cemetery.[517] Funeral services for Willie M. C. Lamb were held from Union Chapel with the Rev. W. H. Moore, pastor officiating. Solos were rendered by Mrs. Davis and Margaret Overton Hill. The deceased was survived by his parents, Rev. & Mrs. Martin Lamb, four brothers, one sister and his grandparents, Mr. & Mrs. Zachariah Bowe.[518]

Funeral services for Mrs. Overton was conducted a Union Chapel Baptist Church. She kept in close contact with the work of the church and gave the best aid she could. Mrs. Overton was survived by one daughter, Mrs. Emma Jane Britton; one brother, Thomas Newby Overton; 10 grandchildren; 10 great grand children and one great-great-grand child.[519] Funeral Services were held for Mrs. Julia Pools from the Union Chapel Church on January 8, 1950 with the pastor Rev. W. J. Moore officiating. Mrs. Poole died on January 5. She had been a member of the church for more than 30 years. Mrs. Poole was survived by her 90 year old father, Ben Skinner; one daughter, Mrs. Alpine Brooks, four sons, Vernard, Henry, Charles Brown, and Fred Skinner, one brother Johnny Skinner, four sisters, Mrs. Emma Riddick, Mrs. Addie Seaile, Mrs. Aaggie Skinner and Mrs. Clara Skinner.[520]

The "devil" got into William Eason on June 19, 1952, according to his own account, and because of it James Shannon, of Weeksville, died. Police reported that Eason and Shannon were working side by side in a lumber mill owned by Arthur Turner. Suddenly, according to the mill owner, Eason turned to Shannon struck him in the head with a piece of lumber, and Shannon's body was dragged toward the circular saw which was in operation. Turner said he rushed to the saw and turned off the power to keep the workman from being sawed in half. There was no quarrel between the men that he could see. Turner told the police, and no words were exchanged before Shannon was struck, he said. Eason, when questioned by the police, allegedly told them he struck Shannon because "the devil told me to hit him." He gave no explanation, according to Sheriff W. L. Thompson. Shannon was examined by a physician and sent home from work. He later developed convulsions and was taken to the Albemarle hospital where he died. Eason, who had been held in the local county jail on charges of assault, was charged with murder following Shannon's death. Mr. Shannon was married to Georgiana Shannon (see picture below). They had two children. Funeral services were held at Union Chapel.[521]

Mr. Butler Sharp and Miss. A. Patterson marriage ceremony was held at Currituck on Thursday afternoon, August 10, 1933. Mr. Sharp has been a deacon of Union Chapel Baptist Church for several years.[522] Mrs. C. V. Boone was given a surprise appreciation service by members of the Union Chapel Church. Mrs. Boone was the oldest member in point of the service of the church's choir. She began to sing for the church at age 12 and continued to retain her fine alto voice. The pastor of Union Chapel, Rev. Moore made the principal address of honor. T. L. Lamb made complimentary remarks referring to Mrs. Boone's unique service record. The senior choir, pastor and members gave the honoree many gifts including an arm chair. Solos were sung by Mrs. Thelma Overton. Among those participating in the services other than those mentioned were Mrs. Minnie Johnson, Mrs. Beulah Williams, Mrs. Mattie Taylor, Mrs. Elizabeth S. Sharp, Mrs. Georgia Shannon, Carre Johnson, Jr., James Shannon, Marion Moses, Willie Mack Johnson, John Henry Williams and Mrs. Bessie Godfrey.[523]

Mr. I. F. Shannon operated the Union School although he had been critically ill with pneumonia.[524] Miss Odessa Owens Holly who was teaching at the Weeksville School returned to Columbia, N. C., for the summer.[525] The 1932-1933 Union Chapel School faculty was composed of A. C. Hill principal, Miss Annie Mourning, 4th and 5th grades; Mrs. Ruth Doxie, 3rd and 4th grades; Miss Mary Grimes of Roper, N. C., and Miss Mary Newby of Whiteville, 1st grade and music.[526] Union Chapel School had two successful Parent-Teacher meetings. Dean S. D. Williams of State Normal School was the mass speaker at the first and Superintendent M. P. Jennings spoke at the second meeting. Both addresses were helpful and interesting.

The Parent Teacher's Association of Union Chapel met last Thursday with a large attendance. On Sunday the teachers and the pupils of the school gave a program. Mrs. Lovey sang a solo; Mrs. A. Mourning recited, and Principal Hill delivered an address. Mss Newby presided at the piano. Mss Mary Grimes was mistress of ceremonies. The first regular session of the parent-teacher Association of the Union Chapel School was held Sunday afternoon, September 10, 1933. After the formal opening the following officers were elected for the tern 1933-1934: president, P. W. Woodhouse; vice-president, S. L. Britton; Secretary, Miss A. L. Mourning; assistant secretary, Mrs. Mattie Taylor, and treasurer, Mrs. C. A. Cabarrus. A committee on programs and refreshments was also named with Messrs. Napoleon Gibson and I. F. Shannon as chairman, respectively. The association was largely attended and each member pledges his hearty support. The 1933-1934 faculty of Union Chapel School was composed of the following teachers: principal and seventh grade, Professor A. C. Hill; fifth and sixth grades, Mrs. Annie Mourning; third and fourth grades, Mss Lennie Lumsden; second grade, Miss Vida Harvey; and first grade, Miss Lucille Woodhouse.

The public school began its session for the 1933-1934 Monday, September 11, 1933.[527] Miss Maude Randall of Norfolk, Virginia spent the past weekend in Weeksville visiting friends. She was a former teacher at the Union Chapel School, but became a faculty member of the Edenton High School.[528] Miss Jessie Welch, a teacher at Union Chapel School and Rev. W. Preston Jones of Princess Ann County, Virginia solemnized their wedding on June 28, 1944 at 8:30 P. M. O'clock at Cornerstone Baptist Church, Elizabeth City.[529]

The Union Chapel School was favored by the Little Jack Health show from the State Health Department at Raleigh given by Miss Ceely and Miss. Ferguson. Also witnessing the show were M. P. Jennings, county superintendent and Miss Stanton, county nurse. Negro History Week was observed Friday morning, Feb. 15, 1946 in the chapel with a program consisting of reports on outstanding men and women given by the 6th, 7th, and 8th grades, Mrs. J. E. Armstrong, teacher.[530] The District PTA was entertained by the parents and teachers of Union Chapel School. The speaker for the occasion was Rev. E. A. Anderson, principal of the P. W. Moore High School. Following the address a turkey dinner was served.[531] The Union Branch Missionary Baptist Church brought the Union Branch School from Pasquotank County North Carolina in 1951 for $1, 200.00.[532]

Mrs. Martha J. Price of Weeksville, North Carolina wrote into the Norfolk Journal and Guide and stated: "I have been reading your paper one year, November (1928) past. I really enjoy reading it. I feel that it is one of the best papers in the country. I believe it gives real news, the best I ever read. I enjoy reading it every week."[533]

The following men have served as pastors of the Union Chapel Missionary Baptist Church: Rev. Eli Mullen, Rev. Joshua A. Faulk, Rev. Zion H. Berry, Rev. C. M. Billups Rev. W. M. Overton, Rev. S. P. Knight, Rev. Lafayette F. Sharp, Rev. Roland C. Lamb, Rev. A. D. Moore Rev. A. B. Askew, Rev. U C. Privott, Rev. E. R. Cooper, Rev. W. J. Moore, Rev. J. E. Barnes and Rev. Charles Sizemore (1987-2010). Union Chapel licensed the following men and woman to preach the Gospel: Llewellyn Billups, Charles Claude, Proctor Freeman, Alexander Green, Joseph Godfrey, A. W. Lamb, D. W. Lamb, Butler Mullen, Kenneth Price, Butler Sharp, Sr. Butler Sharp, Jr. and Willie Olivia Boone-Grey.

The Union Chapel Missionary Baptist Church was totally destroyed by fire on Friday, March 23, 2004. The fire was an accidental blaze, possibly caused by lightning.

Just A Little While

Soon this life will all be over, and our pilgrimage will end.
Soon we'll take our heav'nly journey,
Be at home again with friends
Heaven's gates are standing open
Waiting for our entrance there
Some sweet day we're going over
All the beauties there to share.

Soon we'll see the light of morning then the new day will begin
Soon we'll hear the Father calling,
"Come my children, enter in."
Then we'll hear a choir of angels
Singing out the vict'ry song,
All our troubles will be ended
And we'll live with heaven's throng

Soon we'll meet again our loved ones
And we'll take them by the hand,
Soon we'll press them to our bosom
Over in the promised land;
Then we'll be at home forever,
Thru-out all eternity,
What a blessed, blessed morning
That eternal morn shall be.

Just a Little while to stay here
Just a little while to wait
Just a little while to labor
In the path that's always straight
Just a little more of trouble
In this low and sinful state
Then we'll enter Heaven's portals,
Sweeping thru the pearly gates.

13

THE WEST ROANOKE MISSIONARY
BAPTIST ASSOCIATION

The West Roanoke was born out of the Roanoke Missionary Baptist Association. Its birth arises from the May 3, 1885 motion made by the Association Clerk, T. M. Collins to grant letters of dismissal to the thirty-seven churches listed at the end of this chapter, and to any church petitioning the Association in gospel order. The Reverend William Reid of Murfreesboro, North Carolina was elected as the first Moderator, and one of his first official responsibilities was to agree that all churches which had been legally dismissed from the Roanoke Association should be entitled to seats with this body. Therefore, it can be safely extrapolated that some of the churches which had previously been a part of the Roanoke Missionary Baptist Association had not followed established protocol and received letters of dismissal prior to or shortly after having been dismissed from the Roanoke Association. Hence, Reverend Reid's admonition, "That all churches that can satisfy this body that they have been properly dismissed from Roanoke may be seated in the body." After having settled that matter, it was determined that the first association of the Western Roanoke Association which encompassed the counties of Hertford and Bertie and a part of Northampton, would be held at Zion Grove Church in Hertford County, North Carolina during the week of May 1866. Names of other officers for the First and second annual meeting were lost to the writer, however, the Constitution, and Order of Business and the listings of the early ordained and licensed ministers have survived.

When the Western Roanoke Missionary Baptist Association met in its third annual session on Tuesday, October 9, 1888 with the Swamp Chapel, Northampton County the following officers were selected Vice-Moderator, Rev. A. Cooper of Lewiston, Recording Secretary, J. B. Catus, of Winton, Corresponding Secretary, W. H. Leath, of Windsor and Treasurer, J. J. Biggs, of Roxabel, North Carolina. The Reverends Luke Pierce and G. E. Freeman conducted the Devotional service. Rev. J. W. Ricks delivered an impressive welcome address; the moderator responded. The Introductory sermon was deferred until the afternoon. The pastor and deacons served as the committee on arrangements. He committee of arrangements reported as follows—Time of Opening 9 o' clock A. M.; Close at 4. P.M.; Second Day, preaching in the grove at 11:00 A. M., Reverend Luke Pierce, Reverend W. A. Cobb, and Alternate. Preaching in the grove at 2:00 P. M. Reverend T. H. Wilson, Rev. C. J. White, alternate, and intermission for one hour and a half.

Rev. C. S. Sessions, the Western Roanoke Association State Missionary reported to the Third Annual Session of the West Roanoke Association that he had visited thirty-six churches in the bounds of the Association. Additionally, Sessions stated that: he had endeavored to discharge his duties as a local missionary, though he could not exactly ascertain from the Executive Board what the missionary duties were. Sessions continued, "I merely presumed what my duties were and went to work." He continued, "I am pleased to say our churches are making some progress. Most of them have good Sabbath schools though some fail to have books and papers which they need. Many of the pastors have organized a Foreign Mission Society in their churches. I had the pleasure to assist in organizing one at Sandy branch. The pastor and the deacons seem alive to the cause. Many of the pastors are endeavoring to erect comfortable houses of worship. Most of the houses are very deficient. We have about only four finished churches in the bounds of the Association. I need not name them, as I am aware that the brethren know which they are. I earnestly recommend to the churches to try to secure comfortable houses of worship. I did not always fins things as pleasant as I wish them in visiting the various churches. I was compelled sometimes to make more sacrifices that I desired to make. I have more than once preached in the morning and afternoon without eating anything. I have visited nearly all the pastors' churches in the Association and am sorry to say only one pastor made any preparation for me to get anything to ear or lodging. I have visited 39 churches, preached 32 sermons, delivered 8 lectures, received a total of $37.00 for Foreign Missions, $1.29 for Home missions, $26.31 in the general collection and received $$29.69 for expenses.

The member churches of the newly formed Western Roanoke Association felt as did her parents; the Roanoke Missionary Baptist Association that she should have her own school, thus, the Water's Normal School came into being. Not being satisfied with only one school, the brethren from Bertie felt that the school at Winton in Hertford was too far away for them to enjoy its benefits, and hence they established in the county, and at Windsor, the Bertie Academy. The Northampton people, with a school of high grade at Rich Square, felt that their pro rata should come to them for the support of their school, and this caused the West Roanoke Association to divide its annual contributions with the three schools. The West Roanoke Association raised the largest amount of money raised by any association in the State: as much as twenty-five hundred dollars in an annual sitting.

1888
West Roanoke Missionary Baptist Association
Churches/Pastors/Ministers

Ashland Baptist	Bertie County
1st Colored Murfreesboro	Hertford County
1st Colored Windsor	Bertie County
Chestnut Grove Baptist	Halifax County
Chapel Hill Baptist	Martin County
Conconconary Baptist	Bertie County
Elm Grove Baptist	Bertie County
Hayslett Grove Baptist	Hertford County

Harrellsville Chapel Baptist	Hertford County
Jerusalem Baptist	Northampton County
Jordan Grove Baptist	Hertford County
Mill Neck Baptist	Hertford County
Mount Moriah Baptist	Hertford County
Mount Carmel Baptist	Hertford County
Mount Zion Baptist	Bertie County
Mount Olive Baptist	Bertie County
Mount Pleasant Baptist	Hertford County
New Bethany	Hertford County
New Haven	Hertford County
Nebo Chapel	Hertford County
New Ahoskie	Hertford County
Philippi	Hertford County
Piney Wood Chapel	Hertford County
Pleasant Plains	Hertford County
Popular Point	Martin County
Saint Luke	Bertie County
Saint Mark	Martin County
Saint Simon	Bertie County
Sandy Branch	Bertie County
Solomon Chapel	Bertie County
Spring Hill	Bertie County
Swamp Chapel	Northampton County
Sycamore Chapel	Martin County
Wynns Grove	Bertie County
Weeping Mary	Bertie County
Zion Hill	Bertie County
Zoar	Northampton County

Pastor's Roster	Location
Rev. Calvin Scott Brown	Winton, N. C.
Rev. George Brown	Lewiston, N. C.
Rev. G. W. Brown	Sansouci, N. C.
Rev. A. Cooper	Windsor, N. C.
Rev. Benjamin Clark	Lewiston, N. C.
Rev. T. M. Collins	Winton, N. C.
Rev. H. Clements	Branchville, VA.
Rev. George Freeman	Harrellsville, N. C.
Rev. J. M. Garris	Lewiston, N. C.

Rev. P. Hare	Winton, N. C.
Rev. T. Holly	Mount Gould, N. C.
Rev. B. Mitchell	Windsor, N. C.
Rev. W. H. Morris	Powellsville, N. C.
Rev. Luke Pierce	Windsor, N. C.
Rev. H. Outlaw	Avoca, N. C.
Rev. Andrew Parker	Potecasi, N. C.
Rev. Emanuel Reynolds	Colerain, N. C.
Rev. William Reid	Murfreesboro, N. C.
Rev. C. S. Sessoms	St. John, N. C.
Rev. Thaddeus H. Wilson	Avoca, N. C.
Rev. C. J. White	Windsor, N. C.
Rev. W. A. Cobb	Harrellsville, N. C.
Rev. W. P. Sharp	Harrellsville, N. C.
Rev. Jackson Mitchell	Powellsville, N. C.
Rev. Andrew Hill	Lotta, N. C.
Rev. J. J. Thompson	Lewiston, N. C.

1888 Licensed Ministers

Rev. Rubin Allen	Windsor, N. C.
Rev. A. J. Askew	Winton, N. C.
Rev. H. R. Baker	Windsor, N. C.
Rev. G. Brown	Lewiston, N. C.
Rev. Robert Rush	Roxabel, N. C.
Rev. Byrum Britt	
Rev. John Bond	
Rev. A. J. Cherry	Windsor, N. C.
Rev. H. Cherry	Windsor, N. C.
Rev. H. Epps, Sr.	Lewiston, N. C.
Rev. I. Harding	Rich Square, N. C.
Rev. J. B. Hoggard	Windsor, N. C.
Rev. Charles Harrell	Roxabel, N. C.
Rev. I. Jacobs	Rich Square, N. C.
Rev. M. D. Jacobs	Rich Square, N. C.
Rev. J. M. Jenkins,	Winton, N. C.
Rev. J. Lowe	Avoca, N. C.
Rev. J. Mitchell	Powellsville, N. C.
Rev. D. Moore	Colerain, N. C.
Rev. W. Manley	Bethlehem, N. C.
Rev. F. Powell	Lewiston, N. C.

Rev. William Rascoe	Scotland Neck. N. C.
Rev. R. Smallwood	Windsor, N. C.
Rev. D. W. Steward	Windsor, N. C.
Rev. J. Thompson	Lewiston, N. C.
Rev. J. Vaughan	Lewiston, N. C.
Rev. J. Ward	Windsor, N. C.

"IN TRIBUTE"

Mr. Henry Stewart

Mr. Henry Stewart "known as Father" was born in Bayboro, North Carolina but lived in Norfolk, Virginia since 1868. He was the oldest *Journal and Guide* agent in point of years until he was forced to give up the agency in 1928. He would have been 77 on May 15, 1929. He reckoned his age from the fact that he was three years old when the "big snow fell," in February 1855, he used to say, and also by the fact that he first voted for General Grant as President and had to be 21 years of age to cast his vote.

Mr. Stewart is shown in the picture in his Odd Fellows regalia. He proudly strutted the Odd Fellows insignia. Funeral services for Mr. Stewart were held from Mount Zion Baptist Church. Condolences were read from the following organizations of which he was a member: Children of Israel, Odd Fellows, Missionary Circle, and the Mount Zion Church. An effective solo "Face to Face," was rendered by Mrs. Bessie Jenkins. The sermon was delivered by the pastor Rev. Askew, assisted by the following local ministers: Rev. J. C. Diamond, H. E. Drew, J. E. Rogers, and others. Interment was in Mount Olive Cemetery.

CONCLUSION

The men and women contain in this book were the apostles of liberty, freedom and human development. They possessed qualities of mind and heart that would have made them marked men and women in any country, and would have brought them fame in any career which they may have selected. As a historic fact, charting the progress of the Roanoke Missionary Baptist Association and its Founders, these remarkable men were produced in groups often from the same county or the same city, during the same era. In some regards it may be stated that these founders, pastors, ministers, men and missionaries are no except to the historic rule. These sainted men were from the length and breadth of North Carolina, and Virginia, and from others states within the Union received the sympathies and aid of many Negroes, Afro-Americans, Coloreds and African America, co-laborers and many noble spirits not of his people. It is an honor to present these distinguished men and women, whose fame as orators and earnest and effective workers in the Women Missionary and Education Union in the cause of human liberty has not been confined to one continent, but through the efforts of the Home and Foreign Missions made the Roanoke Missionary Baptist Association known throughout the civilized world. They have at last been brought back into the bright sunshine of 2011.

The Economist, published in 1898, at Elizabeth, N. C., edited by a half educated white man displayed strong views on the Roanoke Missionary Baptist Association and its people. He demonstrated occasional spasm whenever a Negro was appointed or elected to a lucrative office in that state. During March 1893 its editor was recovering from a fit of hysteria over the appointment of Mr. Edward Johnson, a Negro, as assistant district attorney to C. M. Bernard in the first district. "So it goes," stated this editor, "climbing, climbing Negroes, climbing in North Carolina. They are approaching the ermine. A Negro official attorney, and soon a Negro presiding in our courts of justice would have aroused a sentiment of indignation thirty years ago that would have pulled the pillars of the judicial temple. What is to be the out-come? What will thirty years more show? Is not the Negro classed with the mule? Both are necessary to the industrial future of the South. The Negro thinks of liquor not politics. Is this not a white man's government?"

The Founding Fathers of the Roanoke Missionary Baptist Association refuted the views of the Economist and its editor that the Negro was classed with the mule; was necessary to the industrial future of the South; and does not thinks of politics, only liquor. They reacted in part by donning their long dusters and black beaver hats and satchels containing a Bible, a hymn book, and traveling the long winding roads and muddy streams preaching the Gospel to men who had been robbed by slavery of himself and made the property of another. What does it matter that the Founding Fathers lived with the ultimate reality that they were Black and attempted to build their own beloved Black community. What is the meaning of all of this? All of this means that a resurrection was occurring because Free People of Color; and former enslaved Black men were receiving a new vision of themselves. A new vision that their suffering and their humanity and their joy served some great though hidden purpose?

Listen to the screams and groans of the slaves, the sharecroppers, the martyrs and the victims. They did not bleed and did not die in vain during the 73,000 nights of slavery! Listen! What do these things mean? The meaning is History. The history of the North Carolina black man is among other things, the history of a quest for meaning as clearly seen in the lives of the Founders of the Roanoke Missionary Baptist Association. The lives of the Founding Fathers demonstrated that they were aware that the beloved black community could do nothing until Blacks developed themselves; they could do nothing for humanity. They could do nothing until there was a resurrection. Founding Fathers Boon, Flemings, Hayes, Hodges, Johnson, and Reynolds, daily lived and preached as if they were about to live new life, a resurrection life, a life of knowing themselves and others. If one follows this invaluable line of thought, it is evident that the Roanoke Missionary Baptist Association had within it the possibility of setting the members of the Roanoke Missionary Baptist Association member in an entire new light-the light of their creator. They were called upon to see themselves as they were meant to be. This glorification of the 73,000 nights of slavery and the reality that they were Black and attempted to build their own beloved Black community had the potential of setting them at peace with themselves and with the God of the universe; they no longer needed to curse God and die. For their blackness is now-like the rest of their createdness, a sign of His Love and not His anger.

After the Civil War the Founding Fathers freely participated in editing, teaching, and agitating for the rights of their members. They endured their afflictions as men without murmur or complaint and, despite their disadvantages of ignorance and poverty; they have left names worthy of our cherished recollections. Some of the Founding Fathers went into politics. Not because they desired to abandon the pulpit; but, being more intelligent than most Blacks who had no opportunity for education, they were called upon to participate in public matters. A list of those who participated must include the founder, L. W. Boone, J. A. Flemings, Charles E. Hodges, Willis A. Hodges, Caesar Johnson, and Abram Mebane. Many Baptists within the hollow and sacred walls of the Roanoke Missionary Baptist Association were never acquainted with the knowledge that the Founders Fathers of the Roanoke Missionary Baptist Association from the tobacco fields, the rice swamps, the cotton and sugar plantations and the pecan groves in northeastern North Carolina, for almost a century sent up one long agonizing cry for help. They stood on their toes to catch the northern breeze of the first sound of hope, and they waited its arrival with eye and ears and souls expectant. They heard freedom's voice on every wave, and on every sound on every sea. Other political activist among the first generation of ministers include: Prince A. Hinton, George W. Lee, C. S. Mitchell, and W. D. Newsome. The third generation of political activist included: Thomas S. Cooper, B. W. Dance, J. T. Doles, H. L. Mitchell, and Wade H. Owens.

The prayer of these Founding Fathers was "Grant the day Lord when we may worship God under our own vine and fig tree," and this prayer meant to them a separation from the white churches. Crude houses of worship were erected in every section, and where they were unable to erect houses brush arbors were thrown together, and in many instances they were content to worship under the trees. This new privilege was hailed with extreme delight in North Carolina as elsewhere. As time progressed, licenses and ordinations became general, and soon there were many although unlettered who went forth in their rude way telling the joyful tidings of salvation. One of the saddest changes in the history of the Roanoke Missionary Baptist Association was to see with the growth of education and other improvements new demands for a more intelligent ministry, and to see these old landmarks falling out one by one, and men of better training taking their places. Only a few of these old ministers survived in the midst of these changes.

The West Roanoke was born out of the Roanoke Missionary Baptist Association. Its birth arises from the May 3, 1885 motion made by the Association Clerk, T. M. Collins to grant letters of dismissal to the following thirty-seven churches, and to any church petitioning the Association in gospel order.

Rev. I. B. Roach death in 1925 was the last of the Founders to return back to Mother Earth. L. W. Boone died in 1878, Henry H. Hays died 1890; Willis Hodges died 1890; Charles E. Hodges in 1898; R. H. Harper died before 1900; G W. Holland died in 1906; Emmanuel Reynolds died 1906; Joshua A. Flemings died 1910; Caesar Johnson died before 1912; William R. Reid died 1925; Zion H. Berry died before 1913; Rev. Roach's age-mates Eli Thomas died 1912; Rev. James Jenkins 1913; E. H. Griffin 1914; W. T. Askew 1917; L. F. Sharpe 1920; M. W. D. Norman 1927; S. P. Knight, died 1931; and C. S. Mitchell died in 1933. Most of these founders outlived their generations. Some of them lived to see the brush arbor removed, and the log church erected instead, and even the log churches taken away and frame and brick churches erected. Not only did he remove from the brush arbor to the frame church, but from the frame church to the beautiful brick buildings. These men will live in the memory of the older people of our Association. They deserve a place of highest esteem among the Roanoke Missionary Baptist Association. They sleep in their graves, but "their works do follow them." When a more extensive work shall be written much worthy of mention in their wonderful lives will be brought to light. Upon their shoulders at the most critical period rested the destiny of the cause so dear to our hearts, and it may be truly said of them, they bore their burdens, and, like Paul, rejoiced that they were "counted worthy to bear them."

Few in the Roanoke Missionary Baptist Church are aware of these facts about the pre-history and the history of the Roanoke Missionary Baptist Association. They are unaware that the Roanoke Missionary Baptist Association has a history. It is not published in books or taught in schools or colleges; it was not fully printed or accurately published in newspapers. Bits and pieces of the history of the Roanoke Missionary Baptist Association and bits and pieces of the news affecting the Roanoke Missionary Baptist Association communities of churches are printed in the few surviving Annual Minutes of the Roanoke Missionary Baptist Association. However, these bits and pieces of information are not sufficient to reconstruct the glowing history and the heroic deeds done by the Founding Fathers of this Association. In those minutes we read the following request for the membership to subscribe to the following news paper circulations: On motion of Brother A. Reid, *the Baptist Standard* published at Raleigh, N.C., was endorsed by the Association as an exponent of Baptist principals, and its circulation recommended.[534] By motion the Association endorsed *the Elizabeth City Gazette* during its Thursday Morning Session May 20, 1903 session.[535]

"I now call your attention to the *Hertford Messenger*, the organ of this Association. This is your paper by your authorization and as such, it is the duty of every preacher to subscribe and pay for himself, and encourage the members of his church to do the same. Notwithstanding the indifferences of the consistency towards it, *the Messenger* has served a much needed purpose and has been a wonderful help to our work. It is issued at a great sacrifice to the manager; his personal earnings have been lavishly spent to keep it going, not for his own benefit, but for the benefit of the Roanoke Missionary Baptist Association."[536] Rev. B. W. Dance was present and spoke concerning the *Hertford Messenger*. He seemed to have made a lasting impression and to have created much interest,[537] and he also spoke words of encouragement for the paper, endorsing and recommending it.[538]

Brother H. F. Woodhouse spoke in the interest of his paper; "*The Signs of the Times*" A. collection of $1.37 was given him.[539] Bits and pieces of the activities of the Roanoke Missionary Baptist Association were sent to "*The News*," a race paper published in Kelford, North Carolina by Messrs. Brooks and Dudley, or to the Rev. Henry Francis Woodhouse to be published in his weekly Elizabeth City paper, "*The Signs of the Times*", or to The *Norfolk Journal and Guide*.

The Norfolk Journal and Guide was originally christened "*The Gideon Safe Guide*," then it became the "*Lodge Journal and Guide*," and later it emerged from the field of fraternal organs into a secular newspaper as *The Norfolk Journal and Guide*. The paper has never attempted to gain circulation by appealing to the sordid and sensational tastes of people. Its news and editorial policies were steadfastly constructive. "Build up-don't tear down!" remained the admonition of the editor and chief. The Norfolk Journal and Guide provided to be an invaluable resource in the author's effort to reconstruct the activities of the Roanoke Missionary Baptist Association. From its pages were extracted information long forgotten and long removed from the memories of its readership, and form the long term memory of Roanoke Missionary Baptist Association.

Through the decades, the *Norfolk Journal and Guide* newspaper fought for equal employment rights urged African-American participation in politics, and advocated state-funded higher education for blacks. The following people work untiringly with the local Journal and Guide in Elizabeth City and surrounding areas to encourage this action. Mrs. Emmitt Jenkins a popular and active *Journal and Guide* representative in Washington, North Carolina during 1936. She enjoyed a splendid record with the newspaper for more than one year prior. Little Thomas Jefferson Raynor, son of Mr.& Mrs. T. J. Raynor, Sr., 701 Brook Avenue, Elizabeth City, N. C., was one of those hustling carriers who delivered *the Journal and Guide* to readers in Elizabeth City. He built his route up to 150 copies per week and earned enough money to purchase a new fully equipped bicycle. His mother, Mrs. F. B. Raynor was the agent and news correspondent in Elizabeth City. Mr. L. W. Smith of 281 Walnut Street, Elizabeth City, N. C., began his work with the Journal and Guide on January 2, 1932. He was the general agent and distributor for the *Journal and Guide in Elizabeth City.* The patrons of the Elizabeth City area was instructed to send news items through Mr. Smith and to have them in his hands before Saturday noon of each week. The Guide cost 10 cents a copy, $2.50 a year, $1.50 for six months, a$1.00 for three months. *The Journal and Guide* offered sixteen pages of live, stimulating, and interested news, special features and pictures each week. See the tribute to Journal and Guide Agent Mr. Henry Stewart.

Under the leadership of P. B. Young, the "Dean of the Negro Press," The *Norfolk Journal and Guide* became one of the best researched and written newspapers of its era, with a circulation of more than 80,000 by the 1940s. It argued against restrictive covenants, rallied against lynching, encouraged blacks to vote, supported improvements to city streets and water systems, and more. The Journal and Guide campaigned against The Great Migration of Southern laborers to the North. It was one of only a few black newspapers to provide on-the-scene coverage of the 1930s Scottsboro trial, and helped raise legal funds for the nine young black defendants. This Southern-based newspaper had to use a factual, unemotional tone in expressing opinions on social injustice.

Since its inception in 1866 the Roanoke Missionary Baptist Association has been consistent in its belief that discrimination on the basis of color was against God. Its pastors, many of whom were former abolitionist and its ministers demonstrated an ethos that in God's own time, the wicket would cease from their troubling and the weary will be at rest. The wicket was the oppressors and their prodigy. Rev. J. W. C. Pennington, pastor of the Colored Presbyterian Church of New York, placed the Negro's case before the public.

> "Yes, I have shown you a people who are practicing more faithfully than any other, the true Christian law of moral power. I mean the law of forgiveness and endurance of wrong. There is no solitary case on record of a minority, with justice on its side, being crushed, while adhering to the law of forgiveness and endurance. It is not the nature of God's moral government to permit such a thing. On this grand basis the Colored People of America are safe for their future destiny. The American oppressor may destroy himself, but destroy the Colored man he never can. He that reproveth God by taking moral agents which he has made for himself, and reducing them to the perpetual drudgery of brutes, will surely have to answer for it.[540]

The Association remained firm and supportive in her efforts to support the Roanoke Institute at Elizabeth City, North Carolina; and the aims and the objectives of the parent body, the Baptist Convention of North Carolina. The Association celebrated its 100th Anniversary in 1966. She remains an active part of 72 churches located not only in Northeastern, Virginia but in lower Tidewater, Virginia. The Roanoke Association touched every part of the life of its membership. The Association in the absence of other agencies assumed the responsibilities to do more than its duty in taking care of the general interest of its membership.

BIBLIOGRAPHY

1. American Baptist Year Book 1891: American Baptist Publication Society; American Baptist Convention.
2. American Baptist Year Book 1898: American Baptist Publication Society; American Baptist Convention.
3. Caldwell, Arthur Bunyan. A History of the American Negro, North Carolina Edition. A. B. Caldwell Publishing Co. 1921.
4. A Manuel of North Carolina Historical Commission. North Carolina Secretary of State. Legislative Reference Library. 1917.
5. Armstrong, S. C. "From the Beginning; *Twenty-Two Years' Work of the Hampton Normal and Agricultural Institute at Hampton, Virginia: Records of Negro and Indian Graduates and Ex-Students. Hampton: Hampton University,* 1891.
6. Bacote, Samuel Williams. Who's Who Among the Colored Baptist of the United States. Kansas City: Franklin Hudson Publishing Company. 1913.
7. Ballou, Leonard R. Pasquotank Pedagogues and Politicians: Early Educational Struggles. (Elizabeth City, N. C.: Elizabeth City State College, 1966).
8. Bell Jr., John L. "Baptists and the Negro in North Carolina During Reconstruction." North Carolina Historical Review (October 1965).
9. Bowser, Arvilla Tillett. Roanoke Island: The Forgotten Colony. Chesapeake, Va.: Maxmilian Press Publishers, 2002.
10. Brown, Ross D. The Negro and the Next War. Chicago, Ill.: [ca. 1935?]
11. Caldwell, A. B. History of the American Negro North Carolina Edition. (A. B. Caldwell Publishing Company. Atlanta 1921).
12. Cone, James A. Theology/A Black Documented History: One Volume: 1966-1977. (New York: Orbis Books, 1998).
13. Council, W. H. Synopsis of Three Addresses: Building the South, The Children of the South, and Negro Religion and Character No Apology. (Norman Alabama, 1900). 14. Dubois, W. E. B., Dark Water (New York: Harcum, Bruce & Howe, 1920).
15. Eleazer, Robert E. America's Tenth Man: A Brief Survey of the Negro's Part in American History. Commission on Interracial Cooperation; (Atlanta, Georgia, December 12, 1938). 16. Edmonds, George, Facts and Falsehoods Concerning the War of the South 1861-1856. Dahlonega, Georgia: The Confederate Publishing Company. 1904.
17. Emancipation-The Making of the Black Lawyer 1844-1944.University of Pennsylvania Press. (1933)
18. Felder, Jack. Black Origins and Lady Liberty. Dallas, Dallas Challenge, July 16, 1990.
19. Footprints In Northampton 1741-1776-1976, Northampton County Bicentennial Committee, 1976.

20. Gates, Jr. Henry Louis. & Evelyn Brooks Higginbotham, editors, African American National Biography, Volume 5. 2008.

21. Harrell, Isaac S. Gates County to 1860. (Gates County Arts Council 1916)

22. Franklin, John Hope. From Slavery To Freedom: A History of Negro Americans, (New York: Vintage Press 1947)

23. Genovese, Eugene D. Roll Jordan Roll: The World the Slave Made (America, First Vintage Book Edition 1974).

24. Hampton Institute, Hampton, VA. Twenty-two Years' Work of the Hampton Normal and Agricultural Institute at Hampton, Virginia. Records of Negro and Indian Graduates and Ex-Students, with Historical and Personal Sketches and Testimony on Important Race Questions from Within and Without, to Which are Added . . . Some of the Songs of the Races Gathered in the School. Hampton: Hampton Normal School Press, 1893.

25. Gutek, Gerald. ed., "The Civil War, Reconstruction, and the Education of Black Americans," in Education in the United States: A Historical Perspective (Englewood Cliffs: Prentice Hall, 1986).

26. Hardin, Louis R. Editor, Booker T. Washington Papers, Volume 10: 1909-1911, (University of Illinois Press, 1981)

27. Hatcher-Taylor, Annie. Black Cemetery Records, Reunions, Reunions and Personality Sketches of Hertford and Gates County, North Carolina from 1850 to 1988-Volume 1. Winton, N. C. 1988.

28. Haywood, Atticus G. Our Brother in Black: His Freedom and His Future. New York: Phillips & Hunt, 1881.

29. Hutton, Frankie. The Early Press in America, 1850-to 1897. Westport, Ct: Greenwood Press, 1993.

30. Johnson, Karen A. **Uplifting the Women and the Race**: (New York: Garland Publishing, Inc. 2000).

31. Reid Jones, Cornelia. The Four Rooks Sisters The Negro History Bulletin October 1952.

32. Jones, H. G. North Carolina Illustrated, 1524-1984; University of North Carolina Press: Chapel Hill, 1983).

33. Logan, Frenise A. *The Negro in North Carolina, 1876-1894* (Chapel Hill: University of North Carolina Press, 1964).

34. Christopher, Maurine. *Black Americans in Congress* (New York: Thomas Y. Crowell Company, 1976).

35. Mays, Benjamin E. The Negro's God as Reflected in His Literature; (New York, 1969).

36. Munson, Barry. *Afro-American Death Notices from Eastern North Carolina Newspapers 1860-1948.* (2000), P. 46.

37. Newman, Richard. African American Quotations (Oryx Press 1998).

38. Our People: Yesterday, Today & Tomorrow: A Brief History of Union Chapel Missionary Baptist Church; Union Chapel Baptist Church 1990.

39. Paris, Peter J. The Social Teachings of the Black Church (Philadelphia: Fortress Press, 1985),

40. Pegues; A. W. Our Baptist Ministers and Schools. Springfield, Mass. Springfield Printing and Binding Company:1892

41. Pride of the Past-Hope for the Future: Piney Grove-Reynoldson Baptist Church 1827-1977 (Pierce Printing Company., Inc, Ahoskie, N.C. 1977).

42. Reuter, Edward Byron. **The American Race Problem**, (Iowa: University of Iowa Press 1939).

43. Sanneh, Lamin O. Abolitionist Abroad: American Blacks and the Making of Modern West Africa. First Harvard University Press; 2001.

44. Stuckey, Sterling. **Slave Culture: Nationalist Theory & the Foundations of Black America** (Oxford University Press: Orbis Books, 1987).

45. Tannenbaun, Frank. From Slave and Citizen Boston, Beacon Press: 1946.

46. *Taylor, Garfield. "The Windsor Story—1768-1968"—published by Windsor Bicentennial Commission.*

47. The Ahoskie Era of Hertford County. Ahoskie, N. C.: Parker's Brothers, 1939.

48. The Boone Family Reflecting The Past, The Rev. Lemuel Washington Boone Family Souvenir Booklet, Fourth Boone Family Reunion, Holiday Inn-Four Seasons Complex, Greensboro, North Carolina August 13-15, 1982.

49. The History of Blacks in North Carolina Volume 1(The North Carolina African American Foundation in Cooperation with the Delmar Company; Charlotte, North Carolina 1990). 50. The Black Press in Antebellum America: Slavery in America. Judson Press: 2006.

51. The Life of Rev. Lemuel Washington Boone, Unpublished dissertation of Derrick S. Boone, Sr.

52. The Negro in History; (Board of Education, City of New York, 1965).

53. The Works of James McCune Smith: Black Intellectual and Abolitionist; (Oxford: Oxford Univ. Press, 2006).

54. Turner, Joseph Kelly and John Luther Bridges, History of Edgecombe County, North Carolina. Raleigh: Edward Broughton Printing Company. 1920.

55. Villard, Oswald Garrison. John Brown, 1800-1859: A Biography Fifty Years After. Garden City & New York: Double Day, Doran & Company, INC. 1929.

56. Walls, William J. The African Methodist Episcopal Zion Church: The Reality of the Black Church; Charlotte: A. M. E. Zion Publishing House: 1974.

57. Winborne; Benjamin B. The Colonial and State Political History of Hertford County; Issue 3; (Murfreesboro; North Carolina, 1906).

58. Whitted, J. A. A History of the Negro Baptist of North Carolina, (Raleigh, N. C.). Edwards and Broughton Co., 1908).

59. Whitted, J. A. Biographical Sketch of the Life and Work of the Late Rev. Augusta Shepard, D. D., Durham, North Carolina. (Raleigh: Edward & Broughton Printing Company, 1912).

60. Williams, Charles E. History of the Baptist in North Carolina, Raleigh, North Carolina: Edwards & Broughton Publishing Company, 1903).

61. William, M. W. & George W. Watkins. Who's Who among North Carolina Negro Baptist: With a Brief History of Baptist Organizations; 1940.

62. Woodson, Carter G. The History of the Negro Church; (The Associated Publishers, Washington, D. C. 1921).

63. Yarsinske, Amy Waters. Virginia Beach: A History of Virginia's Golden Shore. Charleston: Acadia Publishing, 2002.

PERIODICALS

1. The Southeastern Reporter—Volume 93—Permanent Edition Comprising All The Decisions of The Supreme Courts Of Appeals Of Virginia And West Virginia, The Supreme Courts of North Carolina and South Carolina, and The Supreme Court and Court of Appeals of Georgia With Key-Number Annotations August 4-December 1, 1917.
2. The Crisis 1938, P. 45
3. The Negro History Bulletin October 1952. P 3-8.
4. The South Workman; November 1875.
5. The Southern Workman; May 1899.
6. December 1867 Petition, Letters Received, Headquarters, Records of the Assistant Commissioner for North Carolina, RG 105, National Archives, Washington D.C.
7. One Hundred Ten Years History of First Baptist Hertford North Carolina from 1866 1976. P. 6-7.
8. Public laws of the State of North Carolina by the General Assembly 1969-1870.
9. Insurance Year **Book, June 1907; Volume 40; P. 474.**
10. Dare County Record of Deeds, Outer Banks History Center, Manteo, NC.
11. Anna is Harriett Anna. See 1910 Federal census Record for Belvidere Township, Perquimans North Carolina.
12. Journal of the House of Representatives of the General Assembly of the State of North Carolina by North Carolina. General Assembly. House of Representatives.
13. A History of the Negro Baptist Church: The Reformed Reader.
14. Proceedings of the Forty-Eight Annual Session of the Baptist State Convention of North Carolina held with the Shiloh Baptist Church, Wilmington, N.C., November 14-17, 1915, and of the First Session of the Union Baptist State Convention of North Carolina held with the White Rock Baptist Church, Durham, N.C. Wednesday, January 12, 1916.
15. 1915 Statistics Report of the Roanoke Missionary Baptist Association.

FOOTNOTES

Dedication to William Aldred Boon

[1]   General Affidavit, State of North Carolina, County of Gates; Invalid Pension of William A. Boone; April 18, 1884; National Archives, Washington, D. C.

[2]   General Affidavit, State of North Carolina, County of Gates; Invalid Pension of William A. Boone; May 2, 1884; National Archives, Washington, D. C.

[3]   William A. Boone of the 1. Cav. U. S. C. T. Company Muster Roll.

[4]   William A. Boone of the 1. Cav. U. S. C. T. Company Muster Roll for August 31, 1865.

[5]   William A. Boone Muster Roll Record for August 1864 signed by J. H. Stewart.

[6]   William Boon's Pension Explanation to the Call for History of Claimants Disability; Pension Office, Washington, D. C.; February 2, 1894.

[7]   Reply of William Boon to Call for History of Claimants Disability; Pension Office, Washington, D. C.; January 30, 1894.

[8]   Reply of William Boon to Call for History of Claimants Disability; Pension Office, Washington, D. C.; January 30, 1894.

[9]   William Boon; General Affidavit. State of North Carolina, County of Gates. May 14, 1894.

[10]   General Affidavit, State of North Carolina, County of Gates; Invalid Pension of William A. Boone; February 15, 1904; National Archives, Washington, D. C.

[11]   J. O. Howard, Field Examiner, Pension Administration Office; Washington, D. C., Form 3537-C; July 1932; Examiners Contract Report. National Archives. Washington, D. C.

Introduction

[1]   C. F. Graves; Baptists: State and National; The Baptist Informer; P.5.

[2]   Minutes of the 1906 Annual Session of the Roanoke Missionary Baptist Association. p. 24.

[3]   Minutes of the Fifty-First {1917} Annual Session of the Roanoke Missionary Baptist Association. P. 7.

[4]   "*Church Holds Diamond Anniversary*, Norfolk Journal and Guide, October 26, 1940. P.12.

[5]   Minutes of the Eighty-Fourth Annual Session of the Roanoke Missionary Baptist Association held with Lebanon Grove Missionary Baptist Church Gatesville, North Carolina May 23rd & May 24th & May 25th w1950. P16. Rev. C.C. Boone, Pastor. Rev. J. R. R. McRay, Recording Secretary.

[6]   Minutes of the Ninety-Ninth Annual Session of the Roanoke Missionary Baptist Association held with The First Baptist Church Hertford, North Carolina May 18th, May 19th, & May 20th 1965. P21. Rev. F. L. Andrews, Pastor.

[7]   Minutes of the One Hundred Nineteenth Annual Session of the Roanoke Missionary Baptist Association held with New Chapel Missionary Baptist Church, Plymouth North Carolina May 21st,

May 22ⁿᵈ the, & May 23ʳᵈ 1985. P. 18-20. Rev. A. C. Robinson, Pastor. Mrs. Emma Burke, Recording Secretary.

8   Minutes of the One Hundred and Sixth Annual Session of the Roanoke Missionary Baptist Association held with Galilee Missionary Baptist Church, Weeksville, North Carolina May 18th-May 20th 1972. P12. Rev. W.H. Trotman, Pastor.

9   Minutes of the One Hundred and Eight Annual Session of the Roanoke Missionary Baptist Association held with The Greater Welch's Chapel Missionary Baptist Church Tyner, North Carolina May 21st-23rd 1974. P9. Rev. William H. Davis, Pastor.

10   Ibid. P. 21

11   Ibid.

12   Minutes of the One Hundred Sixteenth Annual Session of the Roanoke Missionary Baptist Church, Edenton, North Carolina held with the Saint John Missionary Baptist Church {May 18th-May 20th 1982} Dr. D. W. Lamb, Pastor. Mrs. H. L. Mitchell, Recording Secretary.

13   Minutes of the One Hundred Eighteenth Annual Session of the Roanoke Missionary Baptist Church, Edenton, North Carolina held with the Haven Chapel Missionary Baptist Church {May 23rd-May 24th 1981} Rev. A. M. Winslow, Pastor. Mrs. H. L. Mitchell, Recording Secretary. J. A. Whitted, *A History of the Negro Baptist of North Carolina*. Carter Godwin Woodson, *The History of the Negro Church* P. 240.

14   Edward Byron Reuter, **The American Race Problem**, (Iowa: University of Iowa Press 1939), p. 255.

15   Johnson, Karen A. **Uplifting the Women and the Race**: (New York: Garland Publishing, Inc. 2000), p.18.

16   Gerald Gutek, ed., *"The Civil War, Reconstruction, and the Education of Black Americans,"* in *Education in the United States: A Historical Perspective* (Englewood Cliffs: Prentice Hall, 1986) pp. 150-172.

17   Carter G. Woodson, the Journal of Negro History, (Washington DC: The Associated Press Publishers,

18   Vol. XI January 1926. Number 1), p.1

19   Frank Tannenbaun, From Slave and Citizen 1946, p. 42

20   *For a history of racism in the United States*, see Paul Jacobs and Paula Landau (with Eve Pell), **To Serve the Devil New York: Random House, 1971}**

The Roanoke Missionary Baptist Association

21   John Hope Franklin, **From Slavery to Freedom: A History of Negro Americans**, (New York: VintagePress 1947), Xii

22   W. H. Council, *Synopsis of Three Addresses: Building the South, The Children of the South, and Negro Religion and Character No Apology.* (Norman Alabama, 1900) P. 8.

23   Robert E. Eleazer, *America's Tenth Man: A Brief Survey of the Negro's Part in American History.* Commission on Interracial Cooperation; (Atlanta, Georgia, December 12, 1938), p. 5.

24   Paul South, *Roanoke Island Fest to Let Freedom Ring, Preaching, Praise, Reunion to Recall Freed Slaves' Colony.* Virginia Pilot May 31, 1996. B1.

25   Ibid.

26   Arvilla Tillett Bowser, *Roanoke Island: The Forgotten Colony*. P. 39.

27   *Arvilla Tillett Bowser, Roanoke Island: The Forgotten Colony*, (Chesapeake, VA, 2001), P38.

28   *The Elizabeth City Carolinian News Paper*; Our Colored People; Volume XXVII; July 24, 1895; Volume 9.

29   Ibid.

30   Minutes of the Roanoke Missionary 1919. p.15.

31   Minutes, 1871 P. 8

32   Proceedings of the Baptist State Convention of North Carolina held with the First Baptist Church in Charlotte, North Carolina. October 20, 21, 22, 23, 1875. P. 8.

33   Baptist Informer *Made from the clay deposits found on the property.* Volume 70 ay, 1948. Number 5. Page 5.

34   Proceedings of the Fourteen Annual Session of the Baptist State Convention of North Carolina held with the First Baptist Church, Warrenton, N.C., October 20-23, 1880. The African Expositor Print 1880.

35   Minutes of the Nineteenth Annual Session of the Roanoke Baptist Association held with the Church of Christ at Zion Hill, Bertie County, North Carolina., and Tuesday after the third Lord's Day in May 1884. P.9.

36   Minutes of the Twentieth Annual Session of the Roanoke Missionary Baptist Association held with the Church of Christ at Providence, Edenton, Chowan County, North Carolina Tuesday after the third Lord's Day in May, 1885 P.9.

37   Ibid. p. 11

38   Minutes of the Chowan Association (1866), 10.

39   Eugene D. Genovese, *Roll Jordan Roll: The World the Slave Made* (America, First Vintage Book Edition 1974), p. 255.

The Haven Creek Missionary Baptist Church

40   Minutes of the Forty-fifth {1910} Annual Session of the Roanoke Missionary Baptist Association. P. 4.

41   Minutes of the 1925 Annual Sessions of the Roanoke Missionary Baptist Association P 13.

42   Minuets of the Forty-Ninth {1915} Annual Session of the Roanoke Missionary Baptist Association. P. 28.

43   Minutes 1878; P. 10.

The Rules

44   Minutes of the 1879 Annual Session of the Roanoke Missionary Baptist Association P. 5.

45   Minutes 1922 Annual Session of the Roanoke Missionary Baptist Association, P. 15.

46   Minutes 1878, P.6.

47   Ibid.

48   Minutes of the 1879 Annual Sessions of the Roanoke Missionary Baptist Association, P 4.

49   Minutes of the 1878 Annual Session of the Roanoke Missionary Baptist Church. P. 5.

50   Minutes of the 1884 Annual Session of the Roanoke Missionary Baptist Church, P. 4.

51   Minutes of the 1879 Annual Session of the Roanoke Missionary Baptist Association, P.7.

52   Minutes of the 1885 Annual Session of the Roanoke Missionary Baptist Church, P. 8.

53   Minutes of the Forty-First {1906} Annual Session of the Roanoke Missionary Baptist Association, P. 29

54   Minutes of 1879 Annual Session of the Roanoke Missionary Baptist Association, P. 4.

55   Minutes of the Thirty-Eight Annual Session. of the Roanoke Missionary Baptist Association P. 22. Minutes of the Forty-Fifth (1910) Session of the Roanoke Missionary Baptist Association, P. 33.

56   Minutes of the Forty-Seventh {1912} Annual Session of the Roanoke Missionary Baptist Association P. 32.

57   Ibid.

58   Minutes of the 1922 Annual Session of the Roanoke Missionary Baptist Association, P. 18.

59   Minutes of the Fiftieth {1916} Annual Session of the Roanoke Missionary Baptist Association, P. 42.

60   Minutes of the 1903 Annual Session of the Roanoke Missionary Baptist Association, P. 19.

61   Ibid p. 30.

62   Minutes of the 1907 Annual Session of the Roanoke Missionary Baptist Association.

The Right Hand of Fellowship

63   Minutes of the Thirty-eight (1903) Session of the Roanoke Missionary Baptist Association P. 19.

64   Minutes of the 1909 Annual Session of the Roanoke Missionary Baptist Association P. 39.

65   Minutes of the Forty-ninth {1915} Annual Session of the Roanoke Missionary Baptist Association P. 48.

66   Minutes of the Fifty-second {1918} Annual Session of the Roanoke Missionary Baptist Association P. 20.

67   Minutes of the 1922 Annual Session of the Roanoke Missionary Baptist Association, P. 16.

68   Ibid.

69   Minutes of the Sixty-first {1927} Annual Session of the Roanoke Missionary Baptist Association, P.8.

70   Minutes of the Fifth-seventh {1923} Annual Session of the Roanoke Missionary Baptist Association, P. 16 & 17.

71   Ibid.

72   Minutes of the Forty-fifth {1910} Annual Session of the Roanoke Missionary Baptist Association, P.3.

73   The Banner-Enterprise Volume III. Thursday, June 7, 1883. Number 15.

74   The Baptist Informer. Volume 68. Number 8. August 46. Page 4.

75   The Elizabeth City Carolinian News Paper. Volume XXVII, Wednesday, September 25. 1895. Number 18.

76   Minutes of the Nineteenth Annual Session of the Roanoke Missionary Baptist Association, P.5.

77   Minutes of the Nineteenth (1884) Annual Session of the Roanoke Missionary Baptist Association, P.6.

78   Ministers of the 1885 Annual Session of the Roanoke Missionary Baptist Association, P.4.

79   Minutes of the 1878 Annual Session of the Roanoke Missionary Baptist Association, P.4

80   Minutes of the Third Annual Session of the West Roanoke Association held in Swamp Chapel Baptist Church, Northampton County, N.C., October 9, 10, and 11, 1888. P.6.

81   Minutes of the Thirty-eight Annual Session, p.10.

82   Ibid. P. 12.

The Dividing Line

[83] Proceedings of the Fourteen Annual Session of the Baptist State Convention held with the First Baptist Church, Warrenton, North Carolina, October 20-23, 1880. The African Expositor Printed 1880. Baptist

[84] Informer Volume 68, October, 1946. Number 10.

[85] Minutes of the Freedmen's Convention, Held in the City of Raleigh, on the 2nd, 3rd, 4th and 5th of October, 1866.

[86] Minutes of the Thirteenth Annual Session (1878) of the Roanoke Missionary Baptist Association, P. 8.

[87] Minutes of 1879 Annual Session of the Roanoke Missionary Baptist Association, P. 13.

The Roanoke Preachers

[88] Minutes of the 1912 Annual Session of the Roanoke Missionary Baptist Association Session, P.12.

[89] Ibid.

[90] Proceedings of the State Baptist Convention in its Sixty-Second Annual Session held with First Baptist Church Goldsboro, North Carolina. October 30th, 1928.

[91] Ibid.

[92] The Baptist Informer. Volume 70; June 1948. Number 6. P.6.

[93] Peter J. Paris, The Social Teachings of the Black Church (Philadelphia: Fortress Press, 1985), pp.57-61.

The Founders of the Roanoke Missionary Baptist Association

[94] Dexter Boone, Lemuel W. Boon (Raleigh, N. C.: unpublished dissertation, North Carolina State University, 1993), P. 9.

[95] Ibid.

[96] Rev. L. W. Boone's marriage record could not be located.

[97] Minutes of the 1878 Annual Session of the Roanoke Missionary Baptist Association, 1878, 9.

[98] *The Boone Family Reflecting The Past,* The Rev. Lemuel Washington Boone Family Souvenir Booklet, Fourth Boone Family reunion, Holiday Inn-Four Seasons Complex, Greensboro, North Carolina August 13-15, 1982, 4.

[99] Proceedings of the First Annual Session of the General Association of the Colored Baptist of North Carolina held with the Church at Greensboro, North Carolina. October 17-191869. (Mills & Hughes,1869), 1.

[100] Baptist Informer, *Made from the clay deposits found on the property.* Volume 70 ay, 1948. Number 5. Page 5.

[101] Minutes of the 1878 Annual Session of the Roanoke Missionary Baptist Association; P.9.

[102] Ibid P.6.

[103] The Banner-Enterprise Volume III. Thursday, June 7, 1883. Number 15.

[104] John L. Bell Jr., *"Baptists and the Negro in North Carolina During Reconstruction," North Carolina Historical Review* (October 1965): 391-409.

[105] *125 Years—Lemuel Washington Boone,* Volume 113. Number 12. Baptist Informer December 1992 (Raleigh, North Carolina: General Baptist State Convention of North Carolina., Inc) Front Page Boone P7.

[106] Ibid.

[107] Arvilla Tillett Bowser & Lindsey Bowser, Roanoke Island: The Forgotten Colony. (Maximillian Press Publishers 2002)-P.8.

[108] *Garfield Taylor. "The Windsor Story—1768-1968"—published by Windsor Bicentennial Commission.*

[109] Minutes of the Eighty-Fourth Annual Session of the Roanoke Missionary Association held with the Lebanon Grove Missionary Baptist Church, Gatesville, North Carolina. May 23rd-25th 1950. Rev. J. R. R. McRay Recording Secretary. Historical Table. Minutes, Proceedings; May 28, 1878.

[110] The Elizabeth City Carolinian Volume XXX February 23, 1899 Volume 10. Page 4.

[111] The Elizabeth City Carolinian Volume XXX May 4, 1899 Volume 50. Page 5.

[112] The Elizabeth City Carolinian Volume XXXI September 7, 1899 Volume 50. Page 16.

[113] The Elizabeth City Carolinian Volume XXXI October 5, 1899 Volume 50. Page 20.

[114] The Elizabeth City Carolinian Volume XXXI April 26, 1900 Volume 49. Page 17.

[115] Our Colored People; The Elizabeth City Carolinian; Number 24.

[116] The Elizabeth City Carolinian Volume XXXI May 3, 1900 Volume 50. Page 16.

[117] The Elizabeth City Carolinian Volume XXXI May 19, 19007, Volume 51. Page 15.

[118] The African Repository, Volume 47 by American Colonization Society, P.147.

[119] Minutes of the 1879 Roanoke Missionary Baptist Association Annual Session P. 3

[120] The One Hundred Forty-First Anniversary Booklet of the Willow Grove Baptist Church. Minutes of the 1903 Annual Session of the Roanoke Missionary Baptist Association; P. 30.

[121] Elizabeth City News; August 18, 1923; Journal and Guide; P8.

[122] Ibid.

[123] *Evangelist In Elizabeth City,* New Journal and Guide; May 9, 1925 P. 8.

[124] F. W. M. Butler, D. W. White & Mrs. L. M. MeBane; Elizabeth City News; Journal and Guide; April 2, 1927; P. 13.

[125] The Southeastern Reporter—Volume 93—Permanent Edition Comprising All The Decisions of The Supreme Courts Of Appeals Of Virginia And West Virginia, The Supreme Courts of North Carolina and South Carolina, and The Supreme Court and Court of Appeals of Georgia With Key-Number Annotations August 4-December 1, 1917.

[126] North Carolina State Board of Health Bureau of Vital Statistics Certificate of Death Gates County Hall Township, June 8, 1918.

[127] General Index to MARRIAGES-Pasquotank County, North Carolina.

[128] The Wilder name is spelled Widdor on Janes Wilder's death certificate. Her last name on the marriage register is spelled Wilder.

[129] Public laws of the State of North Carolina by the General Assembly 1969-1870. 1870 Census Records for Mintonville Township North Carolina.

[130] George Edmonds, *Facts and Falsehoods Concerning the War of the South 1861-1856.* p.231

[131] Public laws of the State of North Carolina by the General Assembly 1969-1870.

[132] Minutes, Proceedings; 1879.

[133] Ibid.

[134] Ibid 1879. P. 12.

[135] W. A. Hodges-The Crisis 1938, P. 45

[136] Frankie Hutton, *The Early Press In America, 1897 to 1850,* ( ) P. 141.

[137] Ibid

[138] Ibid

[139] Oswald Garrison Villard, John Brown, 1800-1859: A Biography Fifty Years After ( ) P. 72. 1878

[140] Minutes List of Elders.

[141] Minutes of the 1884 Annual Session of the Roanoke Missionary Baptist Association, Page 6.

[142] Amy Waters Yarsinske, Virginia Beach: A History of Virginia's Golden Shore P.111.

[143] The Black Press in Antebellum America: Slavery in America.

[144] Micajah Reid was a blacksmith and member of the Militia and Grand Muster in which he played the fife and Drum Corp.

[145] Other Free" Heads of Household in the 1800 North Carolina Census by family name, page 277 Cornelia Reid Jones, *The Four Rooks Sisters* The Negro History Bulletin October 1952. P 3-8.

[146] A. M. Vann, *Important Baptist Meetings Held: Bethany Associations of Virginia and West Roanoke Association of North Carolina,* Volume XVII, Number 3, October 7, 1916, P4.

[147] Minutes of the 1884 Annual Session of the Roanoke Missionary Baptist Association. P.4.157

[148] Ibid. 151

[149] S. C. Armstrong, "From the Beginning," in *Twenty-Two Years' Work of the Hampton Normal and Agricultural Institute at Hampton, Virginia: Records of Negro and Indian Graduates and Ex-Students,*

[150] 1891. p263

[151] The Southern Workman. Volume XXVIII, Number 5. May 1899. P. 185.

[152] Isaac S. Harrell, *Gates County to 1860.* (Gates County Arts Council 1916) P. 16 Ibid.

[153] Ibid

[154] Emancipation-The Making of the Black lawyer 1844-1944.University of Pennsylvania Press. (1933) The Southern Work Man, 1933.

[155] *A History of the Negro Baptist of North Carolina.*

[156] John Riddick, deacon and church historian at the New Pineywood Baptist Church, Powellsville, North Carolina.

[157] Public laws of the State of North Carolina by the General Assembly 1969-1870.

[158] Minutes of the 1884 Annual Session of the Roanoke Missionary Baptist Association. P3. Minutes of the 1885 Annual Session of the Roanoke Missionary Baptist Association. P2.

[159] Minutes of the Forty-First {1906} Annual Session P, 12

[160] Ibid p. 13.

[161] Ibid.

[162] Minutes of the 1885 Annual Session of the Roanoke Missionary Baptist Asociation;. Proceedings.

[163] Minutes, Twenty Annual Session, May 17th, 1885. Proceedings Ibid.

[164] Minutes, Twenty-First Annual Session, May 18th, 1886. Proceedings.

[165] Louis R. Hardin, Editor, *Booker T. Washington Papers,* Volume 10: 1909-1911, (University of Illinois Press, 1981) P. 440.

[166] Suffolk News and Advertisement; Journal and Guide; April 7, 1917;

[167] Article 1-No Title; Journal and Guide; Norfolk, Virginia; December 22, 1928; P.6.

[168] Minutes of the 1912 Annual Session of the Roanoke Baptist Association. P.1.

[169] Ibid p. 3.

[170] Ibid P. 2.

[171] Minutes 1914; P. 40.

[172] News From North Carolina; Volume XVII; Number 24 March 17, 1917; P. 2.

173 *Great Evangelistic Meeting Marks Ground Breaking'* Journal and Guide; August 16, 1924' P. 11. Suffolk News; Journal and Guide, Norfolk, Virginia; September 26, 1925; P.11.

174 *A Trip to Lott Cary Convention;* Journal and Guide; September 18, 1926; P. 9.

175 Ibid.

176 Suffolk; Journal and Guide; 1930; P.9.

177 This date was used as his birthdate date on several documents such as his pension application, Military Records, National Archives, Washington, D. C.; these dates also corresponds with the one on his headstone. However, there is scant genealogical concerning his early life to verify the date.

178 *The Elizabeth City Carolinian News Paper*; Our Colored People; Volume XXVII; July 24, 1895; Volume 9.

179 December 1867 Petition, Letters Received, Headquarters, Records of the Assistant Commissioner for North Carolina, RG 105, National Archives, Washington D.C.

180 Testimonies in Pension applications name Richard's daughters as Onieda, 32, and Maggie, 21, (in 1902), but the head stones in the Etheridge cemetery include only one daughter by the name of Lurena.

181 Minutes of Board of County Commissioners, 1870-1915, Vol. A, Outer Banks History Center, Manteo, N. C. Since the list of jurors does not designate race, there is no way to know how many, if any, of the other thirty-six were black. Minutes 1879, Proceedings.

182 Minutes; 1879; Statistical Table.

183 Dare County Record of Deeds, Outer Banks History Center, Manteo, NC.

184 *The Elizabeth City Carolinian News Paper*; Our Colored People; Volume XXVII; July 24, 1895; Volume 9. Year 1860, Place Pasquotank County, North Carolina; Roll: T624_1124; Page: 14 B; Enumeration District: 78; Image: 439. Year 1880, Place: Newland, Pasquotank County, North Carolina; Roll: T9. Family History Film: 1254976; Page: 366.1000; Enumeration District: 112; Image: 0452.

185 Year 1910, Place Pasquotank County, North Carolina; Roll: M653_909; Page: 1390; Enumeration District: 78; Image: 151.

186 Ibid.

187 Minutes of the Twenty-First Annual Session of the Roanoke Missionary Baptist Association, held with the Church of Christ at Antioch, Camden County, N. C., Tuesday after the 3rd Lord's Day in May, 1886.

188 Proceedings of the Roanoke Missionary Baptist Church, Tuesday Evening. May 18th, 1886.

189 Ibid,

190 Historical Table, Roanoke Missionary Baptist Association

191 Ibid P. 2.

192 Norfolk Journal and Guide December 24, 1955.

193 *Four Generations Attend Griffin Family Reunion,* Norfolk Journal and Guide, July 20, 1970. *Had Nobel Career,* Journal and Guide Volume XXII Number 18 May 6, 1922 P.3.

194 HOUSEKEEPER, 91, NOT ABOUT TO SLOW DOWN NOW, Frank Rabey, Virginian-Pilot, The (Norfolk, VA)-July 9, 2000 Author: FRANK RABEY, STAFF WRITER Edition: Elizabeth City, NORTH CAROLINA Section: LOCAL Edition, Page: Y1, July 9, 2000.

195 Ibid.

196 *Minutes of the Forty-eight Annual Session of the Roanoke Missionary Baptist Association held with Welch's Chapel Baptist Church, Tyner, North Carolina*; R. R. Cartwright, D. D. Pastor; May 20, 21 22. A. D. 1913.; Complied by Rev. C. S. Mitchell, Recording Secretary; P. 10.

[197] ***Monroe Lane-***Amy Dance was the sister of Rev. Benjamin Beverly Dance pastor of Third Baptist Church, Portsmouth, Virginia.

[198] *Funeral Rites Held For Rev. Monroe Lane*; Journal and Guide; June 19, 1943. P. A23.

[199] Minutes of the Annual Sessions of the Roanoke Missionary Baptist Association, 1914 P. 51.

[200] *Retired Minister*, Journal and Guide; June 4, 1938; P. 15.

[201] Elizabeth City News; August 13, 1921; Journal and Guide; P.2.

[202] News From Nearby N. C. Towns; Elizabeth City; January 21, 1922; P.6.

[203] Elizabeth City, N. C.; February 3, 1923; Journal and Guide; P.3.

[204] *Had an Elaborate Jan 1 Celebration*; Journal and Guide; January 26, 1924; P.9.

[205] Elizabeth City News; August 13, 1921; Journal and Guide; P.2.

[206] Elizabeth City Society Page, Journal and Guide; July 25, 1925. P6.

[207] Ibid.

[208] Elizabeth City; Journal and Guide; December 3, 1931. P.3.

[209] Elizabeth City; Journal and Guide; November 12, 1927' P. 11.

[210] Elizabeth City News; Journal and Guide; December 3, 1932; P. A5.

[211] Elizabeth City, Journal and Guide; August 8, 1925; P.8.

[212] *Slaves First Largely Members of Protestants Episcopal Church Later Baptist and Methodist*; Journal and Guide; August 20, 1932; P. 7.

[213] *Her Palm Has A Long Life Line; She Is Now Only 84;* Journal & Guide; July 9, 1932. P.4.

[214] Alnora Etta Falcon, daughter of Rev. Marshall & Sophia Land was a Deacon Sisters at Fist Baptist Brute Street, Norfolk, Va; see Norfolk Journal & Guide; July 22, 1944; P. B 12.

[215] *Mrs. S. A. Land Pioneer Citizen Dies Here at 87*; Journal and Guide; April 13, 1935; P. 2.

[216] Proceedings of the Roanoke Missionary Baptist Association, Tuesday, May 28, 1878. P. 1

[217] Ibid.

[218] *Dr. Hobbs Preaches as Dr. Bowling Marks 30ᵗʰ Year;* Journal & Guide; July 22, 1944; P. B 12. *Baptist Ministers Plan Anniversary on April 30;* Journal & Guide; April 28, 1962; P. 3.

[219] Thomas Dabney; *Norfolk Area Represented*; Journal & Guide; February 14, 1959; P. B17.

[220] *At Shoulders Hill-Centennial Celebration Closes at Union Baptist;* Journal and Guide; December 4, 1965; P D4.

[221] Mrs. Lovie Northern; Berkley Ward Campostella Suburban Norfolk; Journal and Guide; December 24, 1921; P. 7.

[222] *Opening of Schools-A Monster Meeting of the Officials, Teachers and Patrons;* Journal and Guide; September 1, 1917; P.1.

[223] Obituary #3=No Title; Journal and Guide; July 3, 1926; P.6.

[224] Roanoke Missionary Baptist Time Table

[225] Inscribed on a Memorial Tomb Stone acknowledging the founding of the church in 1822 and its former pastors. 110 Years History of First Baptist Hertford North Carolina from 1866-1976. P.6-7.

[226] Minutes 1906 P. 32

[227] American Baptist Year Book 1891: American Baptist Publication Society; American Baptist Convention. P. 159.

[228] American Baptist Year Book 1898: American Baptist Publication Society; American Baptist Convention. P. 182.

[229] Minutes May 28, 1878. Proceeding

[230] Ibid.

[231] Minutes 1879 P. 14.

[232] 1879 Statistical Table 1886 Statistical Table.

233   Register of Deeds; Marriage Records for Washington County, North Carolina. Ibid. P. 8.

234   Minutes 1886 Annual Session P. 8.

235   Minutes of the Forty-second {1907} Annual session. P. 14

236   Marriage Register of Bertie County North Carolina 1869-1872.

237   Ibid.

238   Ibid.

239   Minutes, Proceedings; May 28, 1878.

240   Ibid.

241   Ibid.

242   Record of Colored Marriages in Washington County; P. 72

243   Ibid P.80.

244   *The History of Blacks in North Carolina Volume 1*(The North Carolina African American Foundation in Cooperation with the Delmar Company; Charlotte, North Carolina 1990), P. 93.

245   Frenise A. Logan. *The Negro in North Carolina 1876-1894.* (University of North Carolina Press 1964), P.27.

246   Minuets of the Twenty-First {1886} Annual Session of the Roanoke Missionary Baptist Association. P. 5.

247   Frenise A. Logan, *The Negro in North Carolina, 1876-1894* (Chapel Hill: University of North Carolina Press, 1964): 37; Maurine Christopher, *Black Americans in Congress* (New York: Thomas Y. Crowell Company, 1976): 156

248   *Little Colored Americans*; Colored American; October 12, 1901; Volume 9; Issue 28; Page 3,

249   Henry Louis Gates, Jr. & Evelyn Brooks Higginbotham, editors, *African American National Biography,* Volume 5.

250   *A Manuel of North Carolina*; North Carolina Historical Commission. P. 653 Turner and Bridges, *History of Edgecombe County, North Carolina*; P 270.

251   Minutes of the Freedmen's Convention held in the City of Raleigh, North Carolina.

252   Ibid. P. 8.

253   The North Carolina Historical Review Volume XLIX, January 1972; Number 1; *"Negro Legislators in North Carolina General Assembly July 1868-February, 1782.";*P 25.

254   Benjamin B. Winborne; The Colonial and State Political History of Hertford County; Issue 3; (Murfreesboro; North Carolina, 1906) P. 323.

255   Journal of the House of Representatives of the General Assembly of the State of North Carolina by North Carolina. General Assembly. House of Representatives.

256   Our Colored People; Elizabeth City Carolinian; Volume XXVII; May 29, 2895; Number 1.

257   Elizabeth City Social Page Volume XXI Number 17;

258   Norfolk Journal and Guide; April 16, 1921 P5.

259   Plymouth North Carolina Society Section Volume XXI Number 18

260   Norfolk Journal and Guide April 23, 1921 P.7.

261   News From Nearby N. C. Towns; Elizabeth City; January 21, 1922; P.6.

262   Elizabeth City Society Page; Journal and Guide; October 15, 1932. P5.

263   Mrs. F. B. Raynor; Elizabeth City Society Page; Journal and Guide, April 1, 1933; P.5.

264   Elizabeth City News; W.S. Bowser; Journal and Guide, Norfolk, Va.; Oct 1, 1932. p. 5

265   Our Colored People; The Elizabeth City Carolinian; Volume XXVII; July 24, 1895; Number 9. Elizabeth City; Journal and Guide; December 4, 1926; P.4.

266   Elizabeth City Local News, May 16, 1926.

267   Minutes 1879 P. 7.

268   Proceedings of the Roanoke Missionary Baptist Association, Tuesday, May 28, 1878, p. 1.

269   Minutes, 1879 P. 5.

270   Ibid.

271   Our Colored People; The Elizabeth City North Carolinian; Volume XXX1; Number 16; September 7,

272   1899, P. 16

273   Our Colored People; The Elizabeth City North Carolinian, Volume XXX1 Number 30; December 21,

274   1899, P. 16

275   Our Colored People; The Elizabeth City Carolinian; Volume XXXI; November 30, 1899; Number 28.
Our Colored People; The Elizabeth City Carolinian; Volume XXXI; March 22, 1900; Number 44.

276   Deaths; Mrs. Hester Pierce; Journal and Guide; May 22, 1926; P.2.

277   Several dates are given for Rev. E. E. Randolph's birth date, 1855, 1859 and 1860.

278   Minutes of the 1885 Annual Session Minutes 1885 Statistical Table.

279   Ibid.

280   Minutes of the Thirty-eighth (1903)Annual Session of the Roanoke Missionary Baptist Association held with the First Colored Hertford Baptist Church, Hertford, North Carolina North Carolina Deaths and Burials 1898-1994 for Ned Randolph.

281   North Carolina State Board of Health Bureau of Vital Statistics Standard Certificate of Death. Registration Number 705921 Register Number 33. Minutes 1914, P. 2.

282   The Elizabeth City Carolinian News Paper. Volume XXVII, Wednesday, November 3, 1897. Number 24. Minutes 1913 P. 25.

283   Ibid.

284   Elizabeth City News; Journal and Guide; December 3, 1932; P. A5.

285   *A Day on The Neuse,* The Gazette Volume VIII, No. 5. February 6, 1897.

286   *Crowds Pay Tribute at Brier of Rev. Mr. Thomas Evans'* Journal and Guide; November 20, 1926' P. 11. Ibid.

287   A History of the Negro Baptist Church: The Reformed Reader. A. W. Pegues; Our Baptist Ministers and Schools. P. 435.

288   Minutes 1884 *Proceedings*

289   J. A. Whited, Biographical Sketch of the Life and Work of the Late Rev. Augusta Shepard, D. D.,

290   Durham, North Carolina. (Raleigh: Edward & Broughton Printing Company, 1912) P.10

291   H. G. Jones; *North Carolina Illustrated, 1524-1984* University of North Carolina Press: Chapel Hill, 1983) P. 319. Minutes, P.6.

292   Minutes 1878 P. 13.

293   Ibid.

294   *A Trip to Lott Cary Convention*; Journal and Guide; September 18, 1926; P. 9 Windsor; Journal and Guide; March 28, 1927; P9.

295   *Call To a New Field*, Journal and Guide, December 15, 1923. P6.

296   The Elizabeth City Carolinian News Paper Volume XXVII, Wednesday, January 20, 1897 Number 36. The Elizabeth City Carolinian News Paper Volume XXVII, Wednesday, August 3, 1899 Number 11. Minutes 1915, P. 41.

297   Minutes 1920. P. 11.

298   Minutes 1922; P. 5.

299   *Impressive Rites for Dr. C. C. Somerville, Baptist Leader.* Volume XLIV Number 11. March 11, 1944.

300   Ibid

301   1884 Statistical Table P. 14.

302   News of the Churches; November 18, 1922; Journal and Guide; P.6. Edenton; Journal and Guide; June 2, 1923; P.9.

303   News from City and Towns in N. C.' Volume XXIV; Number 37; September 13, 1924, P. 7. Minutes May 1935.

304   Edenton, N. C.; January 11, 1939; Journal and Guide; P.14.

305   Franklin, Va. Journal and Guide' November 27, 1937; P. 13. Minutes 1950 P. 9.

306   *Leonard R. Ballou, Pasquotank Pedagogues and Politicians: Early Educational Struggles.* Minutes 1879 P. 6.

307   Roanoke Missionary Time Table

President of the W. M. E. U.

308   *Roanoke Institute To The Front*, Journal and Guide September 29, 1917. P. 4.

309   *Woman's Union At Plymouth: Much Money and Enthusiasm for Roanoke Institute.* September 10, 1921. P. 1

310   Florence Rayner, Rites Held For Mrs. Cartwright In Eliz. City; June 23, 1951; P. B3.

311   Mrs. E. Spellman, Elizabeth City; Journal and Guide; July 28, 1962. P. 11.

312   *Florence Raynor; Elizabeth City Resident Feted at Surprise Party*, Journal and Guide; November 5, 1949, P. B4.

313   Florence Rayner Journal and Guide; Journal and Guide, October 18, 1953; P. A4. Ibid.

314   Florence Rayner Journal and Guide; Journal and Guide, October 18, 1953; P. A4.

315   Florence Rayner Journal and Guide; Journal and Guide, November 6, 1954; P. 21.

316   *Queen Contest Featured At Missionary Session* Journal and Guide; November 5, 1960; P. 14.

317   *Women's Mission Group Will Gather In Camden* Journal and Guide; September 23, 1961; P. 14.

318   *The Roanoke Missionary Association Meets May 23-15* Journal and Guide; May 20, 1961; P.3.

319   Mrs. Mary Williamd; *Minister Assumes New Pastorate*; New Journal and Guide, Norfolk, Virginia; June 26, 1954; P. A5.

320   F. Raynor; Elizabeth City News; Journal & Guide; November 29, 1952; P. A4. Baby For You; Journal and Guide; November 12, 1927; P.11.

321   Winfall; Journal and Guide; May 19, 1923; P.3.

322   W. S. Bowser; Elizabeth City; Journal and Guide; August 13, 1931 P.5.

323   Mrs. F. Rayner' Elizabeth City; Journal and Guide, Norfolk, Virginia; May 28, 1932; P.12.

324   Blanche Hinton; In Memoriam; Journal and Guide; June 9, 1934; P. A4.

325   Mrs. F. B. Raynor; North Carolina; Journal and Guide; May 12, 1934; P.15.

326   Mrs. F. B. Raynor; North Carolina News; New Journal and Guide; May 12, 1934; P.15.

327   F. B. Raynor, Elizabeth City News; Journal and Guide; February 14, 1942; P. 16.

328   Black Women in America, Vol. II, pg. 1167.

329   African-American Experience in World Mission: A Call Beyond Community, Volume 1.

330   *Women Doing Fine Missionary Work In North Carolina*; Journal and Guide, Norfolk, Virginia; October 19, 1935; P. 6.

331   N. C. Baptist Contributes $7,000 to Shaw and Missions; Journal and Guide, Norfolk, Virginia; November 19, 1932; P. 4.

332   *N. C. Baptist To Back Dr. G. O. Bullock As Head Of The Lott Carey Meeting*; Journal and Guide, Norfolk, Virginia; August 21, 1937; P. A6.

333   *Liberia Native Is Ordained*; Journal and Guide, Norfolk, Virginia; October 18, 1947; P.B17.

334   *Elizabeth City PTA Gives Cup To Delores E. Owens*; Journal and Guide, Norfolk, Virginia; May 14, 1949; P. B15.

335   Other 8; No Title; Journal and Guide, Norfolk, Virginia; November 10, 1951; P. 11.

336   The Westminster Handbook to Women in American Religious History" Darlene Clark; Facts on File Encyclopedia of Black Women in America: Religion and Community (1977) P. 220.

337   Mrs. F. B. Raynor; North Carolina News, Elizabeth City; Journal and Guide; November 12, 1928; P.14.

338   Elizabeth City Personals; Journal and Guide; February 18, 1950; P. B5.

339   Elizabeth City Personals; Journal and Guide; July 29, 1950; P. B4.

340   Minutes of the One Hundred Thirty Second (1998) Annual Session, P. 4.

341   Mrs. F. B. Rayner; North Carolina; Journal and Guide; April 16, 1938; P.15.

342   Florence Rayner, Elizabeth City; Journal and Guide; October 18, 1952; A4.

343   Elizabeth City; Journal and Guide; December 9, 1922; P.3.

Church Histories

Mineral Springs Missionary Baptist Church

344   *Death of Mrs. Mary E. White*, Journal and Guide; May 22, 1926. P.11. See the obituary at the end of this article.

345   Minutes 1885 Statistical Table.

346   Ibid.

347   *Two Members Honored In Whaleyville Church,* Journal and Guide, December 6, 1969; B19.

348   E. J. Fields, Whaleyville, VA; Journal and Guide; January 21, 1922. P. 3.

349   Whaleyville Notes, Journal and Guide; May 12, 1923; P.8.

350   Whaleyville, November 11, 1933; Journal and Guide, P. A9.

351   *Whaleyville Church Has 71st Observance*; Journal and Guide; November 21, 1942; P. A20.

352   *Congregation Surprises Minister on His 22nd Year*; Journal and Guide; April 24, 1948; P. E5.

Mount Carmel Missionary Baptist Church

353   Minutes the 1903 Roanoke Missionary Baptist Association P. 9.

354   General Education Board S 101 North Carolina. 236. Supervisor for Rural School Reports Box 115-Folder 1043.

355   Rockefeller Archive Center, New York, Report of N.C. Newbold, State Agent Negro Rural Schools for North Carolina. General Education Board 1254, Box 43, Folder 434. Historical Table, Roanoke Missionary Baptist Association.

356   Minutes of the 1868 Roanoke Missionary Baptist Association, p. 7-8.

357   Minutes of the Forty-Ninth Annual Session of the Roanoke Missionary Baptist Association held with the Saint Stephen Baptist Church, Elizabeth City, N. C.,; Rev. J. H. Johnson, pastor; May 19-21 1914. P. 20.

358   Minutes of the Forty-Ninth Annual Session of the Roanoke Missionary Baptist Association held with the First Baptist Church, Hertford, N. C.; Elizabeth City, N. C.,; Rev. G. D. Griffin, pastor; May 18-20 1915. P. 20.

359   Ibid.

360   Minutes of the Fiftieth Annual Session of the Roanoke Missionary Baptist Association held with the Joppa Missionary Baptist Church, Trotville (Hobbsville), N. C.; Rev. J. C. Saunders, pastor; May 21-23, 1918. P. 28. Minutes 1917.

[361] Minutes, Statistics, 1923.

[362] Mrs. E. Spellman; Elizabeth City; New Journal and Guide, Norfolk, Virginia; April 13, 1963; P. A19.

[363] F. Butler; D. White; Elizabeth City; Journal and Guide, Norfolk, Virginia; December 19, 1921; P.3.

[364] Mrs. F. Rayner; *Missionary Women In 7th Annual Meet In Eliz. City*; Journal and Guide; April 21, 1951; P. B 4.

[365] Mrs. Mary Williams; Newland, N. C.; Journal and Guide, Norfolk, Virginia; October 17, 1953; P. A5.

[366] Elizabeth City, Journal and Guide, Norfolk, Virginia; October 15, 1955; P. 5.

[367] *Teacher Ed. Group Cites N.C, College;* Journal and Guide, Norfolk, Virginia; April 2, 1966; P. 10.

[368] Hertford; Journal and Guide, Norfolk, Virginia; September 21, 1968; P. B 27.

[369] Creswell; Journal and Guide, Norfolk, Virginia; October 9, 1968; P. 11.

[370] *Ex-Resident of New Land Dies in Auto Wreck*; Journal and Guide, Norfolk, Virginia; October 30, 1954; P. 22.

[371] See Pasquotank County, North Carolina Deed Book 485 page 895.

Stony Branch

[372] *Pride of the Past-Hope for the Future: Piney Grove-Reynoldson Baptist Church 1827-1977* (Pierce Printing Company., Inc, Ahoskie, N.C. 1977) P.103.

[373] Minutes of the 1869 Annual Session of the Roanoke Missionary Baptist Association, P. 3.

[374] Ibid

[375] Gates County Record of Deed Book 31, Page 31.

[376] Ibid page 32.

[377] Ibid.

[378] 1884 Roanoke Missionary Statistical Table 1885 Roanoke Missionary Statistical Table 1886 Roanoke Missionary Statistical Table.

[379] Roanoke Missionary Baptist Digest of Letter, May 1909. P. 33.

[380] Minutes 1906 P. 40.

[381] Minutes 1907, P.23

[382] Minutes 1920, P.12.

[383] Minutes 1919, P. 44.

[384] Suffolk News & Advertise; Journal and Guide; July 14, 1917 P. 8.

[385] Minutes 1920, P. 43.

[386] Ibid. p. 46.

[387] Minutes, 1922 P. 19.

[388] Ibid, P. 21.

[389] Ibid. P. P. 25.

[390] The Minutes of the Ninety-Ninth Annual Session of the Roanoke Missionary Baptist Association held with The First Baptist Church Hertford, North Carolina May 18-20 1965 Rev. F.L. Andrews Pastor, Rev. J.R.R. McRay Recording Secretary. *The Daily Advance News Paper* Volume XXXVI Number 220, Friday, September 13, 1946.

[391] The Works of James McCune Smith: Black Intellectual and Abolitionist; (Oxford: Oxford Univ. Press, 2006). P. 454.

[392] The Insurance Year Book; Volume 40; P. 461 See the charter located in the Appendix and the list of names affixed to it.

[393] North Carolina Odd Fellows In Annual Session; Journal and Guide; August 27, 1921; P.5. To Lay Cornerstone Thanksgiving Day; Journal and Guide; October 23, 1926; P.11.

UNION CHAPEL

[394] *Our People: Yesterday, Today & Tomorrow: A Brief History of Union Chapel Missionary Baptist Church;* Union Chapel Baptist Church 1990; P.10.

[395] Pasquotank County Deed Book for Union Chapel Baptist Church Filed July 5, 1919.

[396] Mrs Susie Overton; Journal and Guide, Norfolk, Virginia; January 4, 1947; P. B13.

[397] Ibid.

[398] Durant's Neck; Journal and Guide, Norfolk, Virginia; October 27, 1928; P.14.

[399] Minutes of the Nineteenth Annual Session of the Roanoke Missionary Baptist Association held with the Church of Christ at Zion Hill, Bertie County, N. C., Tuesday after the Third Lord's Day in May 1884; P.12.

[400] Historical Table Roanoke Missionary Association

[401] Roanoke Missionary Baptist Association; 1903 Delegate, Clerks and Pastors of Churches.

[402] Sweet Singers Charmed Elizabetg City People; Journal and Guide, Norfolk, Virginia; March 3, 1917; P.8.

[403] F. Butler; D. White; Elizabeth City, N.C.; Journal and Gide, Norfolk, Virginia; July 23, 1921; P. 7.

[404] F.W. M. Butler & D. W. White. Volume XXI Number 30 Norfolk Journal and Guide July 23, 1921 P.6.

[405] F. Butler & D. W. White, Elizabeth City Society Page, Journal and Guide, October 22, 1921. P. 7.

[406] Weeksville; Journal and Guide, Norfolk, Virginia; September 3, 1927; P.11.

[407] BellCross, N. C.; Journal and Guide, Norfolk, Virginia; June 17, 1933; P.11.

[408] Mrs. F. R. Rayner; Elizabeth City; Journal and Guide, Norfolk, Virginia; June 24, 1933; P.14.

[409] Mrs. F. Raynor; Elizabeth City News; Journal and Guide. Norfolk, Virginia; September 9, 1933; P.9.

[410] Elizabeth City News; Journal and Guide, Norfolk, Virginia; September 22, 1934; P. 17.

[411] Ibid.

[412] Mrs. F. Raynor; Elizabeth City News; Journal and Guide. Norfolk, Virginia; October 6, 1934; P.16.

[413] Mrs. F. B. Raynor; North Carolina; Journal and Guide. Norfolk, Virginia; October 6, 1934; P.16.

[414] Elizabeth City; Journal and Guide; Norfolk, Virginia. October 27, 1934; P.16.

[415] Mrs. F. R. Raynor; Elizabeth City; Journal and Guide, Norfolk, Virginia; July 1, 1939; P.15.

[416] Ibid.

[417] Mrs. F. B. Raynor; *Elizabeth City Schools Raises Funds For Improvements*;

[418] Journal and Guide. Norfolk, Virginia; June 16, 1945; P. 18.

[419] *Mrs. F. R. Raynor; Large Crowd Attends Rites For Samuel Edward Norman*; Journal and Guide, Norfolk, Virginia; March 19, 1949; P. C17.

[420] *Union Chapel Church*; Journal and Guide, Norfolk, Virginia; September 3, 1949' P. A19.

[421] Mrs. F. R. Raynor; *Elizabeth City Chorus Marks 2nd Anniversary*; Journal and Guide, Norfolk, Virginia; December 16, 1950; P.A5.

[422] Florence Rayner; Elizabeth City; Journal and Guide, Norfolk, Virginia; August 23, 1952; P. B5A. Elizabeth City News; Journal and Guide, Norfolk, Virginia; October 22, 1932; P. 5.

[423] Elizabeth City News; Journal and Guide, Norfolk, Virginia; October 22, 1932; P.5.

[424] Elizabeth City; Journal and Guide, Norfolk, Virginia; June 17, 1933; P. A10. Elizabeth City; Journal and Guide. Norfolk, Virginia; July 29, 1933; P.11.

[425] Ibid.

[426] Mrs. F. R. Raynor; Elizabeth City; Journal and Guide, Norfolk, Virginia; August 19, 1939; P.15. Mrs. F. R. Raynor; Elizabeth City; Journal and Guide, Norfolk, Virginia; January 25, 1941; P.14. Mrs. F. R. Raynor; Elizabeth City; Journal and Guide, Norfolk, Virginia; July 11, 1942; P.A 8.

[427] Mrs. F. R. Raynor; Elizabeth City; Journal and Guide, Norfolk, Virginia; March 11, 1944; P.A18.

[428]   Mrs. F. R. Raynor; Medaled 92nd Division Soldier Visits Elizabeth City College; Journal and Guide, Norfolk, Virginia; June 23, 1945; P.A17.

[429]   *Peerless Four*; Journal and Guide, Norfolk, Virginia; August 24, 1946; P.A 15.

[430]   Weeksville, N. C.; Journal and Guide, Norfolk, Virginia; December 15, 1928; P.12.

[431]   Pictures from the Union Chapel History Book.

[432]   IBID.

[433]   Elizabeth City News; Journal and Guide. Norfolk, Virginia; July 1, 1933; P.14.

[434]   Mrs. F. B. Raynor; North Carolina; Journal and Guide. Norfolk, Virginia; March 9, 1935. P. 6.

[435]   Mrs. F. Raynor; North Carolina News; Journal and Guide, Norfolk, Virginia; January 28, 1939; P.15. Mrs Susie Overton; Journal and Guide, Norfolk, Virginia; January 4, 1947; P. B13.

[436]   Elizabeth City Deaths; Journal and Guide, Norfolk,Virginia; January 21, 1950; P. B4.